KIWI SCORPIONS

THE STORY OF THE NEW ZEALANDERS
IN THE LONG RANGE DESERT GROUP

KIWI SCORPIONS

THE STORY OF THE NEW ZEALANDERS
IN THE LONG RANGE DESERT GROUP

Brendan O'Carroll

TOKEN PUBLISHING LIMITED

KIWI SCORPIONS

ISBN 1 870 192 41 9

First published 2000

© 2000 Brendan O'Carroll and Token Publishing Limited

Published by Token Publishing Limited, Honiton, Devon EX14 1YD

Typesetting and design by Third Dimension

Printed in Great Britain by Polestar Scientifica, Exeter, Devon

CONTENTS

ACKNOWLEDGEMENTS

This book would not have been possible without the generous support of the LRDG veterans, their families, and the many others who kindly loaned resource material, militaria, and gave permission to publish their photographs, including the Imperial War Museum, London. A special thanks to Merlyn Craw for allowing me to reproduce the poem, *A Dedication To Brave Men*, written by his late wife Elva, and to Alf Saunders for *The LRP Lament*.

I wish to thank Ian Judge, the Secretary of the Long Range Desert Group (New Zealand) Association, who offered much encouragement and provided free access to his records. Along with this came the opportunity to communicate with a number of Association members. I felt privileged in that the following "Kiwi Scorpions" some of whom have since deceased, took the time in sharing some of their wartime experiences with me: Denis Bassett, John Bruce (GB), Eric Carter, Merlyn Craw, Merv Curtis, Merle Fogden, Peter Garland, George Garven, Don Gregory, Buster Gibb, Erl Gorringe, Ray Gorringe, Fred Kendall, Ken Knudsen, Ron Landon-Lane, Charles McConachie, Ian McCulloch, Tommy McDonald, Les Nicholls, Alan Nutt, Derek Parker, Clyde Pickering, Wally Rail, Tom Ritchie, Alf Saunders, Rowley Talbot, Keith Tippett, Clarke Waetford, Frank White, Bill Willcox, Richard Williams and Keith Yealands.

In addition, I am grateful to the following relatives of LRDG veterans who had assisted me with information or made contributions: Mairee Adams, Neil Anderson, Kate Bassett, David Ellis, Nancy Garven, Ken and Jenny Johnston, Irene Jopling, Peggy Judge, Ngaire Lewis, Shaun Moloney, Thelma Mercer, Una Sadgrove, John, Eric, and Michael Shepherd, Joan Svetlik, Charlie Waetford, Warner Wilder and Ceinwen Williams.

I also wish to acknowledge the fellow collectors, amateur historians, and friends, for their help in putting this book together: Andrew Adams, Paul Ackerman, Alan Culhane, Allan Davies, John Daymond, Craig Douglas, Paul Farmer, Kate Foster, Phil Furner, Ian Hamilton, Colin Jansen, Robert Miles, Tony O'Carroll, David and Geoff Oldham, Dave McCann (my Armourer), Jonathan Paynter, Dean Percy, Paul Rourke, Gareth Sangster, Bruce Stewart, Jim Sutherland, Gray Thorp, Jack Valenti of the LRDG Preservation Society, USA, and John Wech.

Finally thanks go to my wife Margaret for putting up with me spending all my time in front of the computer and for the tedious job of proof reading, also my daughter Diana for educating me in computer technology, and to my younger daughter Michelle and son Patrick for enduring the LRDG for the past four years.

THE LRP LAMENT

They wanted soldiers stout and strong to cross the arid lands,
To pioneer the rolling dunes across the Libyan sands,
Where never camels trod, nor Wog, nor Sudanese,
Where never brush nor grass can grow upon the great sand seas.

They wanted men who could, when wished, go short of food and drink,
Be left unshaven and unwashed, yet not so much as stink!
To stand up to the furnace blast of scorching sand and heat,
Which drives into your eyes and mouth, and blisters face and feet.

Now where to find these men made GHQ to wonder,
Till Major Bagnold came along and stole away their thunder.
I n-n-know the men he cried, if you just give me time,
They come from one New Zealand, a land of sunny clime.

And so it was they got us, Tho' Freyberg, much annoyed,
Said, "Why should bloody Pommies send 'my' men to the void?"
However, now we'd started this we meant to see it through,
And soon convinced the older hands we'd thrive out in the blue.

No sooner had we shown them, than it was thought quite fit,
To let the Tommies have a go and leave us in the shit.
To go back to our units was all they told us now,
If you don't, there would be one holy bloody row!

So we'll go back to our units and fight in Greece or Spain,
Or any God Damn country, for preference where there's rain.
But don't forget when e're you read of scraps up on the border,
New Zealanders have blazed the trail, we've carried out an order.

By C.O. "Bluey" Grimsey, December 1940.
Written at the Citadel in Cairo, when the news came through that some members were to return to the NZ Division.

This poem was read publicly for the first time at an LRDG reunion in 1960. Alf Saunders had memorized it from the war. He then gave a copy to Grimsey who had forgotten that he had written it.

A special thank you to Alf Saunders for making the poem available for publication.

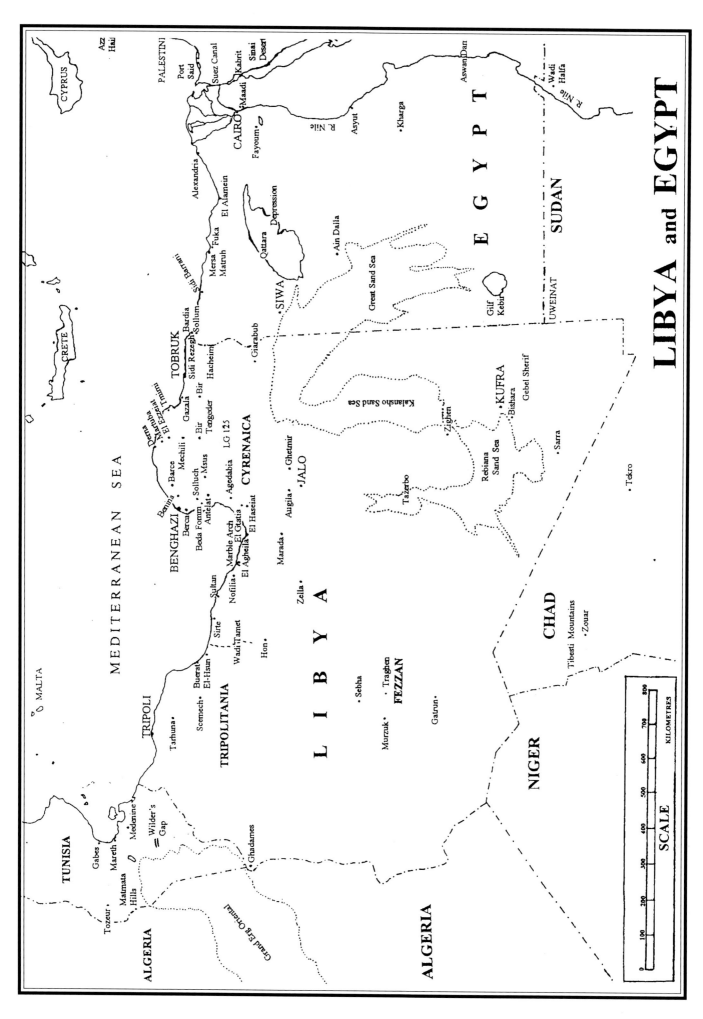

LIBYA and EGYPT

x

INTRODUCTION

The war in North Africa came to an end with the Axis surrender in May 1943. While the opposing armies had advanced and retreated along the Mediterranean coast, the patrols of the Long Range Desert Group had for almost three years, operated behind enemy lines dominating the vast inner deserts of Egypt, Libya and Tunisia.

This special intelligence gathering and reconnaissance unit, first known as the Long Range Patrol, was conceived in 1940 by Major Ralph Bagnold, a British Army Officer and desert explorer. Its initial purpose was to assess the threat to Egypt from the Italians in south-eastern Libya. For the first six months the patrols were nearly entirely manned by especially selected volunteers from the 2nd New Zealand Expeditionary Force. These were self-reliant, hardy men, who were good with vehicles and had adapted well to desert conditions.

Later however, the unit was reinforced with recruits from the British Guards and Yeomanry Regiments, and from Southern Rhodesia. With this it became known as the *Long Range Desert Group*. By 1942 its strength peaked at about 350 personnel, spread over two squadrons, A and B. They were supported by a HQ, and air, signals, survey, repair, and heavy transport sections.

This small, but extremely effective force of Empire troops were experts in navigation, desert warfare, and survival. Their principal objective was to provide by way of ground reconnaissance patrols, detailed charting and information about enemy dispositions from deep behind the lines in the Libyan Desert. Each patrol was a completely self-contained independent body, capable of operating for hundreds of kilometres over barren unmapped country for weeks on end.

They ran reconnaissance and survey patrols with great regularity from Cairo to Tripoli over some of the most difficult and arid terrain in the world. A large percentage of the information the Eighth Army received about enemy movements came via the radios of the LRDG stationed behind enemy lines. By the summer of 1941 they had by way of the Heavy Section established a chain of supply dumps, thereby extending their range of operations to great distances. It was a New Zealand patrol that became the first members of the Eighth Army to enter Tunisia.

The patrols were organised so they could be used offensively if required. They harassed the enemy by attacking their forts, supply dumps, and airfields. Road transport was also disrupted by way of mine laying and machine-gunning. Furthermore, as experts in navigation, the LRDG guided special forces such as the Special Air Service or Popski's Private Army against often superior enemy positions and ensured their safe return. Consequently the Axis had to withdraw badly needed troops away from the front to reinforce and protect their convoys, outposts, and airfields, as they never knew where the raiders were going to strike next. They came and went so swiftly that the Italians called them *Pattuglia Fantasma* (Ghost Patrols). Part of their success was being such a small force that could easily conceal themselves behind enemy lines.

Appropriately the insignia chosen for the LRDG was a scorpion. A potent symbol of power in a small unit, capable of striking suddenly and with great effect. The sting was in its firepower combined with the element of surprise.

The Group also enjoyed much success in their other activities, such as inserting, supplying, and collecting British and Arab undercover agents. Rescuing escaped Allied prisoners of war and recovering downed airmen. Between December 1940 and April 1943, there were only 15 days on which a patrol was not operating behind or on the flanks of the enemy. The unit had lived up to its unofficial motto, as penned by Dr. F. B. Edmundson, New Zealand Medical Corps and LRDG medical officer, "*Not by strength, by guile.*"

The most comprehensive history of the LRDG has been recorded in W. B. Kennedy Shaw's book *Long Range Desert Group* (1945). Likewise, David Lloyd Owen wrote two works, *The Desert My Dwelling Place* (1957) and *Providence Their Guide* (1980) which as well as an inclusive history, covered much of the work of the Yeomanry patrols. The story of the Guards was told in Michael Crichton-Stuart's book *G Patrol* (1958). *Kiwi Scorpions* is not only a general LRDG study, but also the first publication to tell the story from the New Zealand soldiers' perspective, as they were a major element in the force and made a significant contribution to its success.

This book is not intended to be a chronological history of the Group, as that approach has been well covered by the previous publications mentioned. It has been produced as an LRDG reference work with an emphasis on the New Zealand personnel and their activities, without undervaluing the fine accomplishments of the British and Rhodesians. To enable the reader quick referral to the various aspects of interest, the book is set out in topical chapter headings. For example, "Formation", "Transport", "Early Operations", "Desert Life", "Weapons", "Navigation", etc. Also, a number of the notable actions in which New Zealanders took part have been recounted in detail.

Though there are many stories that could be told, much of this work is based on the personal recollections of about ten veterans, thus providing a human face to the history. Officially, patrol members were not allowed to take private diaries or cameras on their trips, but thankfully a number chose to ignore that order and have left a wonderful insight into LRDG life and activities. Their accounts have been reinforced with material from archival and other LRDG information sources.

The LRDG was a British unit, so the qualities of its New Zealand members are best described by those who served with them. Bill Kennedy Shaw explained in his book how he viewed the "Kiwis":

There can be no doubt whatever that much of the early and continued success of the LRDG was due to speed and thoroughness with which the New Zealanders learned desert work and life.

He also mentioned that he felt that the New Zealanders were fitter and possessed a maturity and independence not found in British soldiers of a similar age.

Lieutenant Colonel Vladimir Peniakoff wrote in his book *Popski's Private Army* (1950), his personal observations from working with the Group:

A free, cheerful, tireless, efficient body of bearded men, they were the most pleasant companions I have ever had. I graded their squadrons, drawn from various parts of the Empire, on a scale of human excellence, which ranged from the New Zealanders high on top through the Rhodesians and the British Yeomanry down to the squadron drawn from the Guards Regiments. The New Zealanders, farmers in civil life, took easily to the roaming life in the desert. They had from the first a resourceful, happy assurance and set a standard which the others tried to follow.

The LRDG were never short of recruits and many dropped rank so they could join. For example in December 1940, Bagnold asked General Freyberg, C in C NZ Division, for further volunteers. Of the 800 who applied only 40 were required, so the Group was always in a position to choose the best. The NZ Squadron seemed to attract more mature experienced practical men with rural backgrounds and included several brothers and cousins.

The appeal of the LRDG was the almost complete freedom from drill, guards and fatigues, plus the best army food in the Middle East. It was interesting and often exciting work with the opportunity to prove oneself without the usual regimental constraints. If an individual showed a particular aptitude for the work there was a good chance for promotion. A number of men who had joined as privates finished their service with the Group as senior NCOs or officers.

On the debit side there was the strain of operating for long periods behind enemy lines with very little leave. Suffering the climatic extremes of heat and cold, sandstorms, thirst, anxiety, malaria and desert sores. Also, if sick or wounded, captured or lost, there was little chance of assistance apart from what could be provided from their own resources.

With the loss of transport due to enemy action, or more rarely through serious mechanical failure, it then became a matter of survival. LRDG annals record a number of occasions where men had trekked great distances, sick or wounded, with very little water or rations and had successfully navigated their way to safety. This book recounts in detail three of these great treks undertaken by New Zealanders.

Despite the concerns and hardships of desert life, the men displayed their usual tenacity and stoically got on with the job. The determination and success of this small force is reflected in the fact that nearly a third of its members won decorations.

Special force soldiers are by their nature unconventional, and it was this quality that characterized most of the New Zealand soldiers in the 2 NZEF. They were not regulars but civilians in uniform, because of this they felt they were not bound by "Regulations" (in their eyes anyway). Even the commanders were chiefly temporary soldiers: businessmen, lawyers and farmers who looked at tactical situations with fresh eyes.

Yet most of the men were highly disciplined, because they appreciated that without self discipline they could let down or endanger their "mates". They fully understood the team concept, having in the main played rugby or other team sports, and

providing the officers gave them a fair go they would gain respect in return. The NZ patrols reflected this mutual trust or "mateship" by the officers and men usually calling each other by their first name. The dangerous nature of LRDG operations, along with the high quality of its personnel, meant a good level of esprit de corps always prevailed.

The NZ Squadron's last operation was in the Mediterranean, on the Dodecanese Islands. This sometimes overlooked and ill-fated campaign resulted in more New Zealanders being lost in three months, than during three years in the desert. They had been committed to this area of operations without the knowledge of the New Zealand Government. Thereby after three and a half years "on loan" to the British, General Freyberg ordered his troops to be returned to their original units, though a handful remained and served with the Group in Europe.

Approximately 325 New Zealanders passed through the LRP or LRDG. While some only served a few months, others stayed on for several years. Of that number four were killed in action, two died of wounds, one was listed as missing, and three died while POWs. Including the foregoing, the LRDG's Roll of Honour totalled 37 men.

Finally, what I believe reflects the attitude and feelings of most of the New Zealanders who served with the force, is summed up in the words of A. D. "Buster" Gibb who served in both the LRP and LRDG:

While on the first trip we stopped on an escarpment, and the view in front of us was desert that extended as far as the eye could see. I experienced a prickling in the scalp that was hard to describe. It wasn't fear, it was excitement at the start of an adventure that was to test our Kiwi ingenuity and lead to life long friendships.

This book is a tribute to these men.

A DEDICATION TO BRAVE MEN

In strength they faced a fierce foe of brave and fearless men,
In hope they lived in desert clime, cruel cold and heat and when
In quiet calm obedience they answered every call,
With silence and with fortitude they formed a solid wall.
They fought with resolute and pride, and being oh so strong
That even those who were the best, could never prove them wrong !

They lived a life so hard so long and when the heat was on
The men of the *LRDG* could be depended on.
To fight to live, to fight to die to give their very all,
They never looked at any time that they would likely fall.
Beneath the feet of enemies, who fought with fearless pride,
They only knew their cause was right, and faced them side by side !

If you were a member of the *LRDG* crew,
You had a land to fight for, and were steadfast and true,
You never asked the question you just obeyed the rule,
The strong never falter and they don't run out of fuel.
They learned the hardest lesson in the very hardest way,
That if one amongst them were to fail, the whole crew had to pay !

Not only in the heat and sand but just like spiders' webs,
The work of the *LRDG* spread out like tight strong threads.
To the sea they went to a different world they would not be outdone
They knew they had to forge ahead until the peace was won.
On the slopes of snow white mountain peaks they did their very best,
They practised jumping from the skies, they conquered every test !

The hearts and souls of soldiers are dedicated too,The betterment of
mankind, left to but a few,
Who lived and died for freedom in lands of hostile clime.
Men drawn from far flung countries together for a time,
When nations really needed a group of quiet strong men,
And the world should remember, and thank them every now and then !

The *LONG RANGE DESERT GROUP* recall with honour every year,
Their comrades who have left them, and will no longer hear
The call if it should come again, the memories will not fail
To remind them of their creed which was, "The sting in the tail !"

by Elva M. Craw

FORMATION

The concept of the Long Range Desert Group was devised by Major Ralph Bagnold, a British Army Officer (Royal Corps of Signals), geographer and desert explorer, who with fellow adventureres, charted much of the Libyan desert during the 1920s and '30s in specially adapted Ford Model T and Model A motor cars. He developed the sun compass to assist with his navigation, and steel sand channels, along with canvas sand mats to free the wheels of bogged vehicles. He also designed a condenser that recycled the steam from the radiator, which radically reduced the amount of water needed to be carried in the desert. Bagnold gained immense knowledge of desert life and travel, including the plotting of water holes previously known only to nomadic Arabs. He went on to write two books on his experiences, Libyan Sands, (1935) and The Physics of Blown Sand and Desert Dunes (1941).

When war was declared in 1939, Bagnold suggested to General Sir Archibald Wavell, C in C Middle East, that in the event of conflict with Italy, he could set up a unit capable of operating behind the lines, for weeks on end, reconnoitring and obtaining intelligence of enemy garrisons and movements in the Libyan desert. When Italy entered the war in June 1940, Egypt was considered under threat, so Italian intentions and dispositions in Libya had to be established with some urgency.

The presence of enemy garrisons in Libya with an unknown number of troops and aircraft was disturbing for not only did they possess several motor units specially constructed for desert work, but they had shown by their campaigns of 1929 and 1931, that they had been capable of daring and well executed desert operations. Therefore, a distinct threat existed by both land and air to Upper Egypt, and to Nile Valley communications with the Sudan.

It was imperative to establish what was going on in that vast area behind the sand barrier.

NZ Divisional Cavalry troops line up on the wharf at Wellington, about to embark on the vessel Rangitata for the Middle East, 1940. Trooper J. L. Schaab (behind the man front right) later served with the LRP. Note: In 1940, NZ troops went overseas still issued with WW1 uniform and Pat. 1907 webbing. Photo: Peter Garland.

British Intelligence needed to know if there was a build up of enemy forces in the Kufra area, as it was feared that an attack could be possible through the Sudan. With this, on 23 June 1940, Wavell finally agreed to the formation of a small long range reconnaissance unit to cross into Libya and gather information.

Bagnold, (known as "Baggers" to his men) was appointed its commander and was given six weeks to recruit and prepare the force, which was officially entitled the "No.1 Long Range Patrol Unit" though it was more commonly known (including in despatches) as the Long Range Patrol, or Patrols. LRP was used as both a singular and plural term.

To assist him he chose several fellow desert explorers, including Lieutenant W. B. Kennedy Shaw (Palestine Dept. of Antiquities), whom he appointed Intelligence and Topographical officer; Captain P. A. Clayton (Egyptian Survey Dept.), and Major E. C. Mitford (1st Royal Tank Regt.), were made patrol commanders. Lieutenant T. Heywood (Royal Corps of Signals) was appointed Signals Officer, and Captain R. Harding-Newman (Royal Tank Regt. attached

to the Egyptian Army), used his influence to acquire the unit's vehicles and sun compasses.

Because the LRP needed to be formed as soon as possible, General Wavell gave Bagnold a document of special authority which enabled him to equip his force without suffering the usual administrative delays. Despite some of his requirements being considered unorthodox and difficult to obtain, such as star charts, logarithm tables, theodolites, sandals and sheepskin coats, the necessary equipment was eventually gathered.

The personnel for the unit proved a little more difficult to find, as they not only had to be self-reliant, hardy and accustomed to desert conditions, but also specialists in driving, weapons, mechanical repairs, signalling and navigation. The Australians and South Africans were approached first because they came from hot, dry climates. However, they declined, stating that they were otherwise committed, or didn't want their units under British command. Bagnold then turned to the members of the 2nd New Zealand Expeditionary Force, whose practical temperament appeared suitable for this type of work. They had for the previous six months been training in Egypt, and had shown a remarkable adaptability to desert conditions, far removed from the green coolness of their native land.

On 1 July 1940, Major-General B. C. Freyberg, C in C 2nd New Zealand Division, agreed to loan, "on secondment", specialist personnel, on the clear understanding they were to be returned when needed. Consequently volunteers from the NZ Divisional Cavalry, the 27th (Machine Gun) Battalion, and gunners from the 34th A/T Battery of the 7th Anti-Tank Regiment were supplied.

The majority of these men were not regular soldiers, but had joined up when the war was declared. Many were already accustomed to outdoor life and the handling of vehicles, as they had come from farming, or practical trade backgrounds, therefore they were well suited to the task ahead of them. Later they were to become the first New Zealand troops to see action.

Freyberg appointed three officers: Lieutenant L. B. Ballantyne (NZ Div. Cav.) was made adjutant and quarter-master; Second Lieutenant D. G. Steele (27th MG Bn.) became a patrol commander, and Lieutenant F. B. Edmundson (NZ Medical Corps) as the LRP medical officer. Their first job was to sort out the hundreds of applicants who had volunteered for a "special mission". As the unit was still secret only those who were selected were told of its true purpose. At the request of GHQ Middle East, the 2 NZEF provided a total detach-ment of five officers and 85 other ranks, which included 18 admin-istrative and technical personnel. Over the next five months the O/R's figure varied slightly as men came and went.

Three patrols, designated R, T and W, were formed. Each fielded two officers and 25 men, subdivided into four troops, mounted in a 15cwt Ford V8 pilot car and ten 30cwt Chevrolet trucks. The patrol armament consisted of 10 Lewis guns, four Boys anti-tank rifles and one 37mm Bofors gun, plus a variety of small arms. In addition each truck carried munitions, water and rations for three weeks, and enough fuel for a 2,400 kilometre journey—a total load of nearly two tonnes. There was also a Headquarters unit, and a section of four Ford Marmon Herrington heavy trucks for logistical support and building forward dumps.

The two fighting patrols were commanded by Captain P. A. Clayton, T Patrol, and Captain E. C. Mitford, W Patrol. Second-Lieutenant D. G. Steele commanded R Patrol, which was intended to carry supplies. At first the "Kiwis" were not expected to lead fighting patrols until they gained more familiarity with the desert. Nevertheless, it was not long before

The first two New Zealand patrol commanders, Abbassia 1940. Left, Lieutenant L. B. Ballantyne (NZ Div. Cav.), T Patrol. Right, Lieutenant D. G. Steele (27 MG Bn.), R Patrol. They are driving in R Patrol's Ford V8 15cwt pilot car. Photo: Peter Garland.

they proved themselves as capable fighting commanders.

At Abbassia, the army barracks and workshops just outside Cairo, the men and materials were assembled and the specialised preparations made. Later the LRDG Headquarters were established in the Citadel, an ancient, imposing fort in Cairo. Trooper Dick Lewis of T Patrol, who joined in February 1941, wrote in his diary his impressions of the base:

The Citadel is a very old fortification, everything massive, with the walls several feet thick. You come into the inside, pass through two big archways, dark and gloomy, fitted with tremendous iron studded wooden doors. The whole lot looking ages old, as I suppose it is. Inside are modern buildings, housing the usual amenities an army gathers around itself, such as a NAAFI, barber shop, newsagent, and a picture theatre.

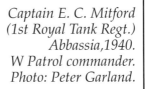

Lieutenant F.B.Edmundson (NZ Medical Corps.) The LRP's first Medical Officer. Photo: Peter Garland.

Captain E. C. Mitford (1st Royal Tank Regt.) Abbassia, 1940. W Patrol commander. Photo: Peter Garland.

Lieutenant R. B. McQueen, 2IC T Patrol. Right, Lieutenant J. H. Sutherland 2IC W Patrol. (Both NZ Div. Cav.) Abbassia, 1940. Photo: Peter Garland.

The bed bugs are very bad. They come out of the crevices in the iron beds we sleep in, and feast on the new arrivals. Some chaps have a terrible time with them. We got going on the beds with blow torches and disinfectant, but the best cure was to take your bed roll out onto the bitumen yard and sleep there.

In July and August 1940, under Bagnold's watchful eye, desert training runs were carried out in all types of terrain, and by the end of August they were ready for action. Captain Clayton led the initial expedition into Libya on 5 August 1940, which was a small reconnaissance force consisting of two trucks and seven men. The LRP's first major task began on 5 September, when Bagnold set out with a column of 14 vehicles to establish forward supply dumps, and to reconnoitre to the north and south of Kufra.

The anticipation and excitement of this first trip is well reflected in the words of Trooper Frank Jopling of T patrol, who wrote in his diary:

5 September 1940: We are all more or less thrilled with the trip and are anixous to get going. Not necessarily because we want to have a go at the Italians, but more for the adventure and excitment of the trip. We are going where no trucks have ever been before, over country that has never been mapped, we will probably see things that have never been seen by white men.

In October Freyberg wrote to GHQ Middle East to request the return of his troops so that the NZ Division could re-commence collective training. Also the commander of the Divisional Cavalry, Lieutenant-Colonel C. J. Pierce, felt his best men had been taken and was demanding them back. It was thought that by this time the reconnaissance mission of the LRP must have been completed. As part of a dispatch dated 11 October 1940, to General Freyberg from GHQ

Middle East, the following was stated:

The Commander in Chief has heard with some concern that you are anxious to withdraw the New Zealand personnel from the Long Range Patrol. He very much hopes that you see your way not to press this request in view of the excellent work this patrol is doing, and the long time it takes to train a patrol. The patrol is definitely carrying out a very important role in our war effort, in that it watches the Western Desert towards the Kufra Oasis.

In reply, General Freyberg wrote a dispatch to Major-General Arthur Smith, GHQ Middle East, 13 October 1940, part of which stated:

The history of this patrol is a bad one. In the first place they immobilised our Divisional Cavalry Regiment by taking all or nearly all its best officers, NCOs and men from it against the CO's wishes. This was under the distinct understanding that they were to be returned to him at the end of one journey. They then came back and I was informed that they had been lent for a year, which is quite incorrect.

As a matter of fact, I have written to Middle East saying I will not raise any more difficulties. My sympathies are, however, entirely with Pierce, my Divisional Cavalry commander, who has had his training gravely interfered with.

. . . Anyway I will not place any more obstacles in the way of the patrol. Lieutenant Colonel K. L. Stewart will see Pierce and arrange to minimise the damage done by substitution, and when they come back you must either take men from depot units or give the Long Range Patrol to somebody else.

Yours etc.

PS. This is a funny war. I feel that what is really wanted is a little more fighting and less patrols.

Finally, after much correspondence, it was agreed that since the New Zealand patrols had pioneered this unit, and what they were doing was such valuable work, they should be allowed to continue for as long as the situation warranted.

The LRP lost its near complete New Zealand identity in December 1940, with the arrival of reinforcements from the Brigade of Guards forming G Patrol, which under the command of Captain M. D. Crichton-Stuart consisted of two officers and 36 men selected from the 3rd Battalion of the Coldstream and the 2nd of the Scots Guards. With this, the force was reformed and became the Long Range Desert Group.

The army base at Abbassia, on the outskirts of Cairo, where the LRP was first established.
Photo: Shepherd collection.

The Citadel in Cairo, the LRDG Headquarters.
Photo: Shepherd collection.

Centre, Captain L. B. Ballantyne with his truck crew. One of his duties was to sift through the hundreds of applicants who volunteered to join the unit, which included a number of brothers and cousins. Left, T Patrol gunner Trooper B. F. "Mick" Shepherd. Right, Trooper W. D. Burnnand, driver. This photo was taken on the occasion of "Mick's" birthday in Cairo 1941. Photo: Shepherd collection.

In regard to this change, Brigadier Bernard Fergusson wrote in his introduction to Michael Crichton-Stuart's book G Patrol the following observation:

It was in the image of the New Zealanders that G Patrol was created; it owed much to their pioneering; yet from the first days in the Citadel it inevitably took on an aura of its own, as units created from the Brigade of Guards are apt to do.

Due to a number of men having to return to their units to go to Greece, W Patrol was now disbanded with its trucks and equipment going to the newly formed G Patrol. The balance of its members were reassigned to R and T Patrols.

In February 1941, the New Zealand Government drew up some conditions with regard to the men of 2 NZEF who were on loan to the LRDG. The first requirement was that 27 men of the Divisional Cavalry were to be returned to Colonel Pierce. Nine immediately, the balance as soon as the situation allowed. Also two patrols at full strength, i.e. a total of four officers and 54 men, plus nine spares, were to be provided, and thus maintained until Tripoli was captured.

The personnel would be supplied by 2 NZEF Base by arrangement between Colonel Bagnold and Brigadier N. S. Falla, Officer in Command of NZEF Base. The period of service for volunteers in the Group was to be limited to six months, after which, in the interest of 2 NZEF they were to be replaced by others. In practice the last condition was not strictly adhered to, as some men had to return to their original units after having only served a few months whereas others spent a number of years in the Group, or rejoined after broken service. Several men such as Ron Tinker, Dick Croucher and Tony Browne, joined in 1940 and left when the LRDG was disbanded in 1945.

Further patrols were added, with the arrival of the Southern Rhodesian, S Patrol (Captain C. A. Holliman) in January 1941, and the Yeomanry, Y Patrol (Captain P. J. D. McGraith), in March. More heavily armed Ford 30cwt trucks, and later new 1942 Chevrolets increased the strength of the force. Field experience showed that a patrol could operate more effectively when split in half, with the smallest sub-unit being two trucks. This was formalised in late 1941, when the patrol was officially reconstituted as one or two officers, and 15 to 20 other ranks in five or six vehicles.

After the new arrivals had completed their desert training, the Group was divided into two squadrons, A and B. By September 1941, after some variation, the composition was established as follows: the four New Zealand patrols (R1, R2, T1 and T2), and the two Southern Rhodesian patrols (S1, S2) made up A Squadron. Major D. G. Steele was appointed its commander. The two Guards patrols (G1, G2), and the two Yeomanry (Y1, Y2), completed B, under Major D. L. Lloyd Owen. Also specialist formations were added to the Group: a Signals, Survey and Light Repair Section, a Royal Artillery Section (for a short time), a Heavy Section (trucks for logistical support), and the Air Section (two light aircraft were supplied for liaison work). Later, the Rhodesians joined B Squadron, leaving A Squadron as a completely New Zealand unit.

In August 1941 Major Guy Prendergast took over the command of the LRDG from Bagnold who was promoted and appointed Inspector of Desert Troops, GHQ Middle East. Prendergast was also a pre-war desert explorer and a skilled pilot, who had done much of his exploration by air. He remained Officer Commanding LRDG to the end of its operations in North Africa. In early 1942 Major C. S. Morris replaced Major Steele as CO, A Squadron. By mid 1942 he in turn was replaced by Major A. I. Guild, who remained to the end of 1943 when A Squadron was eventually disbanded. In October 1943 Lieutenant-Colonel J. R. Easonsmith became OC LRDG, but a month later he was killed in action on the island of Leros, in the Aegean Sea. He was replaced by Lieutenant-Colonel D. L. Lloyd Owen, who commanded the force until it ceased in August 1945.

By March 1942 the Group had grown to its full strength of 25 officers and 324 other ranks, of which 36 were Signals and 36 Light Repair personnel, together with 110 vehicles. Though despite this increase of manpower and equipment, the patrol and half-patrol remained the basic operational unit of the Group during the desert war.

In the meantime, by January 1942, the Indian Long Range Squadron had been formed, which was led by British Officers and senior NCOs. There were also three Indian officers and 82 Indian other ranks. The ILRS included a HQ unit, and two patrols, each of two half patrols, with 35 vehicles similar to those of the LRDG. They came under the command of the Group in October 1942.

When the North African campaign ended in May 1943 the LRDG returned to Egypt to rest and reorganise. From there they transferred to the Cedars of Lebanon, where they trained in mountain warfare, learned to carry heavy packs and to handle pack mules. Their beloved trucks had gone, and the jeeps were now only available if the terrain permitted. The patrols were reorganised in small self contained units of seven to 11 men. After nearly five months in Lebanon they were sent to the Dodecanese Islands in the Aegean Sea to support the British troops based on Leros.

Citadel 1941. General Auchinleck inspects the LRDG. Standing alongside left are Lieutenant-Colonel Bagnold, OC LRDG (partly obscured) and Captain L. B. Ballantyne. Photo: Tom Ritchie.

OGNI GIORNO DI BATTAGLIA
CI AVVICINA ALLA META

The LRDG was employed as coast watchers and garrison troops, and took part in raiding and reconnaissance activities. Their biggest setback was the raid on Levita, which cost the Group 40 men killed or captured, half of them New Zealanders. The whole campaign proved a disaster, as after three months the Germans successfully captured the islands at great loss to the defending British forces.

A Squadron had been committed to this operation without the knowledge of the New Zealand Government, which required that it be consulted first before its troops were sent to a new theatre of war. Thereby General Freyberg decided that his men who had been "on loan" to the LRDG since 1940, should be returned immediately to 2 NZEF. Consequently, on 31 December 1943, A Squadron LRDG was disbanded. Most of its members either went home on furlough, or after spending time at the NZ Armoured Corps Training Depot in Egypt, were posted as reinforcements to the Divisional Cavalry with the 2nd NZ Division in Italy.

This propaganda poster shows that Italian intentions were clear, with the road sign portrayed pointing towards Suez. The caption reads: "Each day of battle brings us nearer to our goal." Brendan O'Carroll collection.

EARLY OFFENSIVE OPERATIONS

Because of a combination of natural and man-made barriers, the Italian garrisons in Libya had good reason to feel shielded from attack from Egypt. Alongside the western frontier of Egypt lies the biggest continuous dune field in the world, the Great Sand Sea (also known as the Egyptian Sand Sea). Both its northern and southern extremities curl round westward in two great arms, as if especially designed to prevent any outflanking movement from the east. This together with forts and 320 kilometres of entangled wire fence stretching from Siwa at the edge of the Sand Sea, on to Sollum near the coast, cut off the interior of Libya from Egypt. In addition, the protection afforded by the enormous distances, the absence of water, and the extreme temperatures which prevailed during the summer months, made the Italians based at Kufra, Uweinat and elsewhere, feel perfectly secure against attack.

Therefore, the early offensive operations across the "impassable" Sand Sea into enemy rear areas came as a shock to the Italian command. The raids from these "Ghost Patrols", as the Italians called them, soon proved so effective that they had to withdraw their badly needed forces away from the front to reinforce and protect convoys, outposts and airfields. It had to be done, as they never knew where the LRDG raiders were going to strike next.

Apart from reconnaissance trips, the LRP's first direct action role was to lay mines on the roads used by Italian convoys. While carrying out such an operation in October 1940, Captain Steele's R Patrol found an enemy bomb dump buried in the sand. Over 700 bombs were dug up and destroyed. Later the same day, on a landing ground near Ain Zwaya, they burned an unguarded Savoia-Marchetti S79 bomber and 160 drums of fuel. After completing further mine-laying, the patrol was spotted by three enemy aircraft that bombed them for an hour. There were no casualties and only minor damage to the vehicles.

Meanwhile, Captain Clayton's T Patrol had laid mines on the Jalo–Ajedabia road, and distributed pamphlets written in Arabic inciting the tribes to make trouble in Libya. On 1 November the column attacked a small Italian fort at Aujila, where after the first burst of Bofors and machine-gun fire, the astonished garrison ran from the fort to a nearby native

October 1940. R Patrol digs up an enemy munitions dump. The bombs were later destroyed.
Photo: Jim Sutherland.

Approaches to the Uweinat mountain, where W Patrol attacked the Italian outpost at Ain Dua. Photo: Jim Sutherland.

village. Clayton captured one Libyan soldier for interrogation, along with two Schwarzloss machine-guns, four rifles and other stores.

In late November, W Patrol led by Captain Mitford visited Uweinat, where for over an hour they were attacked by three enemy aircraft. Though more that 300 small bombs were dropped, skilful driving resulted in no damage being done. The patrol then went on to the Italian outpost at Ain Dua, which at first appeared to be deserted. A round from the Bofors gun was fired which brought an immediate response of enemy rifle and machine-gun fire. The garrison, estimated to be 30 men with three machine-guns, were well established in positions among large boulders, stone walls and trenches. Thereby a frontal attack over the open plain was out of the question.

D Troop, consisting of three trucks and eight men under Lieutenant J.H. Sutherland, moved against the Italian's left flank, while the rest of the patrol gave covering fire. The troop worked its way through the rocks on foot, and despite coming under steady fire drove the enemy up the hill into fresh positions, leaving three casualties including at least one killed.

Two bombers, then later a reconnaissance aircraft appeared, so the patrol withdrew and hid among the rocks. After several hours the skies were clear again and a second attack on Ain Dua was launched. The plan was to attack from both flanks while being covered from the centre. With its Bofors gun in support, D Troop attacked over the ground where it had been before. While one truck and a Bofors gun gave covering fire from the plain the rest of the patrol worked their way around the right flank. Sutherland reached the edge of the fortifications and inflicted casualties with grenades discharged from a rifle cup, only to be then pinned down by return fire. Trooper L. A. Willcox crawled with his Lewis gun to within 18 metres of an enemy machine-gun emplacement, then stood up firing his weapon and killed the crew of four.

W Patrol, 1940.
Back row, from left:
?, L. F. Mather, G. H. Nelson,
A. D. Gibb, A. McCorkindale,
F. R. Brown, A. E. Respinger,
Captain E. G. Mitford,
G. C. Garven, A. M. Saunders,
F. R. Beech, J. W. Eyles.
Middle row: V. C. Spain,
J. Emslie, W. G. Butler,
C. O. Grimsey, A. F. Dodunski,
C. Waetford.
Front row: George Barnes?,
R. O. Gorringe, L. Roderick,
G. C. Parkes, L. A. Willcox,
Lieutenant J. H. Sutherland.
Photo: Buster Gibb.

As Sutherland moved in closer he was again to be cut off by enemy fire. Willcox came to his rescue a second time by silencing a further machine-gun position.

Owing to the almost impassable rocks, the remainder of the patrol was unable to get close enough to engage the Italians. The garrison was well placed, and defended themselves so stoutly that it was impossible to take the position without incurring heavy losses. The New Zealanders withdrew at dusk, leaving six of the enemy killed and at least six wounded without suffering any casualties themselves. As a result of this action Sutherland received the first Military Cross and Willcox the first Military Medal awarded to 2 NZEF.

In December 1940, with the introduction of the Guards patrol, the Long Range Patrol now became known as the Long Range Desert Group. W Patrol was disbanded and the vehicles and equipment went to G Patrol. The men were absorbed into R and T Patrols to bring them up to strength, or returned to their original units to fight in Greece.

In conjunction with the Free French of Chad Province, the LRDG set out on a series of raids on the Italian garrisons of the Fezzan, in south west Libya, a region of sandy and stony deserts, long wadis and fertile oases. The main objective was Murzuk, the capital of the Fezzan which was 2,150 kilometres from the Group's base in Cairo and 560 kilometres from the nearest French post in the Tibesti Mountains. On 26 December 1940, Major P. A. Clayton left Cairo with 26 vehicles carrying 76 men of T and G Patrols and crossed the Egyptian and Kalansho Sand Seas into unknown country to the north-west of Kufra. Though Clayton was the leader, he was also T Patrol's commander, with Lieutenant L. B. Ballantyne as his 2IC. The Guards were led by Captain M. D. Crichton-Stuart. They were also accompanied by Sheikh Abd el Galil,

January 15, 1941

NEW ZEALAND SOLDIERS DECORATED

Lieutenant J. H. Sutherland, of Dunedin, 2nd Cavalry Regiment, N.Z.E.F., Middle East, who has been awarded the Military Cross.

Trooper L. A. Willcox, of New Plymouth, 2nd Cavalry Regiment, who has been awarded the Military Medal.

the leader of the Libyan resistance movement who acted as an interpreter and guide.

To keep their intentions secret, they avoided the routes that led to wells and oases. Clayton left the patrols at a rendezvous about 240 kilometres to the north and took four trucks to Kayugi, in the foothills of the Tibesti Mountains, to collect Lieutenant-Colonel J. C. d'Ornano the flamboyant commander of the Free French Forces in Chad. He was accompanied by Captain Massu and Lieutenant Egenspiler, two sergeants and five native troops. Meanwhile, Lieutenant Kennedy Shaw took three trucks of T Patrol to explore a pass through the Eghei Mountains on the route to Kufra, after which he rejoined the main column.

A New Zealand Weekly News *cutting, mentioning the winners of the first Military Cross and Military Medal in the 2 NZEF. January 1941.*

On 11 January 1941, the now combined force reached the road running southwards form Sebha to Murzuk, which they mined and picketed. At 1300 hours after stopping for lunch, Major Clayton led the LRDG in his Ford 15cwt, T1, Te Rangi towards the fort at Murzuk. Along the way a group of Libyans mistaking them for Italians gave the Fascist salute. A postman, overtaken while cycling to the fort, was forced into the leading truck to supply information and act as a guide. His bicycle was also uplifted and hooked on to the back of Corporal F. R.Beech's truck.

The garrison, some of whom were outside the gates of the fort, was taken completely by surprise as they were machine-gunned from the trucks. Clayton led Lieutenants L. B. Ballantyne and W. B. Kennedy Shaw, along with a troop of T Patrol to the airfield, while the remainder of the force deployed to engage the fort with the Guards' Bofors gun, two two-inch mortars, machine-guns and small arms. The Italians soon recovered from their surprise and offered stubborn resistance, returning heavy fire. Sergeant C. D. Hewson in the truck T3, Te Hai, was shot through the heart when he stood to clear his jammed machine-gun. Trooper G. C. Garven who was beside him, moved the body to shelter and then took over the gun. Four others were wounded, including Corporal L.H. Browne, T Patrol's navigator, who despite being hit in the foot remained at his post during this critical time and kept his Lewis gun in action.

The fort was now successfully contained, and a shot fired by Trooper I. H. McInnes's two inch mortar hit a petrol drum that set the tower ablaze destroying the flagstaff complete with its flag. During the attack a staff car drove up to the gate carrying the garrison commander accompanied by his wife and two children. The vehicle was hit by machine-gun and Bofors fire and the occupants killed. It was not till later that the men discovered who was in the car, which saddened them, though it was considered a foolish thing for the commander to approach the fort while it was still under fire.

Meanwhile, at the airfield, Ballantyne's troop of six trucks including the Bofors gun, opened fire on the men running to the pillboxes and gun pits. Clayton, who was accompanied by Colonel d'Ornano, drove off to encircle the hangar, but as he turned the corner they encountered a machine-gun post at close range. Unluckily their Vickers gun manned by Lance Corporal W. R. Adams had jammed, and before they could reverse d'Ornano was fatally wounded in the throat. An Italian air force sergeant who had been forced to replace the postman as a guide was also killed. The vehicle had received a number of hits, including a bullet just below Clayton's seat and one through the theodolite which was strapped on the running board.

Ballantyne's troop continued to fire on the hangar until its defenders surrendered with 25 prisoners being taken, most of whom were air force personnel. The hangar, which contained three Ghibli bombers, bombs, parachutes, a radio transmitter and other stores, was soaked in petrol and set alight but not before a quantity of rifles and thousands of rounds of .303 ammunition packed in Lewis gun pans were recovered. These weapons were used by the air gunners in the Ghiblis.

Although the airfield had been captured, the garrison in the fort still held out. Nevertheless, the purpose of the raid had been achieved in the destruction of the airfield, so after two hours of fighting Clayton withdrew his patrols. It was estimated that 10 of the enemy had been killed and 15 wounded, while the attackers suffered two killed and five wounded. One of these, the Frenchman, Captain Massu, was hit in the leg where a bullet had passed through his calf muscle. He simply cauterised it with a cigarette end and carried on as if nothing had happened. Troopers V. C. Spain and T. B. McNeil also received slight wounds. Guardsman G. Wilson, with a serious leg wound, had to suffer being transported 1,000 kilometres across country to Zouar before being airlifted out to Cairo. Of the 25 prisoners taken, all except a senior air force officer and the postman were released due to a lack of transport space and rations.

Wrapped in their blankets, Hewson and d'Ornano were buried on the roadside near the town while Major Clayton read the funeral service. Captain Massu drew a picture in his notebook of the single cross made from the wood of a petrol case that marked the shared grave. Someone tacked a brass New Zealand "Onward" badge to the cross, and the words "Mort pour la France" were inscribed below a sketched Free French Cross of Lorraine. After the war the Italians reburied the men in their own cemetery; Massu was there and he honoured Hewson by cutting the rank badges off his sleeve and placing them on the New Zealander's remains.

As the patrols left Murzuk they were concealed by a duststorm that blew down from the north and the enemy made no attempt at pursuit. The next day the force captured two

Carabinieri on camels, who had come from the small town of Traghen, 50 kilometres east of Murzuk. The town was surrounded and an Italian prisoner was sent in to demand the fort's surrender. After a 15 minute wait, Gunner E. Sanders of T Patrol was preparing his Bofors to fire on the post when out of the western gates appeared a strange procession. It was the town headman and elders, leading 50 natives carrying banners and beating drums, followed by two disconcerted looking Carabinieri. They were surrendering the town in the traditional Fezzan manner. The Italians were made prisoners and the fort's munitions destroyed.

The patrols moved on to two other police forts at Umm el Araneb and Gatrun. The first had been warned by radio of the LRDG movements so the garrison was prepared. On arrival the patrols were met by machine-gun fire, and withdrew with some difficulty over the soft sand to a rise some distance from the enemy. It was considered unwise to assault a stone

Below: 5 January 1941, Fezzan campaign. The LRDG meeting with the Free French at Kayugi, in the foothills of the Tibesti mountains.
Left to right: Lieutenant Egenspiler, Lieutenant-Colonel d'Ornano (later killed in action), Major P. A. Clayton, and Captain Massu.
Photo: Shepherd collection.

T Patrol instructing the French in the use of the .303 Vickers machine-gun.
Photo: Shepherd collection.

A rare occasion where the LRDG actually looked liked regular soldiers. Fezzan campaign. Photo: Shepherd collection.

Captain F. B. Edmundson, LRDG medical officer, sitting in the Ford 15cwt "HQ3". He was attached to the Guards' column. Sitting beside him is Sheikh Abd el Galil, the leader of the Libyan Senussi resistance movement against the Italians. Travelling with the doctor, he was taken on the Fezzan operations for propaganda purposes and was well received by the locals. Photo: Shepherd collection.

Dressed against the cold, T Patrol, Fezzan campaign. From left: Signaller A. Pressick, RCS, Trooper E. W. R. Kitney, Corporal L. H. "Tony" Browne, navigator, and Lieutenant L. B. Ballantyne. Photo: Shepherd collection.

fort in unarmoured vehicles, and it was not worth risking lives with little to be gained. They fired a few Bofors rounds and continued south.

The LRDG cautiously approached Gatrun oasis until they were within sight of its fort. Then they made a dash, only to discover it was an empty ruin. From there the patrol moved up a rise on to a landing ground where they met four Arabs who told them that the attack on Murzuk had been reported, and that there were about thirty soldiers in Gatrun. Clayton told the Arabs to ask the garrison to surrender, but when the inhabitants began to leave the village it was realised that the enemy was prepared to stay and fight. The patrols opened fire with all their weapons and the Italians replied with machine-guns. At dusk after some damage was done to the village walls and a machine-gun silenced, the attack was broken off. A plane circled over the force until it was dark and dropped bombs randomly over the scattered trucks, but none hit their target.

On 14 January Clayton ended his operations in the Fezzan and led his patrols southward to Tummo, over rough and broken country by a route which had been considered impassable to vehicles. After a day's halt with the Free French at Tummo, they drove without incident through some of the Vichy territory in the Niger Province. On January 19 the column reached the forward Free French post of Zouar, on the south-west slopes of the Tibesti Mountains in Chad. There they rested for several days.

Bagnold had received orders for the LRDG to co-operate with the Free French Forces in Chad, in an attack on the Italian held town of Kufra. Led by Colonel Leclerc, who had replaced d'Ornano, Clayton's patrols were put temporarily under French command. They left Zouar on 21 January , and travelled over some very difficult country to Faya, on to Ounianga, then Sarra, where G Patrol stayed in reserve while Clayton took T Patrol on to Bishara. They were to act as an advance party for a Free French

column of 100 vehicles, and to reconnoitre to Uweinat.

On 31 January when T Patrol was at Bishara, an Italian plane flew overhead without attacking them. The trucks dispersed and took cover among rocks in a small wadi at Gebel Sherif. There they were camouflaged and the men prepared to have lunch. The aircraft returned and circled over the wadi to which it directed a patrol of the Auto-Saharan Company, the enemy equivalent of the LRDG. The Italians attacked from the rear, entering the wadi from the southern end. The force consisted of 44 men in two armoured vehicles, four SPA trucks with 20mm Breda guns, and a lorry carrying a 65mm gun. They opened deadly, accurate fire from about 200 metres, destroying three out of T Patrol's 11 trucks, and killing Corporal F. R. Beech who was manning his .303 Vickers machine-gun. Two Italian prisoners were also killed, one of whom was the postman, Signor Colicchia, captured at Murzuk. At least three of the attacking party were killed and two wounded.

From the back of his truck Corporal Rex Beech held the attackers at bay until he was hit by an explosive bullet. His steady action pinned down and delayed the enemy long enough to enable most of the patrol to get away. Buster Gibb recalls Bruce Ballantyne, second-in-command, telling him that if it wasn't for Beech's brave stand, the patrol may not have got away at all.

Major P. A. Clayton's Ford 15cwt pilot car Te Rangi bogged in soft sand. Corporal L. Roderick, dressed for the bitter cold, stands in front. This vehicle and its crew were later captured by the Italians.
Photo: Shepherd collection.

Trooper I. H. McInnes, T Patrol, who had won the MM for his effective mortar shooting against the Italian fort at Murzuk, seen here practising with his two inch mortar. Photo: Shepherd collection.

The Italians had only covered one entrance to the wadi, so Clayton took the eight remaining trucks out the other, circled round and prepared to counter-attack. Meanwhile, the machine-guns on Trooper R. J. Moore's truck, one of those hit, provided a short delaying action to help the others to escape. But Moore and his crew soon had to abandon their burning vehicle as the ammunition began to explode. They hid amongst the boulders at the side of the wadi. A truck went back to pick up the other stranded crews who were rescued while still under fire.

Below: The Italian airforce hanger on fire after the raid on Murzuk. January 1941. Photo: Shepherd collection.

The enemy aircraft had now increased to three, and began low-level bomb and strafing attacks. Clayton's car, Te Rangi, received hits that punctured two tyres, the radiator and the fuel tank. The men changed the tyres and refilled the radiator, but ran out of petrol. Luckily for Clayton a bullet had deflected off his steel helmet, but he had been hit in the arm. With the approach of Italian ground forces it was decided that further resistance was useless, so Clayton and his crew surrendered. Lance-Corporals W. R. "Wink" Adams, and L. "Clarrie" Roderick became the first soldiers from 2 NZEF to be captured in WWII. Now led by Ballantyne the other seven trucks dispersed to a pre-arranged rendezvous farther south, then went on to rejoin G Patrol and the French.

Trooper Moore and his crew of three and one Italian prisoner were presumed to have been killed and captured. However, when their truck Te Aroha caught fire and ammunition began to explode they sought shelter among the rocks. Encouraged by Moore, who was wounded in the foot, they decided not to give themselves up, but to follow the patrol southwards in the hope that they might be found. Despite one of the crew, Guardsman J. Easton, being wounded with a piece of metal lodged in the back of his throat, the group set out on an epic 336 kilometre trek, the events of which are recorded in the chapter on "Air Attack" (see page 99).

The patrols rejoined Colonel Leclerc on 1 February, where it was decided that because the Italians at Kufra were now alerted, and in light of T Patrol's losses, to release the LRDG from further service with the Free French, although one New Zealand truck crew remained attached, to help with navigation. Ballantyne agreed to leave his vehicle Manuka, manned by his navigator Lance-Corporal F. Kendall accompanied by Trooper W. D. Burnnand as gunner, along with Driver H. Clarke of the Royal Army Service Corps behind the wheel. Later these men guided the French through the desert for their successful attack on Kufra.

On 4 February the two patrols left for Cairo by way of Uweinat and Kharga and arrived five days later. Since setting out in December 1940, they had covered about 7,200 kilometres with the loss of four trucks by enemy action and two by mechanical failure. One vehicle with a broken rear axle had been towed for seven days from Tummo to Faya, travelling 1,293 kilometres over all types of terrain before it could be repaired. The casualties included three dead, several wounded and three captured, one being the expedition leader Major Clayton, who was subsequently awarded the Distinguished Service Order (DSO). The services of three New Zealanders were also recognised: Corporal Browne who showed coolness and gallantry at Gebel Sherif, as well as at Murzuk, received the Distinguished Conduct Medal (DCM), while Trooper Moore's great trek had also earned him the DCM. Trooper McInnes was awarded the MM for his effective mortar-shooting. These early offensive actions prepared the ground for the many future operations the Group

was to undertake over the next two years. (See Appendix VIII for the breakdown of an LRDG patrol at the time of the Fezzan campaign.)

On 1 March 1941, Kufra fell after an attack by Colonel Leclerc's combined

The damaged hanger at Kufra. A wrecked Caprioni Ca 309 Ghibli light bomber rests in the foreground.
Photo: Fred Kendall.

Some of the Italian prisoners captured in the Fezzan raids.
Photo: Shepherd collection.

Italian prisoners being interrogated by Major Clayton after the Murzuk raid.
Photo: Shepherd collection.

The shared grave of Lieutenant-Colonel d'Ornano and Sergeant Cyril Hewson. The cross was made from the wood of a petrol case, and marked with the Free French Cross of Lorraine and a New Zealand "Onward" badge. Both were killed in the attack on Murzuk, 11 January 1941. Photo: Shepherd collection.

A halt in the column after the Murzuk raid, as Major Clayton (tall man, alongside truck) confers with the French. The bicycle hooked on the back of Corporal Beech's truck, Tirau, was uplifted from the Murzuk postman. Later, at Gebel Sherif, Beech was killed and the truck and bicycle destroyed. Photo: Peter Garland.

force of Free French and Chad native troops. Though the Italians were strong enough to hold out for weeks, they surrendered after a 10 day siege. This ended a decade of Fascist rule over the town. For the next 14 months Kufra became an ideal location as a base for LRDG patrols.

While T and G Patrols were co-operating with the French, R Patrol under Captain Steele assisted a force which included the 6th Australian Divisional Cavalry Regiment in the siege of Giarabub, an Italian occupied town about 260 kilometres south of Bardia. To prevent any supplies reaching the garrison and the enemy from escaping, the Australians watched the northern approaches to the town while the New Zealanders observed the tracks to the west. For

two months R Patrol was engaged in this very tedious task, before it was eventually relieved by T Patrol on 2 March.

In their time supporting the Australians, Alf Saunders of R Patrol recalled one particular highlight. While his patrol was carrying out a reconnaissance of the Giarabub Oasis, they captured an Italian supply convoy in which among other supplies they found several large kegs of cognac. Since they had to report their intelligence-gathering to the Australian Brigade HQ, they decided to deliver a couple of kegs as a gift to cheer up the troops. The cognac was presented and immediately con-sumed by the officers and men, even using hats and helmets as drinking vessels. In a very short time they were "blotto". At this point, the "Kiwis" quietly withdrew. The Australians had planned an attack the next day, but due to the troops not being in top condition it was postponed till the following day.

The Italians, who were supplied by aircraft, continued to withstand the siege until attacked on 22 March 1941. After a fierce assault during a sandstorm the Australians finally took the town. While this was taking place Dick Lewis was with T Patrol watching the road. He wrote in his diary:

March 20: Sitting around just watching the track out of Giarabub. The wind is getting up and it looks like another sandstorm. At mid-night the artillery opened up and is still pounding away every few minutes, the gale is blowing full blast with sand swirling every-where.

March 22: Sitting on our backsides in the driving sand, knowing nothing of what's going on. The first news we got was from Radio Rome on the civilian set, saying that a heavy artillery and infantry attack on Giarabub had been successfully repulsed.

Left: The inhabitants of the town of Traghen surrender to the LRDG in the traditional Fezzan manner, with flags flying and drums playing. Photo: Shepherd collection.

Left: The abandoned fort at Gatrun.
Photo: Shepherd collection.

Above: One of the Carabinieri captured at Traghen stands beside Major Clayton's Ford 15cwt. The Italian was later killed in the crossfire in the ambush at Gebel Sherif. Photo: Shepherd collection.

Below, left to right: Trooper Cyril Eyre, navigator, Corporal Rex Beech, killed at Gebel Sherif, 31 January 1941, and Sergeant A. D. "Buster" Gibb. Mounted on the Chevrolet WB is a .303 Lewis gun, covered to prevent sand jamming the mechanism. Photo: Buster Gibb.

The aftermath of an attack by the Italian Auto-Saharan Company, 31 January 1941 at Gebel Sherif. In the foreground of the top photograph is Tirau, the Chevrolet in which Corporal Rex Beech was killed while delaying the enemy with his Vickers machine-gun. Behind that is Te Aroha, Trooper Ron Moore's truck. It was from this point that he and his crew set out on their great trek. The lower picture shows T Patrol truck Te Paki, one of the three destroyed in the ambush at Gebel Sherif. In front of the vehicle lays an Italian prisoner killed in the crossfire. Photos: Fred Kendall.

At 3pm, our time, we heard from the BBC in London, that Giarabub fell yesterday. That's how we heard, eight kilometres from the scene of operations. Looks as though they just wanted us out of the way while they did the job.

We heard later that the Aussies went in at dawn yesterday, and had the situation under control by 9am. Which wasn't bad in a sandstorm that made machine-guns jam, and

visibility bad. They had about 30 killed and a 100 wounded; a lot of casualties from walking into their own barrage.

When Major Clayton was captured at Gebel Sherif he did not have time to destroy his papers. Therefore all the LRDG codes and cyphers were compromised and had to be changed. Captain Crichton-Stuart of the Guards patrol established a temporary code based on the regimental numbers of various Guardsmen. This remained in place till the patrols returned to Cairo and new codes were issued.

After the impact of the Fezzan campaign, GHQ were no longer in a position to regard the LRDG as a secret unit, so all its activities and deeds were allowed to be published. Their recent exploits were told in various newspapers and featured in magazines such as the *NZ Weekly News, Freelance* and *The Parade*. They were also interviewed for radio programmes. Official photographers were keen to capture these "desert pirates" on film. As Dick Lewis explained in his diary:

March 26, 1941, a few kilometres out of Cairo an official photographer came out and took photos of the trucks on nearby sandhills,

Lance-Corporal L. "Clarrie" Roderick and Trooper Ray Gorringe, December 1940. Note the fighting knife strapped to Roderick's leg. Before the war he was a lightweight Australasian professional boxer. He and Lance-Corporal W. R. "Wink" Adams, who along with Major P. A. Clayton, were forced to surrender at Gebel Sherif when their vehicle was put out of action. Roderick and Adams were the first two soldiers of the 2 NZEF to be captured in the war. Photo: Ray Gorringe.

A captured Italian convoy escort vehicle of the Saharan Tractor Company. The machine-gun in the back is obstructed by a large cask of brandy. Photo: Jim Sutherland.

which could have been a couple of hundred miles out in the desert. They say the camera can't lie, but this one certainly did.

In November 1941, General Sir Claude Auchinleck, C in C Middle East, inspected the New Zealand patrols at the Citadel in Cairo. Stopping and speaking to every man in turn, the General made personal inquiries as to their length of service with the unit, and how they were liking the work. He was particularly interested in Trooper Moore's exploit and asked several questions regarding it. Auchlinleck made a speech, which after expressing his pleasure at the bearing of the men, he went on to say:

I have heard a lot about you, and I am sure I shall hear a lot more. I know the value of the work you are doing. In fact, we could not get on without you. I know that your work has been lonely and dangerous. At the same time, it is on the whole a man's job.

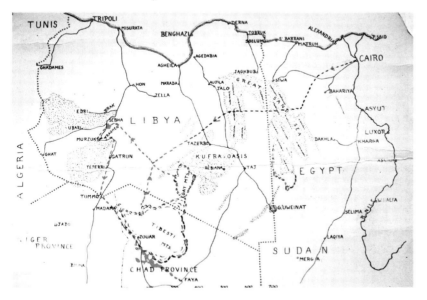

The map that accompanied the operational report on the Fezzan campaign, with the dashed line marking the route taken by the patrols. January 1941. Source: John Daymond.

Above: Part of a captured supply convoy of the Italian Saharan Tractor Company. American D4 tractors hauled three fully loaded ten ton trailers each heavily loaded with a multitude of supplies. After all the useful stores were taken, the balance was destroyed. Photo: Buster Gibb.

Sandstorm at Giarabub, March 1941. R and T Patrols suffered these uncomfortable conditions as they kept a watch on the roads leading in and out of the Italian-held town. The outpost eventually capitulated after a siege by Australian troops. Photo: Shepherd collection.

After the Fezzan campaign the activities of the LRDG were made public. An official photographer took this picture of T Patrol just outside Cairo, March 1941. The trucks are Chevrolet WB 30cwts, apart from the Ford 15cwt commander's car in the middle distance. Patrol members, back row, left to right: F. W. Jopling, R. T. Porter, R. A. Simpson, W. D. S. Forbes, J. P. L. Macassey, L. A. McIver, V. J. Heard, E. C. Stutterd, A. J. Job, R. W. N. Lewis, I. G. McCulloch, T. E. Ritchie, G. T. Smith. Front three, left to right: M. H. Craw, L. Payne, O. W. Wright. Photo: Imperial War Museum.

There will be plenty more ahead. I am sure that we can rely on you to bring back the kind of news we want, as you have done in the past. This winter the people that are behind now will be able to get on a bit too; and as they move, you will be going ahead of them. I want to thank you for what you have done, and I know you will do just as well in the future.

A newspaper article dated 10 December 1941, sourced from the NZEF Official News Service which carried General Sir Claude Auchinleck's speech, also described the parade:

It was early on an autumn morning and the long row of stockily-built trucks with the men standing smartly at post made an impressive sight. Some of them were wearing their desert headgear and sandals, which gave them a wild, Arab appearance.

Their trucks too, were ready for the desert road at a moment's notice.

Well armed against attack from the air or from the land, they had an air about them of mobile security. Veteran vehicles of rolling wastelands, they had proved their suitability, as had those who rode in them, for the tough job they had to do.

Later, the unit's romantic concept also attracted the attention of Captain Peter McIntyre, the official NZ war artist. He spent three weeks with the LRDG, enjoying the beauty, colours and formations of the inner desert. During which time he painted or sketched many images of personalities, patrol life and desert landscapes.

Captain Peter McIntyre, the official NZ war artist (left), has lunch with Lieutenant J. R. Talbot, R Patrol (centre), and Captain Chevalier. Photo: Richard Williams.

General Auchinleck with Captain Ballantyne, LRDG, talks to Corporal Ron Moore, DCM, next to him is Trooper Alan Nutt. Citadel parade, November 1941. Photo: Tom Ritchie.

NAVIGATION

The LRDG operated in the Libyan Desert, which covers western Egypt, north-western Sudan, and practically the whole of Libya. It stretches 1,600 kilometres southwards from the Mediterranean Sea and more that 1,600 kilometres westwards from the Nile Valley to the hills of Tunisia, an area roughly the size of India. It features some large rock formations, plains broken by deep wadis, and scattered settlements around oases. Much of the inland desert was unmapped, featureless terrain, such as vast seas of sand which are ribbed with long parallel dunes that followed in succession like waves, often over 100 metres high. For example, the Great Sand Sea stretches nearly 1,300 kilometres of continuous and seemingly impassable yellow rolling dunes, with an average width of about 240 kilometres.

The absence of recognisable landmarks made it necessary for the patrols to navigate as if at sea: by compass, sun and the stars. The navigators were trained by Lieutenant W. B. Kennedy Shaw and Lance-Corporal C. H. B. Croucher (later Captain), a British born New Zealander who had a Mate's ticket in the Merchant Marine. Every truck was equipped with either a sun, aero, or magnetic compass, and all carried maps of their transit and operating areas so they could get home independently if necessary.

The sun compass consisted of a horizontal circle, divided into 360 degrees, with a central needle which cast a shadow across the graduations. By rotating the circle every 30 minutes throughout the day to correspond with the sun's movement across the sky, the shadow was made to indicate the true bearing on which the car was travelling. These devices were mounted above the dashboard, and were usually fitted to two vehicles in each half patrol, as well as to the patrol commander's car. Every man was expected to know how to use the device, note bearings and distances, plot the course with protractor and scale, and know the speedometer correction for his vehicle. To ensure that in an emergency they could find their way alone, those not fitted with sun compasses, carried magnetic or aero compasses. The magnetic compass was inaccurate when used within a vehicle, so it had to be employed some distance away.

Typical desert terrain over which the LRDG had to learn to navigate. Four trucks are camped in the shadow of a wadi. Photo: Jim Sutherland.

Lance-Corporal C. H. B. Croucher (left) and Lieutenant J. H. "Sahara" Sutherland, 1940. Croucher, being ex-Merchant Marine, helped to train the LRP navigators. He went on the first LRP trip, and was later commissioned and became a patrol commander. By the end of the war he was the LRDG Adjutant and Intelligence Officer. Sutherland was second-in-command W Patrol, and at Ain Dua in the Uweinat he won the first Military Cross awarded to 2 NZEF. Photo: Alf Saunders.

In the height of summer the sun compass could be ineffective for several hours around midday, where the sun was directly above and would not cast a shadow. The patrol would usually stop and rest under the shade of their trucks, while the navigator would obtain a bearing from his prismatic compass using it away from the vehicle, at the same time being careful not to carry any steel objects like knives and pistols.

Sometimes the sun compass was used at night when the moon was up and not to high in the sky. In that case the sun compass ring was set to the azimuth of the moon as measured directly with a prismatic compass, instead of the azimuth of the sun as taken from the navigation tables.

Navigation in the desert had two parts: a "dead reckoning" course by sun compass and speedometer, and an "astro-fix" by observations of the stars with a theodolite to check the accuracy of the "D.R." position. In dead reckoning, a line from the point of departure to the objective was ruled on the map. The patrol followed the general direction of that line, but deviated from time to time as required by the terrain and other considerations. The navigator recorded the times, sun compass bearings and the distance travelled on each bearing by speedometer reading, and plotted the data on the map at each halt. The final point on the map arrived at by that method was the "dead reckoning position".

With good dead reckoning navigation, the error at the end of a day's run of 200 kilometres should not have been greater than 4 kilometres. The principal source of error was the variability of the distance reading according to load, speed and "going".

Learning to operate the sun compass. Invented by Major Bagnold, it helped to solve the problem of desert navigation. Photo: Shepherd collection.

More accuracy was needed when finding or establishing dumps and making rendezvous among high dune regions. In these cases the position may have had to been confirmed either by the sun, or by the stars at night.

Each patrol had a senior navigator who plotted the course and compared it with a second check navigator who travelled in a different vehicle. As soon as it was dark the navigator, with a star atlas by his side, set up his theodolite and "shot" the stars. First an assistant noted the sixth "pip" of the Greenwich time signal with his stop-watch, then with the aid of the timekeeper who noted the exact second, detailed readings of certain stars were recorded, after which some time was spent trying to convert the readings to longitude and latitude to establish a position. This was done with reference to the astronomical navigation tables, and it was often a struggle trying to work out the complicated arithmetic in the cold and dark. The result was then reported to the patrol commander.

Position finding involved a knowledge of Greenwich Mean Time to within an error of half a second. The senior wireless operator with each patrol assisted the navigators by being responsible for the care of the chronometers, and for keeping a log of their errors from daily wireless time signals. The navigator usually travelled in the wireless truck behind the commander's vehicle.

Frank White of T and R Patrols

recounted some of his navigation experiences:

After dark you could drive by navigating by the stars. You used to set up your theodolite and shoot yourself in. One night, a fellow "shot" himself in the middle of the Indian Ocean! What you did, was to set it on a certain star that you knew. There was a fellow on the wireless which was tuned into Greenwich Mean Time and you'd say, "Coming up, coming up, up". Directly you said "Up!" he had to have the time. Then you took another star and did exactly the same thing. When you had all the times and everything, the tables indicated where the two lines crossed and what your position was.

The Italians' maps were shocking. Six to eight miles out at least, that sort of thing. So we navigated by sun compass. We had Air Force Navigation Tables to work from for each month. The needle mounted on the compass showed the shadow, and the tables told you how much to turn the circle round. You could drive in a straight line or so, for a hundred miles all day, by just following the shadow. It was really quite simple.

Accurate navigation was essential for successfully completing a mission and desert survival. Bagnold stressed this in his LRDG Training Notes written in January 1941:

SAFETY RULES
The danger of getting separated from the rest of the party is real. The sudden realisation that one is alone and does not know how to rejoin the party causes such a shock that one is apt to lose one's head—to start moving in some random direction and thereby reduce the chances of being found to a minimum.

The following rules must never be broken:
(a) When on the move every member of a party must know

(e) In the event of a party suspecting that they don't know their position on the map, or that their navigation has gone wrong they will halt at once and will on no account move again until the situation has been thought out quietly and deliberately. The error in position or navigation will nearly always be spotted, the necessary correction can then be made and the party can proceed. If however the sense of being lost still remains, the party must remain where they are until found.

(f) If for any reason a truck becomes stranded the crew must remain within sight of it.

(g) Every truck must have on board three days emergency rations including water.

The LRDG became the Middle East experts in navigation. Bagnold wrote two training manuals on the subject, and Group members sometimes conducted courses on navigation for officers and men from units of the Eighth Army. The skill of this work was recognised in 1942, when the War Office approved a new army trade, Land Navigator, earning an extra pay of a shilling a day. However, it appeared that this may not have applied to the New Zealand navigators with the LRDG, as Trooper Frank Jopling of T Patrol explained in his diary:

9 April 1942: About a week ago, it came out in routine orders that in future all navigators are to receive a shilling a day extra pay. So Bing Morris went to see the New Zealand Administration Office and they told him that the New Zealand Government wouldn't pay extra pay for navigators. So the position at present is that all Tommy navigators are getting an extra shilling a day, while we don't get any extra pay, which seems to be a very unsatisfactory state of affairs to me.

T Patrol members, Troopers H. D. "Paddy" Mackay (left) and Jack Davis, plot their position with the aid of a theodolite.
Photo: Tom Ritchie.

where the next rendezvous is to be and must have a map and compass handy to get him there independently of the others.

(b) No vehicle must operate by itself unless under special orders from the patrol leader.

(c) No man must ever be left alone by himself without transport, out of sight of an obvious landmark whither he knows he can go if he wants help.

(d) No man must ever be parted from his waterbottle.

RECONNAISSANCE AND SURVEY

The primary role of the LRDG was reconnaissance and intelligence gathering while operating behind enemy lines. Offensive actions were secondary to this purpose unless specifically ordered, or opportunistic without compromising their intelligence gathering ability. Survey and pathfinding were to establish the "going" (the nature of the terrain), and to improve the mapping of areas likely to become the scene of future main force operations.

On 7 August 1940, Captain P. A. Clayton led the first Long Range Patrol incursion into Libya. He was to reconnoitre the Jalo–Kufra track by which the Italians took supplies from Benghazi to their garrisons at Kufra and Uweinat. With no radio, Clayton set out in two Chevrolet WB 30cwt trucks, loaded with stores and mounting Lewis guns for self-defence. He took with him an Arab servant and six New Zealanders whom he generally described as "Enormous and terrifyingly fit". They were: Lance-Corporal C. H. B. Croucher, who assisted Clayton with the navigation; Lance-Corporal W. J. Hamilton and Private J. Emslie, gunners; Privates R. A. Tinker and R. O. Spotswood, drivers; and Private M. W. Curtis, Clayton's driver/ mechanic. Abu Fudail was Clayton's servant who, before the war, had been found near death on the Kufra–Sudan track, a victim of Italian aggression against the Senussi.

Merv Curtis related how he came to be on the first LRP mission. He was an Ordnance Corps Fitter/Mechanic attached to the 27th Machine Gun Battalion, and had recently finished a course with the Royal Army Ordnance Corps at Abbassia when he received a visit at Maadi Camp by a NZ Ordnance officer accompanied by a British officer. Merv was told that they were looking for a mechanic for a special project and he had been recommended by NZ Ordnance. *"Would you volunteer Curtis?"* they said, *"Course you would! Get your gear and we will take you with us."*

He became Clayton's driver/ mechanic and was ordered to prepare the vehicles and spares for a journey that could involve several thousand kilometres, though no mention of destination was made. Security was so tight that for a while Merv thought he was going to Ethiopia. To ensure the incursion into Libya was not detected by the enemy, measures were taken such as using Italian newspapers as toilet paper, and by entering misleading dates in the men's paybooks.

The two trucks set out towards Alexandria, then left the road near El Alamein and headed south into the Qattara Depression. They arrived at Siwa on 9 August, and spent the day with the Egyptian Frontiers Administration. The next day, so as to enable a forward dump to be established for Clayton's patrol, the EFA provided six light trucks to carry petrol, manned by Sudanese crews under an Egyptian officer. They went south through the Egyptian Sand Sea and dumped the fuel at Two Hills, then returned to Siwa.

From the Big Cairn (erected by Clayton in 1932), a point near the Libyan frontier, the LRP struck out westwards into unexplored territory. A level gravel plain was found that stretched for about 160 kilometres to the west of the Egyptian Sand Sea, which the Italians had not shown on their maps and Clayton was unaware of.

One of the two Chevrolet WB 30cwt trucks used in the first LRP incursion into Libya, August 1940. This nine day trip was successfully completed without a radio, and no sand mats or sand trays to ease them over the soft terrain.
Photo: Merv Curtis.

Near the western end ran the Jalo–Kufra track, which was marked every kilometre by tall iron posts. The men spent three days there enduring the hottest weather of 1940, keeping a 24-hour watch for traffic, with nothing being seen. Unknown to Clayton at the time the Italians had moved the track further west, as the surface of the original route was so badly cut up.

After the watch was completed they recrossed the Sand Sea and headed south to Uweinat, a 2,000 metre mountain on the Egyptian–Libyan–Sudan borders, where they briefly stayed to examine some ancient rock paintings. As their journey continued they had made a number of interesting observations, such as when the patrol crossed the wheel tracks made by Bagnold's expedition in 1938, and the sighting of bones, both human and animal left by the Senussi tribes in their flight from the Italians. Also not far from their watch the men discovered "Fright Rock", which was an isolated large flat-topped rock, that in the heat haze could look like a truck, thus causing a fright to the patrol when sighted. This large outcrop provided welcome shade to enjoy lunch by in the middle of the day. Throughout the trip the midday heat often taxed the vehicle engines, as the water boiled and the petrol vaporised in the system. It also caused the men to seek shelter under their transport for at least four hours a day, resting, or having long discussions.

On 16 August they had returned to Siwa, and logged their position to GHQ by telegram. By the 19th, they were back in Cairo after a 13 day, 2,574 kilometre journey, which included a three day watch. Though they had not observed the enemy their mission was still a success, as Clayton had charted unmapped territory and discovered the gravel plain route protected in the north by the horseshoe formation of the Egyptian and Kalansho Sand Seas. This was to become an established path for future LRDG operations. The significance of the first LRP incursion into Libya was duly recognized by GHQ, with General Wavell giving Bagnold his fullest support. To mark the event, Anthony Eden, the British Foreign Secretary, who visited Egypt in September, presented a special LRP badge to all those who went on the first trip.

The Italians, after three months of hesitation, had decided to press across the Egyptian frontier to Sidi Barrani. It was assumed that the enemy might also be on the move in the inner desert, so a reconnaissance of all the Italian supply lines leading to Kufra had to be undertaken. On 5 September, 1940 the Long Range Patrol set out from Cairo on their first major task. Bagnold led a column of 14 vehicles, which comprised of detachments of T, W and R Patrols. He was accompanied by a small HQ party, including Lieutenant Kennedy Shaw and Flying Officer Farr of the RAF, to survey for possible landing grounds.

They drove across the Egyptian Sand Sea from Ain Dalla to Big Cairn, where the dune ranges ran for hundreds of kilometres and often rose 150 metres from trough to crest. The best routes were through the gaps in the dunes and on the firmer "going" in the valleys. However, the trucks sometimes got stuck and much time was spent in the heat trying to extract them. At Big Cairn Captain Mitford's W Patrol unloaded extra petrol and water, then returned to Ain Dalla for further supplies. They marked the route permanently with petrol cans and stones collected from Big Cairn. Wind would eventually obliterate the tyre marks, but the stones would remain uncovered and visible on the surface of the smooth sand for up to 200 metres. While W Patrol was ferrying supplies from Ain Dalla, Captain Clayton's T Patrol and Lieutenant Steele's R Patrol moved about 30,000 litres of petrol through the most difficult part of the Sand Sea, south from Siwa to Big Cairn. With forward dumps now in place the three patrols separated: W to reconnoitre to the north of Kufra, where the desert was pinkish in colour and full of amazing rock formations, T to the south, and R Patrol went back to Siwa for another load.

W Patrol crossed the gravel plain where it was possible to travel at 80 to 100 kilometres per hour, then struggled through the Kalansho Sand Sea to the Jalo–Kufra track. During a sandstorm they visited two enemy emergency landing grounds and wrecked fuel tanks, pumps and wind indicators. From the wheel marks on the Jalo–Kufra track they were able to estimate the amount of traffic use, after which the patrol went further west to examine the Taiserbo–Marada track, and then south towards Kufra.

At a landing ground about half way between Taiserbo and Kufra, they encountered two Fiat six-ton lorries belonging to the civilian firm of Trucchi Co. who ran a fortnightly supply convoy to Kufra. A burst of Lewis gun fire brought the trucks to a sudden halt. The LRP's first prisoners consisted of two Italians, six arabs and a goat. Their only weapons were a shotgun and an old Austrian pistol. The booty consisted of various stores, 11,000 litres of fuel, and of more interest, a bag of official mail from Uweinat and Kufra. This proved valuable intelligence, as it gave details of Italian dispositions in the inner desert. Because the captured lorries were almost out of diesel fuel they were hidden in the Gilf Kebir at the southern tip of the Egyptian Sand Sea. Later, Heavy Section fitters were sent out to recover them, but on the way back, due to burnt out clutches and rough going, the Fiats had to be abandoned.

The three patrols then came together at a rendezvous near Uweinat, where amongst the huge granite boulders at the base of the mountain were springs of good water, two of which, Ain Dua and Ain Zwaya, were in Italian territory. At each of them the enemy had located an outpost and landing ground. The distance from Uweinat to the Nile was only 500 kilometres of easy terrain, hence it would make a useful base for the Italians to launch an attack on Wadi Halfa, yet a reconnaissance of the surrounding desert showed that enemy forces had not ventured into the Sudan.

The first Heavy Section party who supplied the LRP's forward supply dumps, September 1940. The job was done with 6 ton Ford Marmon-Herrington trucks as seen in the background. The men are all New Zealanders apart from W. B. Kennedy Shaw, the Intelligence Officer. From left to right: J. Zimmerman, F. D. Rhodes, A. W. Hood, A. F. McLeod, W. B. Kennedy Shaw, E. T. Russell, and J. L. Schaab. Note the rum jar in the foreground, an essential for every desert trip. Photo: Jim Sutherland.

Some of the beautiful desert rock formations encountered by the first patrols. Photo: Jim Sutherland.

In the month of operation over 241,000 truck kilometres were covered without serious mechanical trouble, apart from a torn clutch plate which was replaced by the fitters. One truck had overturned on a dune, but was soon righted having suffered little damage. Forward dumps were now in place, maps were updated, the "going" and possible RAF landing grounds had been noted. In addition, Italian dispositions had been revealed and a number of suitable places for laying ambush were plotted. The lessons learned from this first major reconnaissance had prepared the ground for the many other LRDG operations that followed.

Apart from a garbled radio message, GHQ Middle East had not heard from the patrols for a month, so they had been given up for lost. Consequently, when they did eventually arrive in Cairo it caused much excitement. Unwashed and bearded, the men were nevertheless in good spirits, bringing in prisoners and important information.

The LRP had proved its worth. The story of their successful mission soon spread throughout the clubs and service messes, though after some time became exaggerated, but their reputation had been made. General Wavell sent Bagnold a letter of congratulations.

In October 1940, as part of a mission to gain more information about enemy ground and air patrols between the Ajedabia–Kufra–Uweinat roads and the Egyptian frontier, the LRP had the assistance of the RAF. Attached to the patrols was an obsolete Vickers Valentia transport/bomber aircraft, from No. 216 Squadron, RAF. It was piloted by Flying Officer Farr, who had travelled previously with the LRP searching for landing grounds. His crew consisted of a second pilot, two radio operators, a fitter and a rigger. His passengers included Major E.C. Mitford and the LRP medical officer, Captain F. B. Edmundson, with first-aid supplies.

Crossing the Sand Sea, September 1940. Lieutenant D. G. Steele's Ford 15cwt pilot car sunk to the running boards. Note the R Patrol commander's pennant, the aero compass below the driver's seat and the EY grenade launching rifle next to the pith helmet. Photo: Jim Sutherland.

Arabs working for the Italians, some of the first prisoners captured by the LRP. September 1940. Photo: Jim Sutherland.

Huge boulders at the base of the Uweinat mountain. This area contained a good water supply and an Italian outpost. Photo: Jim Sutherland.

The Valentia was fitted with long range tanks and was refuelled from three dumps previously laid by the LRP for that specific purpose. It carried sufficient food for eight men, plus a reserve supply in case of an emergency. Because of load concerns it was impossible to carry enough water for the whole operation, so it was supplied by the ground patrols when they made contact with the aircraft. The Valentia communicated with the RAF at Ismailia several times each day and at set times with the patrols.

During this mission R and T Patrols mined roads, captured a small fort at Aujila and destroyed unguarded enemy dumps, along with a Savoia-Marchetti S79 aeroplane. With the aid of the Valentia more geographical information was obtained about the recently found Kalansho Sand Sea. In other areas, the "going" was plotted for future mapping and further landing grounds were located. The aircraft flew eight missions that covered a distance of 3,070 kilometres, with a total flying time of nearly 25 hours.

This reconnaissance was to be one of the first long range topographical explorations behind enemy lines, the type of work in which they were to become specialists.

Captain L. B. Ballantyne led one party of T Patrol and Captain W. B. Kennedy Shaw (Intelligence and Topographical Officer) and Lieutenant E. W. Ellingham the other. They left Tazerbo on 20 July for the desert to the south of the Gulf of Sirte.

They crossed the Marada track at a point where 18 months later Captain L. H. (Tony) Browne of R Patrol guided the NZ Division round to outflank Rommel taking El Agheila. The patrol then split in two parties, Ballantyne taking a southern route, while Kennedy Shaw and Ellingham took the northern one. Between them they gathered information that proved very useful to Allies over the next two years. Several weeks later S Patrol made a similar reconnaissance farther without discovery by the enemy.

In 1941 the Group's Survey Section was formed under the command of Captain Ken Lazarus (Royal Engineers), a New Zealand born surveyor who had worked in Rhodesia before the war. The Section's role was to reconnoitre and survey uncharted areas of the Libyan Desert that were likely to assume strategic value. The Italian maps were assumed incorrect until proved otherwise, for even their charts of quite large areas in the coastal belt were found to be inaccurate in longitude. Two or three trucks were used for this work, one being fitted with two sun compasses, one for the driver and one for the use of the surveyor. They divided the desert into different topographical areas and each land type was described and delineated. The position of oases and other man-made or natural features were also fixed.

This task entailed travelling thousands of kilometres behind the lines, for weeks on end, and was done

Top picture, taken in October 1940, shows the Vickers Valentia of 216 Squadron RAF. This obsolete and vulnerable aircraft flew eight missions in conjunction with the LRP for mapping and reconnaissance work. In the lower picture the Vickers Valentia is flying over an LRP truck. A Wyndom aerial has been erected to improve radio communication. Photos: Jim Sutherland.

They were lucky they had not encountered enemy aircraft who would have made short work of such a lumbering target. The patrols returned to Cairo after a successful 15 day, 3,450 kilometre journey.

In July 1941 in anticipation of a British advance into Tripolitania, GHQ required information about the "going" for wheeled and tracked vehicles, sites for landing grounds, and the local supplies of water. Details were needed such as to how fast columns could travel over certain terrain, and whether movement was possible on a wide or narrow front. Mapping also had to be accurate, especially of any impassable obstacles and of landing grounds.

without the surveyors ever being disturbed by the enemy. Valuable charts were produced which proved essential for the Eighth Army's future operational planning. At the base of the maps were printed the words "Surveyed by the LRDG".

In addition to the work of the Survey Section, every commander made their own contribution towards charting. At the end of each mission a full detailed report was submitted to Captain Kennedy Shaw, who would extract the relevant information. He would then pass it on to GHQ in Cairo, who in turn would use this data for the correction of old maps or the making of new ones.

Reconnaissance behind enemy lines always had its dangers. In September 1942 Lieutenant J. R. Talbot's R2 Patrol was watching the northern approaches to Jalo when six Stukas attacked with bombs and machine guns, the trucks returned fire and swerved to avoid the bombs. They dispersed over a flat gravel plain and within an hour had covered 40 kilometres by the time the planes had left. However, they had lost contact with each other. Talbot, being unable to find the rest of his patrol, returned to Kufra, locating two of his trucks on the way.

Eventually all six trucks reached base, but not without incident or casualties. While swerving to avoid a bomb the R2 wireless truck overturned, injuring a British signalman. The vehicle was righted but had to be towed until it could be put in running order the next day. During the air attacks the following New Zealanders received wounds: Sergeant L.A. Willcox MM, Lance-Corporal A.D. Sadgrove and Troopers L.A. Ellis, E.J. Dobson, and M.W. Stewart. Finally, on the way back to Kufra a truck capsized over a sand dune, injuring Private J.E. Gill and Sergeant Willcox who had already suffered wounds.

On another occasion, in December 1942, Captain Tony Browne was leading his R1 Patrol reconnoitring the country beyond Wadi Tamet when his jeep struck a land mine. Browne was injured and a South African survey officer travelling with him was killed. With Second-Lieutenant K. F. McLauchlan now in command the patrol continued its reconnaissance. But later, on the 27 December near the Gheddahia–Bu Ngem track, they were ambushed by two German armoured cars. The wireless truck with its crew of three New Zealanders (Lance-Bombardier C. O. Grimsey, Private K. C. Ineson and Trooper R. D. Hayes) and an Englishman, were captured along with a jeep carrying a South African officer and his driver. The rest of the patrol managed to evade the enemy.

In preparation for the Allied advance into Tunisia the Group was required to reconnoitre the country's southern approaches through which a column, outflanking the German-held Mareth Line, would have to pass. In January and February 1943 the LRDG and Indian Long Range Squadron explored the territory to the south and west of the range of hills extending southwards from Matmata.

As they progressed the patrols signalled HQ daily, reporting the "going", obstacles, cover, water supply and sites for landing grounds. On their return the commanders conferred with Captain Tony Browne (now LRDG Intelligence Officer) at the NZ Division HQ, where a model was made to demonstrate possible lines of advance.

On 12 January 1943 T1 Patrol under Captain N. P. Wilder crossed the frontier and became the first troops of the Eighth Army to enter Tunisia. They found an uncharted pass south through the Matmata Hills, which became known as Wilder's Gap. It was by this route two months later that the NZ Division executed its "left hook" round the fortified Mareth Line.

Other patrols explored the country farther to the west, T2 in the area to the south of Djebel Tebaga, between

*T Patrol officers, 1941.
Captain L. B. Ballantyne (left)
and
Lieutenant E. W. Ellingham.
Photo: Tom Ritchie.*

Matamata area and T2 to examine the "going" in the direction of Chott Djerid.

On their return Tinker rejoined "Popski" at Ksar Rhilane, where they learned that the base camp had been strafed the previous morning by three Messerschmidts, and that within 10 minutes nine vehicles of the LRDG and PPA had been destroyed. The PPA had planned raiding operations behind the Mareth Line, but now all their explosives and supplies were lost. Also two New Zealanders, Lance-Corporals R.A. Ramsay and R.C. Davies were both wounded in the legs, and several others suffered superficial burns while trying to salvage essentials from the burning trucks. The wireless jeep had been left untouched until a blazing petrol can, projected from one of the trucks, landed on the jeep and burnt it out. Local Arabs had betrayed the patrol's position to the enemy.

Sergeant George Garven of T2 and Captain Bob Yunnie of the PPA along with two of his Senussi guides stayed on at the camp. The men remained to warn the Rhodesian S2 Patrol, who were due in the area soon, of the Arab treachery. The other survivors moved on to Ksar Rhilane where a mixed group of 51 men had gathered: PPA, LRDG, six Free French and two British SAS men who had been stranded because their transport had broken down. Altogether there were five serviceable jeeps, but not enough fuel to take them all to safety. So Tinker with 13 men including the wounded set out for Sabria, an oasis near Chott Djerid, in three vehicles and enough petrol for a 250 kilometre journey. The other 37 men formed a walking party led by "Popski". They were accompanied by two jeeps that mounted Vickers K machine-guns, mainly as protection against hostile Arabs. The vehicles also carried supplies and acted as a relief for the walkers.

The plan was for Tinker to quickly seek proper aid for the wounded, to send back assistance for the other

Matmata and Chott Djerid, a high salt marsh, and G2 in the area between the Chott and the Grand Erg Oriental, an impassable sand sea extending into southern Algeria.

While on this reconnaissance operation T2 Patrol under Lieutenant R. A. Tinker, accompanied by Major V. Peniakoff and his men of Popski's Private Army, set up a base camp south of Ksar Rhilane. From there Tinker and Peniakoff, each in a small party of two jeeps, went north towards Djebal Tebaga where a natural corridor extended to the Matmata Hills towards the coast at Gabes—this was the Tebaga Gap through which the outflanking of the Mareth Line was to be done. After a while the men parted company to continue with separate tasks: the PPA to carry out demolitions in the party, and because there was no radio, to report the result of their reconnaissance to HQ as soon as possible. If Sabria was not held by the French he would have to proceed on to Tozeur.

Sabria was occupied by the Germans so Tinker had to bypass it, but he had insufficient petrol to complete the journey around the shore of Chott Djerid to Tozeur. He decided to cross the salt marshes by camel track to Nefta, a village about 25 kilometres from Tozeur. When the going was firm they were able to drive at top speed, but where the water seepage had formed a quagmire the jeeps lurched through muddy pools onto solid lumps of sand and coagulated salt. They were the first vehicles ever to cross the Chott.

At Nefta, Tinker arranged by telephone for the French to supply petrol from Tozeur. Two of the jeeps, now refuelled, were sent back to find the walking party, except this time they avoided crossing the Chott. Tinker went on to Gafsa, 100 kilometres to the north-east of Tozeur, to obtain transport from the US First Army and to report his situation by wireless to HQ. The Americans were unable to help and told him to go to Tebessa, 160 kilometres to the north-west in Algeria. When he arrived the US command, though uncertain about Tinker's story, agreed to loan him two jeeps and to send a message to the Eighth Army.

He then went back and found "Popski's" men who had walked 240 kilometres over six days, and took them to Tozeur. The jeeps sent earlier from Nefta had missed the walkers only to arrive at Tozeur a day after the others. Sergeant Garven's group had met up with the Rhodesians. Their warning about the Arabs was not in vain, because the patrol had been sniped at all the way from Ksar Rhilane to Tozeur and suffered some casualties.

Tinker returned the vehicles to the Americans where he received orders

from Eighth Army HQ requesting his immediate return by air, along with the vital maps of his recent reconnaissance. He left his patrol in the hands of the local Allied forces and, accompanied by Corporal R. F. White, they flew from Tebessa to Algiers, then on to Tripoli, where he reported to HQ to assist in planning for the "left hook" around the Mareth Line. For his determination and courageous leadership Tinker received the MC and was promoted to Captain.

The final task assigned to the LRDG by the Eighth Army was the navigation of the New Zealand Corps during the outflanking of the Mareth Line in March 1943. Appropriately the work was performed by New Zealanders: Captain Tinker with three men from T2 Patrol in two jeeps. The New Zealand Corps passed through Wilder's Gap and remained at an assembly area while the route was plotted to the north west. A wadi with steep, rocky escarpments presented a very difficult obstacle, but Tinker, accompanied by Captain J. A. Goodsir of the New Zealand Engineers, found a place where tracks could be constructed with road making machinery to get the heavy transport across.

After the war, Winston Churchill in volume IV of his *The Second World War* histories, gave full credit to the LRDG

T1 Patrol, 12 January 1943. The first troops of the Eighth Army to enter Tunisia. Left Back: Lieutenant E.Y.M. Hutchinson, H.D. Mackay, W. Morrison RCS with (spectacles), K. E. Tippett, N. W. Hobson, (with pipe), R.W.N. Lewis. Middle: Captain N.P. Wilder, A. Vincent, J.L.D. Davis, W.H. Rail, Dr. Holywood RAMC. Front: S.D. Parker, E.J. Dobson, R.D. Tant, D.P. Warbrick. Photo: Ngaire Lewis.

Trooper Andy Crawford (left) alongside Sergeant George Garven, MM, T2 Patrol, 1943. Note the water condenser in the foreground. Photo: Imperial War Museum.

for their role in this operation, in the following words:

The route had formerly been pronounced by the French as impossible for vehicles, but had been reconnoitred in January by the Long Range Desert Group and declared feasible, if very difficult. Here was not the least valuable of the many services rendered throughout the African campaign by this hardy and highly mobile reconnaissance unit.

Meanwhile, the T2 navigator, Corporal D. M. Bassett, DCM, guided a New Zealand Provost party marking the "Diamond Track", using cut out drums enclosing candles or lanterns which would light the line of advance at night. As the Corps left the assembly area on 19 March, in recognition of Bassett's navigational skills which made this operation possible, General Freyberg invited Corporal Bassett to sit alongside him in his jeep to watch the progress.. The following day the Eighth Army launched its frontal attack on the Mareth Line. From there they moved forward to Tebaga along the route reconnoitred by the Group and made contact with the enemy on the 21st. Eventually the Axis forces were driven back into a corner of Tunisia.

There being no further scope for the LRDG they were released from the Eighth Army and returned to Egypt to rest and reorganise. The war in North Africa ended with the Axis surrender on 13 May 1943.

Corporal D. M. Bassett, DCM, T2 Patrol navigator. He and Captain R. A. Tinker guided the NZ Corps in the outflanking of the Mareth Line, Tunisia, March 1943. Photo: Denis Bassett.

TRANSPORT

For the rigours of desert patrol, Bagnold needed strong reliable vehicles with a long range and a heavy load capability. He decided on the 1939 Chevrolet WB 30cwt two-wheel drive, light commercial truck, 14 of which he was able to obtain from the Egyptian Army, and a further 19 from a branch of General Motors in Alexandria. In addition, seven 1938 Ford 01 15cwt V8s were acquired, three as scout cars for the patrol commanders, and the balance for HQ.

To help reduce weight and make them desert worthy, windscreens, (replaced with aero screens), doors and cab tops were removed, springs strengthened, 10.50x16 sand tyres fitted, various brackets for sun and aero compasses, gun mountings and sand channels and mats were installed. Also wireless sets with extra batteries, water containers and condensers for radiators were added.

In March 1941, after the Fezzan campaign, where the trucks had "clocked up" over 7,200 kilometres in very rough terrain, they were in need of urgent replacement. All that was available to the Group at that time were the four-wheel drive 70 Ford F30 4x4 30cwts. These were much heavier than the Chevrolet WBs, and used twice as much fuel, thus drastically reducing the effective range of a patrol. They were also distinctive in that their radiator grills and bonnets had been removed to assist cooling. Also the Fords were not as popular with the drivers as the Chevrolets, because the V8 motor was mounted between themselves and the front passenger, so it got very hot, plus the engine was awkward to work on in a hurry. The New Zealanders used the F30s for about 12 months.

The Ford 15cwts were now past their best and were returned to HQ for base transport. Further vehicles were obtained in December 1941 with the issue of 25 Chevrolet 1311X3 4x2 15cwts. In March 1942, to replace the Ford F30s, a consignment of 200 specially-ordered Canadian Chevrolet 1533X2 4x2 30cwt trucks had arrived. Though they were only two-wheel drive, an extra low ratio of gears along with a six cylinder engine

producing a lower petrol consumption, made them ideal for desert work.

By July 1942 Willys MB 5cwt jeeps were being issued as pilot cars, prior to that the odd example had been "acquired" from the SAS when the opportunity arose. The patrols were now generally reorganised on a basis of two jeeps and four 30cwt trucks, either Fords or Chevrolets. By May 1943, as the desert campaign had come to an end, the requirement for 30cwts had diminished, so they were replaced by jeeps. Of these A Squadron had 26, with each patrol being entitled to six.

The trucks of the Heavy Section, whose primary role was to establish and provision forward supply

Top picture shows a 1939 left hand drive Chevrolet WB 30cwt 4x2, Rotowaro of R Patrol, 1940. These early trucks had the option of a canvas hood to protect the driver from the sun, though it wasn't used when operating a sun compass. Amongst other stores the Shell petrol cases are stacked high in the back.
The lower photograph shows the Headquarters truck, Matai, stuck in the sand. Note the strongly contrasting camouflage pattern.
Photos: Jim Sutherland.

Top: A close up view of the Chevrolet WB, with the rolled up sand mat in its cradle on the mudguard. A Lewis gun is mounted on the door pillar and a Boys anti-tank rifle in the rear. Trooper R. J. Landon-Lane of R Patrol stands alongside. Photo: Jim Sutherland. The lower picture shows two Ford 01 15cwt V8s, Fezzan campaign, 1941. These American left-hand drive vehicles were used by the patrol commanders as scout cars. The model was based on a commercial light pick-up, the tray sides being wood and the floor pressed metal. To assist in cooling the engine, the side front of the bonnets have been cut out and replaced with mesh. Both vehicles are mounting Vickers heavy machine-guns. Photo: Shepherd collection.

regularly transporting fuel, water, food, munitions and equipment to forward dumps, or between supply depots to LRDG bases. Often these journeys were adventures in themselves, involving both navigational and desert driving skills over great distances. For example, to keep the base at Kufra supplied, a regular 2,250 kilometre haul from the depot at Wadi Halfa was required. They encountered, and had to resolve, many of the same difficulties as the patrols.

On one trip a Marmon Herrington cracked a cylinder block, a repair that was a laborious job that took eight hours to complete under very trying conditions. On another journey a combination of rough terrain and a heavy load resulted in a broken chassis. This was also repaired after many hours of hot, exhausting work.

Each patrol had a fitter's truck, which always travelled at the rear of the column to deal with any breakdowns. It carried the necessary tools and spares such as extra springs, clutches, fanbelts, plugs, carburettors, water pumps, coils, etc–all the parts vital for running repairs in the field. They often had to improvise parts or "cannibalise" written-off vehicles to bring their transport home. On one occasion a pipe mounting for a machine-gun was used to replace a smashed driveshaft. Another time a lost distributor rotor arm was effectively replaced with the aid of a beer bottle cork and safety pin.

As the trucks were loaded to top capacity and driven hard over all types of country, mechanical failures were expected. Common problems were burnt out clutches, punctures and bent tie rods, along with broken fan belts, steering boxes and springs. Sometimes repair work had to be done while under fire. Private F. R. Brown of T2 won the MM for saving a truck and its equipment while making repairs as they withstood an enemy attack north of Melchili. His efforts enabled the patrol to success-fully complete its mission.

dumps, began with four 6 ton Ford Marmon Herringtons supplied to the LRP from the Southern Mediter-ranean Oil Company. These six wheel drive vehicles were good in the desert, and could carry about 144 cases of petrol each, as well as their own fuel and spare parts. When one was stuck in the sand it could be cleared by the other. Later these were replaced with four 10 ton Whites. In spring 1942 they in turn were replaced by an equal number of Mack NR9s, then soon after 20 Ford F60 CMP trucks were added. The Group also occasionally utilised captured Italian vehicles, notably the four wheel drive Fiat Spa AS37 light trucks. These were used in a variety of roles, including training and supply.

To help maintain the Group's long range capacity many LRDG officers took a turn in the Heavy Section,

Very seldom did transport have to be abandoned because of irreparable mechanical failure. In the Fezzan campaign, a Ford 15cwt with a broken rear axle was towed for seven days, travelling 1,293 kilometres from Tummo to Faya over all types of country before it could be repaired. The loss of a truck was almost invariably the result of enemy action. To enable the patrols to journey beyond the range of assistance, the maintenance of the vehicles was always of the highest standard. As soon as a patrol returned to base the trucks were handed over to the Light Repair Section, who would ensure that they were ready to go out again at short notice. Each vehicle was overhauled every six months, and engines usually did between 19,000 and 26,000 kilometres before they were replaced. One New Zealander, Staff-Sergeant A. F. McLeod, who served first as a fitter with the Heavy Section, then was later in charge of A Squadron workshops at Abbassia, received the British Empire Medal (BEM) for his diligence in the repair and maintenance of the Group's equipment.

The respect the New Zealanders showed for their transport, apart from it being vital to the unit's survival, was reflected in the words Kennedy Shaw wrote in his book on the LRDG:

Many were owner-drivers at home and therefore naturally disposed to taking care of their cars, regarding them as a thing to be preserved rather than, as was sometimes the British attitude, as the property of an abstract entity, "the government", whose loss or destruction was of small concern of theirs.

A Ford F30 that had been backed into a well, 1941. The four-wheel drive ability of the vehicle was useful in extracting itself when stuck. This truck has the metal frame in place for a canvas canopy. It was rarely used, but sometimes the frame was erected on the ground and served as a useful shelter. Photo: Ian McCulloch.

The skill and resourcefulness of the fitters was legendary. It has been recorded on at least two occasions that LRDG fitters had found bananas to be a useful asset in times of crisis. The first incident was when a patrol was crossing terrain where the sand covered large pieces of rock. The going was very difficult, so it had to be undertaken in low gear. A truck dropped hard on a rock, cracking its differential housing and crushing the cover plate, resulting in a total loss of oil. Neither spares nor the correct oil were carried on this trip.

First, chewing gum was used to seal the crack in the housing but the problem was replacing the oil. They did not want to abandon the truck and

A Canadian right-hand drive Ford F30 4x4 30cwt truck, Te Anau T11 of T Patrol. To assist in cooling the V8 engine the radiator grill and bonnet were removed. These vehicles weren't popular with the drivers because the cab was over the engine, thereby the heat generated could cause much discomfort to themselves and their passengers. Photo: Ian McCulloch.

A newly-issued Canadian right-hand drive Chevrolet 1533X2 4x2 30cwt truck of R Patrol. It is stacked with stores and equipment, ready to set out. These vehicles were the mainstay of the LRDG patrols from March 1942 till the end of the desert campaign.
Photo: Imperial War Museum.

it would have been impossible to tow it the 1,600 kilometres back to base, so a solution had to be found. Then someone had an idea. Included in the patrol's rations were bananas, and it was suggested that they should be packed, complete with the skins, into the differential. The cover plate was hammered out to as near its original shape as possible, then bolted in place. A trial run of about 8 kilometres was completed, after which the differential housing remained relatively cool and there was no noise so they continued their 1,600 kilometre journey back to base, stopping every 80 kilometres to check for overheating and noise. They reached their destination without further incident.

Another occasion was when the patrol was returning from a road watch. One of its trucks hit a rock, ripped off its exhaust and badly cracked the gearbox. The exhaust

system was easily fixed, but with the gearbox losing oil there was a danger it may seize within the next 30 kilometres, so they camped for the night to study their problem.

The next morning they spotted a Bedouin driving his flock of sheep and goats. One of the men who spoke the language, found that the Arab was carrying a supply of bananas, so an exchange was made of tea and flour. The patrol ate the fruit as the top of the gearbox was being removed and they stuffed the skins into the cavity. This measure proved effective enough to enable the vehicle to continue motoring for almost 1,450 kilometres, before a new gearbox was fitted at base.

In July 1941, as part of an official dispatch concerning an appreciation of LRDG activities, General Wavell gave special praise to their fitters:

Their exploits have been achieved only by careful organisation, and a very high standard of enterprise, discipline, mechanical maintenance and desert navigation. A special word of praise must be added for the RAOC fitters whose work contributed so much to the mechanical endurance of the vehicles in such unprecedented conditions.

The fitters in the British patrols were specialists from the Royal Army Ordnance Corps. The New Zealanders usually supplied the fitters from their own units. Their skills were reflected in an allowance of an extra shilling a day.

Above: A Chevrolet 1311X3 15cwt unloading stores from a Bristol Bombay transport, R2 Patrol, Kufra 1942. These vehicles eventually replaced the Ford 15cwts as light transport.
Photo: Sharon Palmer.

Centre: A Willys MB jeep of T2 Patrol at the water point in Kharga, 1942. Note the water condenser mounted on the front bumper connected by a hose to the radiator. Also part of the grill has been cut away to assist cooling. The jeeps took over the role as patrol pilot cars from the 15cwts.
Photo: Ian McCulloch.

Left: A Heavy Section Ford Marmon-Herrington 6 ton truck, 1940. It is being driven at speed over firm ground by Trooper Joe Zimmerman.
An improvised water condenser has been fitted using a 4 gallon tin with a hose connected to the radiator.
Photo: Clarke Waetford.

Above: A fully-loaded Marmon-Herrington bogged, 1940. Its six-wheel drive capability often made extraction easier than it looks. These vehicles did essential work by establishing forward dumps for the early patrols. Photo: Jim Sutherland

Right: Trooper Norm Campbell stands alongside a White truck of the Heavy Section. Photo: Tom Ritchie

Credit must also go to the fact that the Chevrolets supplied to the LRDG were well built, robust American designs, as Buster Gibb recalled:

Those Chev trucks stood up to the extremes wonderfully well and survived being literally rolled down sand dunes, bounced over obstacles, and crash landed time after time. The longest jump on the flat over a sand ripple was with a Chev, that flew 14 metres from take off to landing. A bent tie rod was the only damage. A greater distance was achieved with a Ford F30 four wheel

drive. It leapt 16 metres, though all the bolts of both front wheel housings sheared. The Ford's four wheel drive saved no end of digging, but didn't compare with the Chevs.

In 1941 there was friendly competition among the patrols as to who held the record for the longest leap over a sand dune, which was usually attained by accident. The record for a "jump", originally held by R Patrol using a Ford P30 truck, had stood at 16 metres. This was later bettered by T Patrol while they were returning to Cairo after a trip. Merlyn Craw was operating a movie camera from the back of his truck as they were travelling over a series of very large dunes, 60 metres high. He wanted to get a shot of the trucks crossing them, so he left his vehicle and jumped into the back of *Te Rangi II* the Ford V8 pilot car that was leading the column. It was driven by Captain Bruce Ballantyne with his gunner Trooper "Mick" Shepherd sitting alongside. They drove up the side of a dune doing about a 100 kilometres per hour, this being easy because the sand had been compacted by the wind. But Ballantyne failed to slow down as he neared the top, then suddenly the vehicle became airborne, crashing 18 metres further on, caving in its front end assembly. The record was broken, but so was *Te Rangi II*, which had to be unloaded and trucked back to the workshops of Cairo.

Amazingly, apart from Shepherd chipping his front teeth on the aero windscreen, the men escaped injury. The Ford was later rebuilt, but Dave Burnnand who was the usual driver, was speechless with rage at the loss of his truck. Experience proved that dunes had to be transversed with care, especially the razor-back. These men were lucky, whereas others had been badly injured in tumbles or crashes.

Driving skills were an integral part of a successful patrol. To reduce the chances of getting bogged, various procedures, such as partially deflating the tyres, helped to improve the traction over soft ground, and by keeping to the upper edges of the

Captain P. L. Arnold of the Heavy Section takes a break while on a trip to supply a forward dump, 1942. He and his driver were later killed when their vehicle ran over a mine after setting up dumps for the Barce raid. Photo: Ngaire Lewis.

Private C. B. McKenzie of T Patrol, working on the engine of his Chevrolet 1533 X2 Breda gun truck. The maintenance of the vehicles was always of the highest standard. Photo: Ian McCulloch.

For transport to the workshops, a broken down Ford F30 truck is loaded on to the back of a Heavy Section White truck, marked HS 4. Sand trays and ammo boxes are being used as a ramp. Photo: Shepherd collection.

The A Squadron Light Repair Section. Some of the workshop fitters who kept the transport in top condition, 1943.
Back row, left to right: W. R. Bambery, J. P. Gilmore, C. I. McConachie, I. C. McCallum, F. R. Stone, D. A. Lewis, D. Farmer.
Front row: N. W. Gedye, N. J. Parker, R. H. Crabbe, L. D. Dalziel.
Photo: John Daymond.

dunes it ensured they could turn downhill when they hit a bad patch. When they stopped or started on dunes or drifts, it was always done very gently. Many sand surfaces, though just strong enough to carry a vehicle running steadily over them, collapsed under wheels that suddenly braked or accelerated. Going over the tracks of a previous vehicle had to be avoided, as the disturbed sand could cause the truck to stick. To enable the patrols to progress over unstable ground they travelled on as wide a front as possible.

If one truck became bogged the others might still get through and be in a position to assist. Adherence to these procedures all helped to keep the patrols mobile, over sometimes very arduous terrain.

The New Zealand drivers adapted well to the conditions, and most notably it was their proficient use of the gears that helped to ease the trucks over difficult country. A typical example was Tom Ritchie of T1 Patrol, who never got stuck once on his first drive across the Sand Sea. Gear changing was not synchronised as in cars, so the clutch had to be let out as the gear lever passed through.

T Patrol driver I. G. "Snowie" McCulloch stands alongside his Ford F30 with its radiator removed, 1941. The drivers and fitters in the field had to be highly skilled and able to improvise. The survival of a patrol often depended on their ability in keeping the vehicles running under very difficult conditions.
Photo: Ian McCulloch.

A short-wheel-based Ford F40, Te Rangi III T1, also known as "Stinker". It was used for a time as a pilot vehicle by Captain L. B. Ballantyne and driven by Trooper W. D. Burnnand (in photo). This vehicle may have been the only one of its kind employed by the LRDG, as the author has sighted no other reference or photo of similar transport. It mounts a shrouded Vickers machine-gun and is equipped for desert work.
Photo: Shepherd collection.

To negotiate the soft patches often a driver had to apply a technique of moving from high to low gear in one change, while at the same time revving the motor at the appropriate speed. According to one new Zealand veteran, initially the English drivers operating under similar conditions tended to get stuck more often because they would drive in the usual way, by changing from top to second then low, in which time the truck had become bogged.

The "going" had to be carefully judged to keep the vehicle moving, but even the most experienced driver could not always distinguish the patches of dry quicksand, soft sand or the sporadic salt marsh. If he became stuck, first the tyres were deflated to improve traction, then the hard labour of having to dig troughs under the wheels began, before the 1.8 metre perforated steel channels could be laid and every man pushed. On particularly bad stretches lines of channels were laid to make a kind of railroad, though sometimes on very hot days these were difficult to handle because of the heat absorbed in the

steel. Further ahead men waited with channels ready to be thrown under the rear wheels as soon as they were seen to start to spin in the sand. The art of channel throwing required skill and the few who mastered it were in constant demand. Also as part of this process the canvas and slatted wood sand mats were unrolled and placed under the front wheels to help to ease vehicles out of soft sand, and were often used over extensive areas of unstable ground.

Ford F40 Te Rangi III with Captain Bruce Ballantyne (left) and the driver Trooper Dave Burnnand. A Vickers K machine-gun is mounted in the front position.
Photo: Shepherd collection.

Ford 15cwt Te Rangi II crashed landed after flying 18 metres over a razor back dune, 1941.
Photo: Shepherd collection.

Damaged after crashing over a dune, Te Rangi II had to be returned to the Citadel workshops in the back of a Ford F30 truck. Trooper Dave Burnnand stands alongside.
Photo: Shepherd collection.

The names were painted along the side of the truck bonnets in white letters, usually against black, though with some LRP vehicles it was against dark green. Replacement trucks often used the same name, so they became Te Anau II or Te Paki III. By 1943 the naming of new trucks was discontinued.

Other insignia painted on the front of the truck bonnets was a black Kiwi on a green base, as displayed on T Patrol vehicles. Whereas R Patrol featured a green Tiki (a Maori idol) with a red tongue.

With the formation of the LRP it was decided to give the patrol vehicles Maori names, thinking it would help to confuse the enemy. This task was achieved after Lieutenant Jim Sutherland with instructions from Captain E. C. Mitford, asked Trooper Clarke Waetford, the only Maori in the unit at that time, and Trooper Alf Saunders to assist him in the naming of the trucks. The preference was to use Roto to begin the name of R Patrol vehicles, T Patrol Te, and W Patrol with Wai; e.g. Rotoma, Te Hau, and Waikato. There were a few exceptions though, such as Taipo and Wanaka. LRP HQ and Heavy Section vehicles bore names starting with "M", for example, Manuka and Matai.

Further markings were the black stencilled "INSPECTED" and WD numbers, along with vehicle numbers such as R2 or T6. Occasionally LRDG artwork such as a scorpion, or a caricature, appeared on trucks, but these were rare. The commander had the authority to paint his vehicles as he thought fit, according to the availability of paint colours. This resulted in trucks being finished in a variety of paint colours. In the early days, combinations of paint colour types such as Light, Portland or Grey Stone or Slate, with Purple Brown or Desert Pink were used. Later Canadian or Desert Sand colours were more common.

Each truck usually carried a crew of three: the truck commander, a driver

The burden of desert travel, 1942. An R Patrol crew dig under the wheels of their badly stuck Chevrolet 30cwt. Note the back of the truck jammed with stores and the "bail out" kits hung by the driver's position.
Photo: Richard Williams.

and a gunner, who may also have been a cook or medical orderly. Every patrol also included a navigator, a radio operator and a fitter. The truck commander was responsible for the packing of the interior of the truck, including knowing the contents and placement of every case. He also had to report the quantities on board to the patrol leader to keep a constant look-out for enemy aircraft and ground forces, to keep station and pass on movement orders to the driver; and was responsible for the tactical handling and extraction of his truck if it got stuck.

The driver was responsible for the whole of his truck, except the interior of the body, and for all tools and fittings apart from the armament. He had to keep his truck mobile at all times by ensuring regular maintenance, such as checking the oil, water and tyre pressures. In the morning, with the cooler temperatures, the tyres would be half flat, whereas after an hour's motoring heat expansion could cause over-inflation. With the heavy loads carried the tyre

pressure checks were very important and conducted at every halt. Air was provided by a hose attached to an automatic air pump run from the vehicle's engine. The drivers also had to be alert to the avoidance of hitting rocks and getting stuck in the sand.

The selection of the actual track lay directly with him, but the commander was primarily responsible for maintaining the correct speed and direction

A right-hand drive Ford 15cwt pilot car, 1941. This is unusual, as most of these models were left hand drive. The rear wheels are deeply bogged in soft sand. Often the stores had to be unloaded before the hard labour of extraction could begin.
Photo: Shepherd collection.

A 1942 Chevrolet of R Patrol showing the use of sand mats to ease the front wheels over soft sand. Note the Tiki painted on the bonnet. This symbol was displayed on all R Patrol vehicles.
Photo: Imperial War Museum.

R Patrol sleeping arrangements, Libyan Desert 1941. An uncoiled sand mat, acting as both a windbreak and headrest, lays against the side of the Chevrolet WB Rotowai R4. Private E. T. Russell rests in the centre. The mats were not only used for negotiating soft sand, but also doubled as air recognition panels, with the inner surfaces being painted red and white.
Photo: Bill Willcox.

T Patrol members and some friendly Arabs pose against Te Aute, a Chevrolet WB30. Behind that is the commander's Ford 15cwt. It appears to have a set of antlers in the back next to the machine-gun, 1940.
Photo: Peter Garland.

T patrol letter. The LRP was organised on Divisional Cavalry lines, so the troop leaders would carry coloured flags as follows: Green, A (HQ) Troop; black, B Troop; yellow, C Troop; red, D Troop. With the formation of the five truck patrols the use of the flags was limited to the green patrol flag being flown on occasion.

When it became necessary to depart from an intended route, or in the event of enemy action, patrol movement was controlled by blue and white signal flags or hand signals. Typical signs were such as when the enemy was in sight the flag would be waved vertically up and down, and dispersal was indicated by two horizontally held flags being waved up and down. Another sign, without flags, was when two men stood on the body of a truck. This indicated a mechanical breakdown and not just being stuck.

One of the more unusual aspects of Group transport was the Air Section which consisted of two American built WACO (Western Aircraft Corporation of Ohio) biplanes (types ZGC7 and YKC) purchased from Egyptian businessmen in April 1941. The section was established because Major Bagnold often had difficulty in persuading the RAF to fly to many of the remote places he wanted them to go, either because they didn't have suitable aircraft to do so, or were not prepared to set out when Bagnold wanted them to. He stated these concerns to his superiors and after much debate was granted permission to form his own LRDG "air force".

The planes were flown and regularly maintained by Major G. L. Prendergast, an experienced pre-war desert flyer, and Sergeant R. F. Barker

and for choosing the route over which the truck was going to travel.

The gunner was not only responsible for the care and maintenance of all armament, but was also available to assist with any other duties as directed by the commander. Every patrol member was trained to be a competent gunner, including the medical orderlies. All the crew were expected to be able to take over each other's responsibilities if required.

The patrol commander led the unit in a 15cwt pilot car (later jeeps) and ranged ahead to select the best route. The second in command travelled at the rear to keep a watch on the formation. He also acted as transport officer and supervised maintenance. In the days of the 11 truck patrols, the commanders and their 2 ICs flew a green flag displaying a white W, R or

(NZ Divisional Cavalry, later Captain), a qualified New Zealand pilot who at one time flew support aircraft for the Australian aviator Sir Charles Kingsford-Smith. An Egyptian aircraft company, Misr Airways, or occasionally the RAF, were used to attend to the routine inspections and major repairs. Known as the "big" and "little" Wacos, they were numbered AX697 and AX695 and cruised at about 140 (122 knots) and 115 (100 knots) miles per hour respectively. Both were single-engined cabin machines capable of carrying four or five men.

These aircraft were sturdy and reliable, capable of landing almost anywhere. They were used for

Above: The Kiwi insignia on the bonnet of Te Aroha III indicates it's a T Patrol vehicle. Note the sun compass in the centre above the dashboard. The gazelle trophy is all that remains after the rest of the animal was consumed by the patrol. Photo: Keith Tippett.

Left: W, T and R Patrol vehicles all bore Maori names beginning with the patrol letter. Lined up is a selection of T1 Patrol truck names, 1942. Photo: Shepherd collection.

Trooper W. R. Bambery (left) and Trooper H. P. Hewetson with a restored Ford V8 15cwt pilot car, November 1943. This was done up at the workshops where a scorpion insignia was painted on the mudguard. It was unusual to see LRDG vehicles with unofficial markings. Photo: John Daymond.

The picture at far right shows an R Patrol column of Chevrolet WBs halted after the 13 kilometre climb in low gear up the escarpment from Kharga oasis. The rear truck displays some individual artwork featuring a crying skull, 1940. Photo: Jim Sutherland.

reconnaissance, delivering mail and essential spares in the field, moving key personnel, short-range casualty evacuation, and liaison between the Group's bases and Middle East HQ. The aircraft displayed RAF roundels and below the cockpit appeared the LRDG initials. Also to the rear of the engine cowling was painted a black Kiwi insignia within a shield.

There was no radio or direction-finding equipment carried, so to assist when required two truck navigators were trained in aerial work. If they were ever uncertain about their position they would just land and check their calculations with the aid of a "sunshot". The Wacos flew great distances above vast wastelands in all conditions, over dust or sandstorms and in desert haze, with their careful navigation bringing them to an appointed rendezvous.

Despite often not having meteorological or topographical data to rely on, they never got lost or had an accident. Though they were in equal danger from Allied fighters or AA gunners who at a distance could have easily mistaken a Waco for an Italian CR42 biplane they also managed to avoid any encounters with enemy aircraft or had an accident. The Air Section proved a success due to the solicitous handling, planning and maintenance procedures employed by two very skilled pilots.

In 1980 a long lost piece of LRDG history was found: a truck from one of the early patrols of the LRP was located in the Egyptian Desert by geologists about 650 kilometres south of Cairo and north west of Bir Tarfawi. The vehicle was a Chevrolet WB 30cwt, WD number 8302, still in good condition and it carried the name Waikaha of W patrol, with the designation W8. This patrol was disbanded in December 1940 and its equipment handed over to the Guards who had joined the unit when it became known as the LRDG. Since its discovery there has been much conjecture as to how the truck came to be abandoned, because wherever possible the Group always endeavoured to recover its transport. Alf Saunders, veteran of W Patrol and driver of the wireless truck W2, Waitemata, explained to the author the reason why Waikaha was left behind.

Trooper Saunders was part of a four truck reconnaissance patrol trying to find a way through the centre of Gebel Uweinat and thereby into the rear of the Italian fort at the south end of the mountain. This was the place where earlier Lieutenant Sutherland and Trooper Willcox had won their decorations during a frontal attack against the enemy position. The

patrol was led and navigated by Lieutenant W. B. Kennedy Shaw, but as they got within the northern perimeter of Uweinat he became very ill with yellow jaundice. His condition deteriorated, causing him to suffer delirium for most of the time.

It was decided to cancel the mission and get Kennedy Shaw back to Cairo as soon as possible. On the return trip one of the trucks, Waikaha, got stuck on a very high sand dune. After a great deal of effort the Chevrolet was finally rolled down the hill but during a gear change the gear-box jammed and though the truck continued to slide to the bottom it was now immobile.

The men examined the gearbox but being only a small patrol were not equipped with suitable spares to carry out the necessary repairs. The option of towing the vehicle was discounted due to the priority of obtaining medical treatment for their commander without further delay. Waikaha was stripped and left to be recovered at a later date.

The site was not far from the route taken by the Heavy Section to a forward dump at Gilf Kebir, so it was thought that on one of their return trips they could either uplift the truck or provide spares to get it running again. Alf Saunders doesn't know why the truck was not recovered. It was possibly because a few weeks after that the LRP had ceased to exist and when it reformed into the LRDG it shifted base to Siwa. Also W Patrol was now disbanded and a number of men were returned to their old units.

With all this change the recovery job for Waikaha was probably overlooked until it was picked up 43 years later! In 1983 an expedition led by Tony Pearce of the Grange Cavern Military Museum in Wales, with support from Major-General David Lloyd Owen, Chairman of the LRDG Association, recovered Waikaha and brought it to Britain. When it was discovered the speedometer read 40,000 miles, there was no rust in the body, and the wood and tyres were still in good condition although Arabs had removed the radiator, most likely for its copper,

The "Little" Waco YKC four seater liaison plane of the Air Section. It was fitted with a 225hp 7 cylinder Jacobs L4 engine and cruised at 115 miles per hour. Registered AX695, this aircraft was damaged beyond repair when it swung on landing at Heliopolis on 24 April 1942. Along with the "Big" Waco, these aircraft did much useful work in supporting the patrols. Pictured is the LRDG Medical Officer Captain R. P. Lawson, who won the MC on the Barce raid in September 1942. Photo: Ngaire Lewis.

One of the important roles of the Waco aircraft was evacuation of the sick or wounded. In this picture are Trooper H. D. Mackay (left) and Trooper A. Vincent. Laying in the stretcher is Trooper P. J. Burke, who broke his leg when his truck ran over a mine. Standing is Dr. R. P. Lawson, RAMC. Note the Kiwi insignia within the shield and LRDG initials on the side of the plane. Photo: Jim Sutherland.

Below is the "Big" Waco ZGC five-seater plane being serviced by T Patrol members. It was powered by a 285 hp 7 cylinder Jacobs L5 engine and cruised at 122 miles per hour. The aircraft was registered AX697 and served the unit up to 1944. Trooper I. G. McCulloch stands in the foreground. Photo: Ian McCulloch.

and the glass from the headlight. The carburettor was also missing and a 1942-dated .303 round was found, probably dropped by a Bedouin. It is the only original LRP truck known to survive; after having been displayed at Grange Cavern for a number of years it can now be seen at the Imperial War Museum, London.

In the 1960s, an RAF unit called the Desert Rescue Team operated in Libya. They not only served in their rescue role but also reported, and sometimes recovered, relics from WWII desert battle sites. One of their most significant recoveries was the No. 2 engine and other artefacts from the B-24 Liberator bomber "Lady Be Good". This team had also covered much of the ground originally travelled by the LRDG and recorded two interesting discoveries. The first was at Ain Zwaya, where in October 1940 R Patrol destroyed an Italian Savoia-Marchetti S 79 bomber. Its burnt out skeleton still remains there today. The other was at Gebel Sherif, where T Patrol was attacked by the Italian Auto-Saharan Company in February 1941. Three burnt out Chevrolet WBs, complete with their blackened supplies and equipment, still remain as they were left after the battle. Nearby lay two graves, believed to be those of Italian prisoners killed in that action. It was from this place that Trooper Ron Moore began his famous 336 kilometre trek.

In 1969 Colonel Gaddafi overthrew Libya's monarch, King Idris, and declared a Republic. He expelled the British and American forces who had bases there. The desert was then closed off to foreigners, which may ensure that these relics will remain intact to be rediscovered by future adventurers.

EQUIPMENT AND SUPPLIES

For communication with HQ and other units, each patrol was equipped with the low powered Army No.11 wireless set. They had been used in tanks until the army replaced them with the No.19 set, and had proved very robust under all the conditions experienced. It had been designed for a range of only 15 kilometres, but when employed with Wyndom aerials that were slung between 5 metre poles, transmissions over great distances could be achieved. When not in use the support poles were stowed strapped in sections at the top of the body side of the truck. For signals up to 800 kilometres a 1.8 metre rod aerial was adequate. Also a Phillips Type 635 receiver was carried for the GMT navigation time check, listening to music and the regular "news". The Chevrolet WBs mounted their radios inside the body of the truck, whereas in all the later vehicles they were accessed from the outside.

It was remarkable what long range communications were obtained with the low powered No.11 sets. For example, during the Murzuk raid in January 1941, contact was made over 2,400 kilometres between G and T Patrols in Zouar, Chad, and the LRDG HQ in Cairo. The greatest distance ever recorded was by the Indian Long Range Squadron, who were able to transmit between the Damascus area and Benghazi, a range of over 2,500 kilometres.

Each patrol included a radio truck which always travelled behind the commander, thereby usually bearing the number 2, such as R2 or W2. It carried a fully trained signaller while at least one other qualified operator travelled in a different vehicle. In the LRP most of the operators were New Zealanders, but with the formation of the LRDG they were all drawn from the Royal Corps of Signals. They not only had to be highly skilled, but had to have exceptional technical ability so that they could keep their equipment working for weeks without any help from the outside. Only on four occasions (other than enemy action) had a set broken down and left a patrol out of touch with HQ. Almost invariably the operators were able to fix a fault within a day or two. The radios were powered by batteries charged by the truck. On road watches charging sets could be used but they were noisy, so some commanders preferred to take extra batteries.

Lance Corporal A. Pressick, a British signalman of the Royal Corps of Signals attached to T Patrol, February 1941. In the Chevrolet WBs the radio was fitted inside the truck, whereas in later vehicles it was accessed from the outside. Behind him is a .55 Boys anti-tank rifle mounted on a steel cross bar. Photo: Imperial War Museum.

Signalman T. Scriven, RCS, attached to T2 Patrol, 1942. His job wasn't over at the end of the day, as he would be employed for several hours in the evening transmitting all the latest information gathered. The No. 11 radio was operated in the Ford F30 in the manner shown. To gain access the whole side panel had to be dropped, whereas with the 1942 Chevrolets there was a special access panel. The wireless truck was the most important vehicle in the patrol, and if it was put out of action the mission was usually aborted. Photo: Denis Bassett.

Because security was vital in LRDG communications, all transmissions were passed in code; when in the field signals were destroyed every 12 hours, as were any working papers immediately after use. The Group as a whole used a system whereby frequencies were changed twice daily, with the call sign being altered at the same time. The patrols were expected to report to base at least once a day, usually in the evening or at meal times. After use the dials of the set were always tuned to zero, in case the radio was captured and a frequency compromised.

T1 Patrol listening to the "news" on their Phillips receiver, 1942. Captain Nick Wilder stands next to the vehicle. Note the camouflage net helping to conceal the truck Photo: Tom Ritchie.

To maintain their long range patrols the trucks carried nearly 2 tonnes of stores. This included petrol in four gallon (18 litre) tins, packed two to a wooden box, bedrolls, tarpaulins, camouflaged netting, spare wheels, tyres and springs, munitions, and most importantly, water, rations and a rum issue. Apart from the normal allocation of supplies, each vehicle also carried three days emergency rations, including water. Slung near their stations were the crew's "bale out" kits. These were individually made up haversacks, which usually contained personal items, a small scale map of Libya along with a compass, a waterbottle, emergency rations and cigarettes. The packs were placed within easy reach, to be grabbed in case the vehicle had to be abandoned in a hurry.

The members of the Group were probably the best fed troops in the Middle East. From the beginning the LRDG was placed on a special scale of rationing, distinct from that provided for troops of the Eighth

Army and on base installations. To enable the men to cope with severe conditions for long periods, without fresh meat, vegetables or bread, and very little water, they were issued with food of high calorific value and with as much variety as possible.

Below R2 Patrol are sorting out stores in preparation for a trip, Kufra, 1943. Photo: Merle Fogden.

Abbassia Barracks, October 1940. The trucks are lined up ready to receive their very carefully calculated supplies, packed in wooden boxes. This is prior to departing on the second LRP incursion into Libya. Photo: Peter Garland.

A cosy shelter erected alongside a Ford F30 truck of T Patrol, 1941. Lieutenant Walter Ellingham rests amongst the clutter of stores and equipment. The bandage on his knee covers a desert sore, a common affliction on long patrols. Photo: Ian McCulloch.

Most food was canned, which included such luxuries as salmon, herrings, NZ steaks, meat and vegetable stew, fruit and vegetables, as well as the more mundane like bully beef and baked beans. In addition there were onions, lentils and haricot beans, along with dried food, such as large ship biscuits, oatmeal, rice, spaghetti, flour, fruit and condiments. Sometimes, if the patrol was within range, the Waco would fly out and deliver fresh bread. Coffee, tea, condensed milk, lime juice and rum were also supplied.

Cooking was done in two gallon cauldrons, or in four gallon tins that had been cut to shape. Either primus stoves, broken up wooden petrol cases, or petrol poured into a hole in the sand and ignited, were used for heating. Fresh meat was provided when a gazelle was sighted and could be brought down with a suitable weapon fired from the back of a fast moving truck, as Jack Davis recorded:

27 Jan. 1943: We had some grand shooting with our sub-machine guns among gazelle in herds of 20 to 50 at a time. Of course we could not miss. Besides giving us good practice, it provided us with plenty of fresh meat to take back to base. Gazelle is a rather tasty meat when properly cooked; thoroughly enjoyed liver with our tinned bacon.

Alfred "Buster" Gibb, one of the originals from W Patrol, relates his story about supplies in the early days:

My task at this stage was under the guidance of Dr. Edmundson, to draw bulk rations and break them into daily lots. The doctor along with Bagnold, had worked out a diet suitable for the conditions we would be working under. Separate rations for breakfast, lunch and dinner had to be compiled. For the 28 members of the patrol, one day's rations fitted compactly into a Benzine case. Some rations considered hospital comforts, were carried separately, such as tinned Irish potatoes, red beet, fruit, etc. Everyone also received a daily ration of a small cake of chocolate. From the Army supply stores, I had to draw 68 gallons (308 litres) of rum. Each man was entitled to a gill measure a day (about 140mls). For a start, I had difficulty attempting to draw this issue. I was "palmed off" from a sergeant, to a lieutenant, to captain, then colonel, via a major. The colonel set me on the grade down, and when I got back to the captain, I asked to use the phone. I rang Colonel Bagnold at HQ, and explained the situation. After he

had finished with them I could have collected anything I required, even without a chit.

In 1940, Gibb drew rations for the three patrols, but as he was appointed to W Patrol, his main concern was for their supplies. He continues his story:

A problem developed during one trip, where the rations included tins of herrings in tomato sauce. Unfortunately, the fish when canned, still had the roes in them. Half the blokes wouldn't eat what they described as "pregnant" herrings, and wanted something else. I wasn't too popular when I refused to broach next day's rations. This would have meant that we would have finished up only with herrings. As it was, we ended up with a surplus of this ration.

On 20 September 1940, the LRP made its first enemy contact when W Patrol captured two Italian trucks, along with their valuable cargo, it was also Buster Gibb's birthday. He sought permission to issue extra rum to celebrate the double occasion. In addition, they had acquired from the enemy loot a number of bottles of Chianti. That night the potent combi-

Filling the 4 gallon tin "flimsies" at the water point at Ain Dalla. Water flowed continuously through a four-inch pipe protruding from the sand from a subterranean water supply, then disappeared back into the ground. All the patrols replenished their supplies at this point before crossing the Egyptian Sand Sea. A wooden box carried two tins, with the screw caps being soldered in place to prevent leakage.
Photo: Jim Sutherland.

nation of red wine and rum led to an over-indulgence and much exuberance, with one member performing for hours, until it took four men to hold him down before he finally flaked. The next morning while nursing a hangover, Corporal Gibb was informed by Captain Mitford that because of the ill discipline, he faced a court-martial when the unit returned to base.

After the battle at Ain Dua in the Uweinat the patrol set out for Cairo, but before they left the Sand Sea they decided to ensure they would not return any rum, in case they were issued with less on the next trip— thereby they emptied the spirit into four gallon tins, topped it up with lime juice, and celebrated their successful trip. By this time Mitford had mellowed, and dropped the charges against Gibb.

Establishing a camp site, 1941. Water is being raised from the well in the foreground. The trucks are Ford F30s of T patrol.
Photo: Ian McCulloch.

T2 Patrol Christmas dinner at Kufra, 1942. The LRDG enjoyed the best rations in the Middle East.
Photo: Denis Bassett.

Water was carried in cased four gallon (18 litre) tins, with the caps being soldered in place so they would not loosen with the motion of the vehicle and cause wastage. For more ready use, apart from personal water bottles, it was also carried in two gallon (9 litre) containers with handles and screw tops. After a hot day the water was warm and unpleasant to drink. One way to bring its temperature down was to put the liquid on a plate and place it under a truck, where the shade and breeze helped to cool it down.

The summer ration was 4.5 litres per man per day. This was for all purposes, including vehicle radiators. Water saving techniques, such as heating tinned food by standing it in the liquid that was used for making tea, and cleaning food utensils in drifts of blown sand, all helped to reduce consumption. No water was to be drawn from any container except under supervision, at regular issue times. On arrival at a waterhole all containers were to be filled before washing or any other activity was started.

The distribution of rum, water and rations was strictly controlled by the patrol commanders through their quartermasters (usually the second-in-command) and senior NCOs. At the end of a day's run one of the first duties of the 2 IC was to take stock of all remaining supplies and report to the commander their condition, how much further the patrol could travel, and for how long.

Later in the desert campaign the more robust German designed "Jerricans" were adopted to carry fuel and water. These eventually replaced the four gallon tins ("flimsies"), which tended to leak or puncture with rough handling. GHQ Middle East once stated in a report that, due to the inadequacy of the flimsy square tins, there was a 30% loss of petrol between base and the consumer. The LRDG were among the first units to be issued with jerrycans for general use, these were either captured examples or the

British made copies. The containers had a special lining which enabled them to be used for petrol or water. They did not leak and their shape made for easy storage and handling. The only drawback was that the empty jerrycans had to be returned to base, whereas the "flimsies" were squashed and buried.

When the Ford F30 4x4s were employed, they used twice as much fuel as the Chevrolets, thereby the quartermasters had to take special account of supplies required for a trip. In order that additional petrol could be carried, water and rations had to be carefully calculated in relation to the proposed distance of travel. Consequently the vehicles became overloaded, which resulted in tyres blowing more often, requiring extra spares to be carried. The Ford's four wheel drive was handy at times, but the truck was prone to overheating which led to greater water consumption. They were also slower than the Chevrolets that were considered the better vehicle for desert work.

Not all the equipment supplied proved suitable for the purpose intended. In the early patrols each truck was issued with eight lengths of hessian scrim, 1.8 metres wide and 9.1 metres long. The idea was to drape them over the vehicle as camouflage and make it appear like a mound of sand. One day Buster Gibb

An R Patrol Chevrolet WB camouflaged with scrim with a few rocks to keep it in place. Later, when viewed from the air, it was found that the scrim contrasted greatly with the desert terrain, so its use was soon discontinued. The Lewis gun is mounted in a ready anti-aircraft position. The resting crew are, from left: Trooper M. E. Hammond, Private E. Harcourt and Private F. R. Brown. Photo: Jim Sutherland.

was given the opportunity to view the effect from the air. He found that the scrim was obvious, and stood out, in his words, "Like a boil on a baby's bum", a complete failure. Gibb had also observed that where footprints or tyre marks were swept over, the change in the colour of the sand surface was dramatic. The sand, having been burnt by the sun for thousands of years, took on an even sunburnt look, so when the surface was disturbed it revealed a different colour. This variation was clear from any height or distance.

Needless to say the scrim was not used for camouflage purposes again. But it did become an ideal medium for packing between the loads on the trucks to prevent vibration, which also helped to overcome a previous problem with the loss of fuel and water. Sometimes leaks developed when the tins rubbed against the sides of their wooden packing cases. This,

combined with blown sand, acted like a grinding paste, producing small holes that led to the loss of contents.

The organisation involved in the distribution of supplies to the Group was complex and created special problems for the quartermaster. From late 1941 to February 1943 Captain D. "Shorty" Barrett was the Quartermaster LRDG, as well as Adjutant. He received the MBE in recognition of his efficiency in keeping the patrols operational and well provisioned. The LRDG seldom dealt directly with base ordnance depots, as this usually involved too much delay. Because their supply requirements had to be met almost immediately, the demands were made directly to GHQ Middle East Forces, who placed them on a high priority. Supply was maintained by the Heavy Section, who ran a regular schedule from depots to bases, usually bringing in a month's supply in one trip.

R2 patrol view the welcome sight of the arrival of their Waco aircraft. Where possible these planes delivered mail and supplies and equipment such as fresh bread, or urgent spare parts. On the outward journey they could take return mail and the sick or wounded. Photo: Sharon Palmer.

WEAPONS

In the beginning the patrol's primary purpose was reconnaissance, with weapons only being carried for self defence or for use in small scale attacks against supply convoys and lightly defended Italian emplacements. Gradually, as the Group took on a more aggressive role, the firepower increased. The first patrols each carried ten Lewis guns, four Boys anti-tank rifles and one especially adapted 37mm Bofors anti-tank gun. In early 1941 the armament had improved, with four Lewis guns being replaced with .303 Vickers Mk.1 water cooled machine guns, in addition there were also several .50 cal. versions employed. To overcome the shortage of water these weapons were sometimes cooled with Hypoid oil. Vickers tripods were also carried, so the guns could be dismounted and operated from the ground if necessary.

Gunner Tom Walsh of T Patrol directs his .303 Lewis gun against enemy aircraft. The weapon's exposed magazine base was sometimes a disadvantage in the desert, as wind blown sand could cause a jam. It was practice to cover the guns when they were not required for immediate action.
Photo: Tom Ritchie.

T1 Patrol Chevrolet 1533X2 shows off its weaponry. Manning the Lewis gun is Trooper Euan Hay, behind the wheel is Driver Gerry Gerrard with his .303 Lee Enfield service rifle clipped in position by his side. Corporal Merlyn Craw is at the ready with his .303 aircraft Browning. This was put together from the guns of a wrecked fighter (note the crude shoulder stock). Later, the single gun was replaced with a pair of Brownings, which in tandem produced devastating firepower. Photo: Imperial War Museum.

The 37mm Bofors, (also referred to as a 2 pounder) was mounted on a 360° turntable fitted to a steel trestle bolted to a reinforced truck chassis. Ammunition boxes carrying 90 rounds were attached to the floor. When the gun was fired, as protection from the muzzle blast, a thick rubber flap was used to cover the vehicle's dashboard. Though the Bofors was fitted for an anti-tank role it was probably never used as such because the patrols rarely encountered armoured vehicles with whom they would choose to confront. These single shot breech loading weapons were initially manned by two gunners recruited from the 34th A/T Battery of the 7th NZ Anti-Tank Regt. and were mainly used against Italian forts and positions. Buster Gibb viewed the gun as *"A bloody useless thing, that nearly lost us the war!"*

In the Fezzan campaign the truck-mounted weapon was put to good use, but being a heavy vehicle it had its difficulties. While Gunner E. Sanders was pounding an Italian fort a shell jammed in the breech. As he and a fellow gunner tried to clear it, their vehicle came under enemy fire, so the driver attempted to withdraw. However, the recoil of the gun had caused the back wheels to sink in the sand up to the axle. Fortunately the

fire was sporadic, so the crew reached for shovels and sand trays and after much toil extracted their vehicle. It had received few bullet holes and though the men were exhausted they came through unscathed.

Another time the patrol was spotted by a Ghibli reconnaissance aircraft which dived down to investigate, whereupon Gunner Sanders quickly backed his truck up a dune to gain elevation for his gun and fired a couple of rounds at the plane. This in combination with Lewis gun fire proved sufficient enough to scare it off. Later that day when three bombers appeared Sanders did the same trick again, causing the aircraft to gain height, thereby becoming less of a threat to the patrol.

By March 1942, with the introduction of the new Chevrolet trucks and the halving of the patrols, each was now armed with five Lewis guns, one .303 Vickers Mk. 1, three .303 air cooled Vickers Ks, on single or twin mounts (these eventually replaced the Lewis guns), two heavy .50 cal. water-cooled Vickers, and to replace the Bofors and Boys, a more versatile, dual-purpose Italian 20mm Breda anti-tank/anti-aircraft cannon, mounted on the back of a truck.

The patrols could now produce more firepower than the original unit of twice the strength. This was further increased when .50 cal. Browning HB Air Pattern machine-guns were later issued. In addition, sometimes these and other weapons were collected from crashed aircraft, wrecked vehicles, or from the enemy, and fitted to the vehicles.

The light Italian Breda 20mm gun was mounted on a carriage turntable which was bolted through the rear deck onto the truck chassis. Operated by a crew of two, the weapon was very reliable and efficient, capable of transversing 360° horizontal and 180° vertical. It was fired by a foot trigger, leaving the operator free to transverse the gun. Fed by a 10-round clip, it could be loaded with a mix of ammunition to suit the target. The skill of the loader dictated the rate of fire. In July 1942 Gunner Saunders displayed the effectiveness of the Breda by knocking out four German vehicles in pursuit of his patrol. It also proved to be a useful weapon for shooting up enemy convoys. But the gun trucks, due to weight and storage factors, had little room to pack their own supplies, so these had to be distributed amongst the rest of the patrol. They also mounted single or twin machine-guns in the passenger's

position, to be used at the times when the gun was not required.

Merlyn Craw of T1 Patrol, recounted the story of how he came to fit additional firepower to his truck *Te Paki III*. It began when he and Trooper Frank White were recovering from malaria at Siwa. The men had to remain at the hospital, while the rest of the patrol moved on to a new base at Jalo. In a hut they found 12 Browning .303 aircraft machine-guns which had been recovered from a crashed Hurricane fighter. To help pass the time they chose two of the guns and decided to make a twin mount to fit on a truck.

The armament of T11 Te Anau, a Ford F30 of T Patrol 1941. Mounted on the back is a .303 Vickers Mk. 1 machine-gun. A tripod was also carried so the gun could be operated from the ground if necessary. The other weapon is a .55 Boys anti-tank rifle. Photo: Ian McCulloch.

A Vickers .303 Mk. 1 water-cooled machine-gun. Several Vickers in .50 cal. were also employed by the patrols. These weapons were sometimes cooled with Hypoid oil to overcome the shortage of water. A .303 Lee Enfield service rifle rests in a bracket on the inside of the truck. In the background, General Claude Auchinleck inspects the LRDG at the Citadel in Cairo, 1941. Photo: Tom Ritchie.

The Brownings were fired electrically when used in aircraft, so it was only after much experimentation that the men managed to get them to fire in unison. Eventually they were mounted on *Te Paki III*, and soon proved formidable weapons. The rate of fire for each gun was 1,200 rounds a minute, fed by linked metal belts of 1,000 rounds a piece. Other belts were simply attached by clipping them on with one round. The ammunition was obtained by the the RAF, who supplied them loaded in a sequence of tracer, incendiary and armour piercing. The belts produced a high and constant rate of fire, whereas with the Vickers K the 100 round drums had to be changed.

In addition to the twin Brownings, which produced a combined rate of fire of 2,400 rounds per minute, Craw's truck also carried a .50 Browning Air Pattern machine-gun that fired at a rate of 850 rounds a minute. This was the firepower of only one truck, which in combination with the guns of five or six other vehicles, virtually disintegrated their targets. When T1 raided the Barce airfield in September 1942, the patrol carried three pairs of .303 Brownings as well as twin Vickers K and .50 Brownings. It was the skill of the drivers who got them through the operation in the dark, but it was the gunners who made it a success. Most of the enemy aircraft, transport and equipment, were destroyed by volumes of accurate and steady machine-gun fire. Airfield defence positions were suppressed in the same way, or forced to fire erratically. Against the light of the burning aircraft and fuel dumps, the trucks should have been easy targets. Yet it was the combined ability of the drivers and gunners, along with some good luck, that enabled T1 to escape the airfield without loss.

By 1942/43 the truck mounted weapons had also proved devastating against concentrate enemy targets, such as convoys.

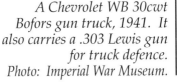

A Chevrolet WB 30cwt Bofors gun truck, 1941. It also carries a .303 Lewis gun for truck defence.
Photo: Imperial War Museum.

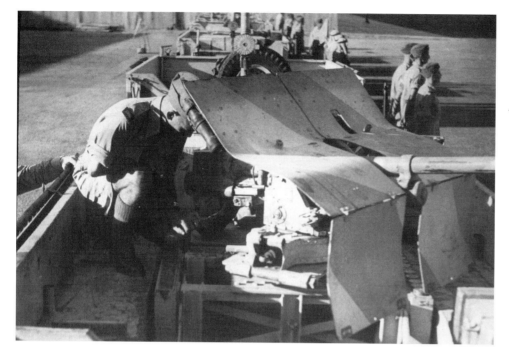

One account recorded in Kennedy Shaw's book on the LRDG described the armament as used in an attack by Captain Timpson's G1 Patrol:

> *Driving with the headlights on we came to the Road House, and passing by slowly, opened up on men and vehicles. The blaze of fire was tremendous, the first three trucks firing with one Breda 12.7 (tracer, incendiary, A.P. and H.E.), two Vickers .303, three Vickers K, one twin Browning, one single Browning and a Lewis. In fact there was too much fire, for the rear trucks were blinded by the light of those ahead and the multi-coloured ricochet of the tracer. Six large trucks were parked by the roadside and into these we poured ammunition.*

Of the variety of machine-guns adopted, the most widely used and effective was the lightweight, air cooled Vickers K. These aircraft guns, obtained from the RAF as they had become surplus to its requirements, were supplied to the LRDG, SAS and PPA. The weapon's high rate of fire of 950 rounds per minute, fed from 100 round flat drum magazines, made them ideal for hit-and-run raids, especially when they were used on twin mounts. They stood up to desert conditions extremely well, whereas the heavier Lewis gun, whose 47-round ammunition pan had an exposed base, tended to jam if subjected to wind blown sand. Later in the desert campaign a few .303 Bren guns fitted with 100 round drum magazines for sustained fire were also used.

One of the first Vickers K machine-guns used by the LRDG was responsible for shooting down a German aeroplane. Pilot Officer Rawnsley of the RAF travelled with T Patrol in December 1941 as an observer. He had brought with him a Vickers K, which he left behind after he returned to his squadron. Sergeant I. H. McInnes later adopted the gun and mounted it on his truck. One day while on patrol supporting the Eighth Army, six Me 110 fighter-bombers suddenly swept over them, flying very low. Merlyn Craw, who was with McInnes, rushed for the Vickers, but the planes were gone before he could fire. Then he saw another Me 110 following behind, trailing smoke. As it passed overhead Craw fired the whole pan of a hundred rounds of tracer ammunition at the Messerschmitt, plainly seeing the bullets ripping into its belly. Craw thought his effort with the Vickers caused the aircraft to stall as it endeavoured to get out of the line of fire. The plane crash-landed further ahead of the patrol.

Kufra, 1942. A Chevrolet 1533X2 30cwt gun truck of T2 Patrol, mounting an Italian 20mm Breda gun. This replaced the 37mm Bofors, and proved to be a very effective and reliable weapon. The gunner is C. A. Dornbush, with A. G. Ferguson (centre) and K. Kelly. Photo: Ian McCulloch.

Two-inch mortars were carried, though rarely used. During the attack on Murzuk in January 1941, Trooper I. H. McInnes of T Patrol set up his mortar about 360 metres from the town's fort. His first two bombs fell short, but after adjusting his sights he sent a further 18 into the enemy position. A fuel drum was hit which set the tower ablaze, destroying the flag and its pole, while black smoke engulfed the building causing much alarm amongst the defenders. McInnes' mortar shooting won him the Military Medal.

Also carried were the strengthened SMLE No. 1 Mk. III .303 EY (Extra Yoke) rifles fitted with discharger cups that projected a No. 36M (Mills) grenade set to a 7-second fuse. These saw good service in a number of actions. At Ain Dua, Lieutenant J. H. Sutherland won the Military Cross after dislodging enemy positions with grenades fired from a rifle cup. During the Barce raid Sergeant J. Dennis of the Guards caused havoc by discharging grenades through the windows of the Italian barracks. At El Ezzeiat, Trooper Springford of Y Patrol was responsible for the capitulation of a small Italian fort. He used the rifle cup to lob a Mills bomb into the fort's tower. This skilful shot knocked out a machine-gun and killed two soldiers. The garrison of 20 thought they were facing heavy calibre weapons, so they surrendered, along with quantities of stores, ammunition and three machine-guns, all at no loss to Y Patrol.

Alf Saunders of W Patrol recounted a story about a close call they had while undertaking rifle grenade training at Jalo oasis. The lesson was being conducted by Lieutenant Jim Sutherland, who was demonstrating a live firing exercise in front of about 12 men who formed an arc around him. He first fused a Mills bomb and placed it in the rifle cup, then inserted the special blank firing cartridge into the breech. With the rifle prepared he accidentally slammed its butt hard onto the ground. The resulting jar caused the weapon to fire, sending the grenade discharging vertically above the heads of the men. Someone shouted *"Run!"*, and the group dived for cover behind the nearest sand hammock they could find. The bomb exploded on the spot where the party had just been standing, showering the sheltering men in sand, with shrapnel whistling close by.

Front view of T10, the T2 Patrol Chevrolet 30cwt Breda gun truck. A captured Italian machine-gun is mounted on the front for personal defence. The driver is Trooper C. B. McKenzie.
Photo: Ian McCulloch.

Another view of the Breda gun truck. Trooper A. P. Renwick of R Patrol stands beside his Breda gun truck. The belts of 20mm ammunition draped over the truck were as supplied by the RAF. The individual rounds were removed from the belts and fitted into 10-round clips for use in the gun. This automatic weapon operated as fast as the loader could change the magazines. A light machine-gun was usually mounted by the passenger's seat as an additional weapon. Photo: Richard Williams.

Fortunately no one was hurt, and as the men scrambled to their feet they started to chuckle at the sight of the lieutenant's ashen face, as he realised how close he had come to wiping out half of his patrol. Alf Saunders said without thinking, *"Whose side are you on? The Germans!"* He got no reply. In jest, the men ensured it took Jim Sutherland a long time to live that one down. His proficiency in using this weapon against the enemy though, was well proven.

Mines and explosives were used as the need arose. From the beginning, mine laying was a common and successful practice for the LRDG. One night in December 1941, Corporal George Garven of T2 Patrol won the MM by destroying at least seven pursuing enemy vehicles by laying mines. He didn't have time to dig holes to bury the devices, so he placed them just below a rise where the headlights of the enemy transport would overshoot them. Before too long the patrol had counted seven explosions.

Gunner Edgar "Sandy" Sanders of T Patrol, 1941. Probably the LRDG's most remarkable gunner. He saw long and distinguished service in the unit, operating both the Bofors and Breda. In 1942 Sanders won the MM when he proved the effectiveness of the 20mm Breda by knocking out four German vehicles in pursuit of his patrol. Captain Peter McIntyre, the official NZ war artist, sketched Sanders and described him as, "One of the toughest men I have ever met." In 1938 Sanders saw action in the Spanish Civil War. After leaving the LRDG in 1943, he joined Popski's Private Army and fought in Italy as a patrol sergeant.
Photo: Ian McCulloch.

Buster Gibb described the result of one of his mine laying jobs:

We laid six mines across a track we suspected the enemy of using. Some considerable time later we revisited the area and found a large Lancia truck immobilised there. It had hit a mine with the front right wheel, which was blown off, and a part had gone through the sump.

The vehicle evidently continued on, and the left dual wheel was blown after the second mine had exploded. Evidence showed it carried on just past the row of mines, and some unfortunate jumped off the rear of the truck on to a third mine.

Merlyn Craw was T1 Patrol's explosive expert who had learned his skills by blowing up tree stumps on

his father's farm. Later with the LRDG he was sent on a demolition course, and used his knowledge in creating the bombs employed in the Barce raid. He was responsible for the destruction of ten Italian bombers. Plastic explosive was hard to obtain at the time, so he had to use Noble's gelignite or "808". A half kilo of this was mixed by hand into a ball with an equal amount of aluminium turnings. The incendiary part of the bomb consisted of beer cans of petrol which would ignite and scatter the aluminium turnings that spread the fire. Inserted into the explosive was a detonator on the end of an 8- second fuse. On the end of that was another smaller detonator which was struck from a spring loaded pin attached to a string. This was pulled when the bomb was placed on the aircraft. To ensure total destruction the devices were laid against the bomber's fuel tanks. Craw said they were lucky at Barce, because the planes were full of aviation fuel and not with bombs. Otherwise the explosions would have provided a greater danger than already existed.

Included in the original plan for the Barce raid, Merlyn Craw was to use his expertise to blow the town safe for Major V. "Popski" Peniakoff. It was thought to contain valuable information as well as a large amount of money to pay Peniakoff's Arab agents. However, prior to the raid the idea was scrapped.

Bomb making had certain drawbacks, as Frank Jopling of T Patrol wrote in his diary:

> *4 May 1942: Today four of us were shown how to make bombs, and this evening we started to make them ourselves. After using Nobles 808 for a while the man who is handling it gets a severe headache. Each of us has to make six bombs, and this evening I made my sixth, and believe me I certainly developed a headache, as did everybody else who had made their sixth bomb.*

Each truck had a designated gunner who usually had the position in the back, where he had to make himself as comfortable as possible sitting amongst the loaded stores. He was responsible for the maintenance of the weapons, fittings, mountings and ammunition supply. The machine-guns, though frequently covered to protect them from the sand and dust, had to be ready for instant action whenever needed, hence they were test fired every couple of days.

Personal weapons consisted of .38 Webley or Enfield revolvers, Lee Enfield .303 service rifles, .45 Thompson sub-machine guns and Mills grenades, or anything useful they may have taken from the enemy. It could be an advantage using the enemy's weapons while operating behind their lines, as it usually ensured a ready supply of ammunition.

The gunners often worked closely with the fitters in installing special mounts for "acquired" weapons, or improving the firepower. A number of guns similar to Merlyn Craw's twin Brownings were tested and put together in Archie McLeod's workshops at base. Because many of these weapons came from aircraft they relied on air speed for cooling. Though when tested, it was found that after firing 1,000 rounds the barrels became white hot, yet they still continued to operate without stoppage. The workshops skilfully installed special mountings to fit these and other weapons to the trucks.

In 1941, T Patrol fitter C. A. "Dorny" Dornbush tried to improve the rate of fire of his .303 Lewis gun by placing rubber bushes in the mechanism to make the bolt return faster. He tried it out once when his patrol was attacked by an Me 110 fighter-bomber. The only disadvantage was that the higher rate of fire meant the 47-round magazine had to be changed more often, which put the gunner at greater risk, especially while under air attack. Later this difficulty was overcome when belt- and 100-round drum-fed weapons replaced the obsolete Lewis. Another development was the use of graphite in machine-gun mechanisms. This resolved the problem of normal lubricants attracting sand and jamming the guns.

With the trucks heavily loaded, carrying fuel and munitions, there was always the danger of accidental fire or explosion. One incident occurred when Don Steele, the commander of R Patrol, was travelling about 2 kilometres ahead of the rest of his men in his Ford 15cwt pilot car. He was carrying bundles of scrim camouflage netting, mines in metal cases, and grenades and ammunition in wooden boxes. Both he and his driver were pipe smokers and travelling in an open vehicle caused the tobacco to burn quickly, eventually the glowing dottle would pop out. Which is what happened on this particular day, setting the scrim alight. As the wind fanned the flames the occupants were totally unaware of their predicament.

Following behind, Sergeant Gibb had observed the smoke trailing out of the back of his skipper's vehicle, so he told his driver to accelerate to warn the men. But the fully loaded 30cwt Chevrolet could only do 110 kilometres per hour on good "going", so they had no chance of catching the 15cwt. Gibb stopped his truck, loaded a magazine on his Lewis gun and fired a long burst alongside the Ford.

That startled the men who looked around and saw the fire. Instead of abandoning their vehicle, Steele and his driver stopped and immediately unloaded the truck. This was considered a very brave response, as the mine cases were red hot, the wood on the grenade cases was burning, and most of the scrim had gone. Despite the fire, everything was still serviceable.

R Patrol members showing off belts of .50 cal. ammunition. By 1943 the firepower of the patrols was devastating, especially against concentrated targets such as enemy convoys. Photo: Denis Bassett.

DRESS & INSIGNIA

The men who joined the LRDG supplied their own uniform and personal equipment as issued by their parent units. This basically consisted of greatcoats, battledress and khaki drill wear. The Group supplied leather sandals *(chapplies)*, which were more suitable for movement in the hot, soft sand than Army boots, and in 1941, the *keffiyeh*. This was a mustard coloured Arab headdress that was kept in place by a black, rope-like *agal*. Originally the patrols wore the topee pith helmet, being at that time the official desert issue. Though used for a while, they were considered a nuisance, and usually ended up rolling around the bottom of a truck until they finally became crushed and discarded.

It was after an officer from the Palestine Defence Force was taken on a trip as an observer that the idea of the *keffiyeh* was born. On their first night back he attended the mess in his full dress uniform, which included an Arab headdress. When Colonel Bagnold saw it, he declared that was what he wanted for his troops, so by early 1941 it had become LRDG issue. They were worn as parade dress (though such occasions were rare), and at other times as a matter of individual choice. When wrapped around the face they gave good protection from the cold, sun and flies, and were very useful in a sandstorm yet they could be stuffy in hot weather, and apt to become entangled in engines or heavy weapons. Dick Lewis of T Patrol recorded in his diary, his thoughts on the *keffiyeh*:

> *30 April 1941: We have been issued with Arab headdresses, forget what they are called, but it's the double ring holding on a square linen shawl affair folded into a triangle. Very good for travelling in a duststorm and things like that, but a nuisance for working at odd jobs. Probably the reason why Arabs never work at odd jobs.*

It tended to be worn more often at base, than in the field. By 1943, the *keffiyeh* had been replaced by the black RTR (Royal Tank Regt.) pattern beret as the official headdress.

T Patrol members Trooper B. F. "Mick" Shepherd (left) and Gunner E. C. "Lofty" Stutterd, showing off their newly-issued keffiyehs and LRDG shoulder titles, 1941. Photo: Shepherd collection.

An inspection at the Citadel in Cairo, November 1941. General Claude Auchinleck, accompanied by Captain L. B. Ballantyne, review T Patrol members wearing parade dress. The LRDG issued the Arab headdresses, shoulder titles and leather sandals. The trucks are Ford F30s mounting .303 Lewis guns and a Boys anti-tank rifle.
Photo: Tom Ritchie.

Trooper Clarke Waetford of R Patrol, the unit's first Maori soldier, poses for a studio photo dressed as an arab, Cairo, 1940.
Photo: Clarke Waetford.

Many New Zealanders, especially those who went overseas with the First Echelon in 1940, often wore First World War pattern greatcoats. Sometimes these still displayed the large early type distinguishing patches of their original units, sewn on the upper sleeves. For the cold weather, as an alternative to the greatcoat, a British "Tropal" sheep-skin-lined coat, or a locally-acquired "Hebron" sheep or goatskin coat, were also supplied.

A. D. "Buster" Gibb, of W Patrol, related his experience of the "big smelly" sheepskin coat:

> *The impression one got was that they had been roughly removed from a long tailed, long wool sheep, dried, then roughly cut to shape, sleeves added and then issued to us. They still had their dags and pizzles on. I never wore mine, but it made a lovely mattress on the sand.*

Personal equipment consisted of 1937 pattern web sets with cartridge carriers, along with the side and back packs. Revolvers were carried in either the web RAC pattern open top, or a flap type case, though sometimes leather holsters were also used. Apart from when armed with revolvers, most of this equipment was stowed in the vehicle, available within easy reach.

R Patrol members Trooper M. E. Hammond (left), Private E. Harcourt (centre) and Private F. R. Brown, display their issue sheepskin coats, 1940.
Photo: Jim Sutherland.

While on patrol the men dressed according to the climate. In colder conditions and especially at night they would apply layers of clothing that included New Zealand woollen underwear, battledress, jerseys, leather jerkins, sheepskins, greatcoats and balaclavas, with shoes or ankle boots. During winter they could remain dressed as such both day and night. Dick Lewis wrote in his diary: *"To see us, one would think we were in the polar regions instead of the desert."* In the summer as the day warmed up the layers were unpeeled, and by midday they would be down to shorts and sandals. On the early operations overalls were often used as everyday dress, notably by the fitters.

For LRDG personnel on campaign "Dress Regulations" did not exist. Comfort was the main consideration. Water rationing prevented shaving, so this along with the state of their dress often made the men look like a band of wandering vagrants. At times it was an advantage to be wearing nondescript clothing, especially when spotted from the air.

R Patrol members looking like a band of vagrants, as they are dressed against the bitter winter cold. Their truck behind them has been completely camouflaged in scrim. 1940.
Photo: Jim Sutherland.

Typical LRDG summer dress. Trooper Ian "Snowie" McCulloch of T Patrol stands beside his Ford F30 truck, 1941.
Photo: Ian McCulloch.

Trooper C. B. MacKenzie T2 Patrol, 1942. He displays his LRDG badge on the agal of his keffiyeh. He is also wearing the combined NEW ZEALAND/LRDG slip-on shoulder title.
Photo: Jim Sutherland.

R2 Patrol after two months behind the lines, and now looking like a group of Victorian seafarers. RTR Pattern berets are much in evidence.
Back row: E. J. Dobson (captured on Levita October 1943, died while POW 6 May 1945), A. Boys.
Middle: A. P. Renwick, L. T. Campbell, L. A. Ellis, J. B. Magee, ?, H.L. Mallet (killed in action, Levita 24 October 1943).
Front: J. E. Gill, R. R. Williams, F. D. Rhodes, M. W. Stewart
Photo: Richard Williams.

By waving at enemy aircraft, they could possibly be seen as Axis troops driving captured Allied vehicles.

The headdress was as varied as the clothing. The individual wore what he liked. Apart from the *keffiyeh,* Field Service and Service Dress caps, "Lemonsqueezer" felt hats, topees and the black RTR pattern berets were all in evidence. These could be worn showing the badges of their parent units (in the case of the New Zealanders, the "Onward" badge) or the LRDG badge, or no insignia at all. Knitted cap comforters or balaclavas, occasionally worn with badges, were also favoured. Steel helmets were carried in the trucks, though more often worn on the early operations, they saw little use later except when coming under heavy fire.

LRDG insignia consisted of shoulder titles and a cap badge. The usual shoulder title was a fabric slip-on type, with woven red letters (the weave of which often varied in shape and style) on a navy blue to black background. For the New Zealanders and Rhodesians this was sometimes incorporated with a national title, e.g. "NEW ZEALAND" (white letters against black). There was also a brass LRDG title, and cloth, black letters against khaki, slip on type, but these appear less common. No shoulder titles were worn in the LRP.

The first insignia to mark the LRP was in the form of a commemorative badge, presented to those who went on the initial incursion into Libya, in August 1940. Only seven were issued, and were awarded at a special parade at Abbassia by Anthony Eden, the British Foreign Secretary who visited Egypt in late September 1940. Private Merv Curtis, a New Zealander, who received one of these, recalls how on the night of the parade he had run short of money, therefore sold his badge to a British soldier for £3 10s.— a considerable sum at the time. Later, Bagnold got to hear about it and was furious. Merv provided a drawing of how he remembered this extremely rare item.

A drawing of the commemorative Long Range Patrol badge presented to those who participated in the first incursion into Libya, August 1940. Only seven were issued and were awarded at a parade at Abbassia by Anthony Eden, the British Foreign Secretary. Drawing by Merv Curtis.

T1 Patrol, Benghazi, March 1943. Dressed for winter, but now looking less like vagrants and more like soldiers.
Photo: Keith Tippett.

Apart from the special presentation, the unit's badge was produced in two patterns. The first was unofficial and made for those who served with W, R and T Patrols of the LRP. It was introduced to mark the existence of this near complete "Kiwi" force, before the Guards joined in December 1940 and it became known as the LRDG. The insignia was designed by Corporal C. O. (Bluey) Grimsey, an LRP recruit from the 7th NZ Anti-Tank Regt. He was later captured by the Germans in December 1942.

The badge was struck, made of silver and brooch mounted, it exhibited a fat scorpion enclosed in a circle that represented a wheel. Below this on separate scrolls was "LRP/NZ/LRDG". Because the scorpion was disproportionate it looked more like a beetle, so it was often referred to as the "scarab" badge. The scorpion was said to be modelled on the one that had stung Grimsey three times. He survived, but it died, and was kept pickled in a jar of spirit.

In early 1941, Issac Faber, a French jeweller, was contracted to manufacture the badges. He had a little shop in a narrow lane among other small traders, at the top end of the Fauad, in Cairo. Eric Carter of T Patrol said it cost £10 to have the die made, and the men purchased their own badges. Being silver, some were stamped on the reverse with either two or three Arabic hallmarks, whereas others were not stamped at all. Examples sighted show a variation in marks, some of which are indecipherable. Buster Gibb recalls the initial order was for 68 to be struck, yet up to 87 may have been manufactured before the men destroyed the die themselves. Though those who served in the LRP were entitled to the badge, a number were bought by men who had joined the unit a short time after the LRP had ceased. This was as a memento, because no other LRDG insignia existed at the time, apart from the shoulder titles.

A good proportion of the badges were made featuring a gilded scorpion, but as it was only a gold wash it quickly wore off. This would account for why most of those examples seen today now only show traces of gilding. Though some were worn as hat badges while at base or on leave, they were rarely displayed, if at all, in the field. Eventually, most were sent home to friends or family.

The second and official LRDG badge was adopted in early 1942. It was made of brass for O/Rs, and either blackened brass or bronze for officers, though they could wear either type. Still based on the original design, the scorpion was thinner and more

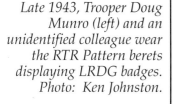

Late 1943, Trooper Doug Munro (left) and an unidentified colleague wear the RTR Pattern berets displaying LRDG badges. Photo: Ken Johnston.

Trooper Alf Saunders (centre) displays his LRP badge on his Lemonsqueezer hat. The photo was taken in early 1941 at a Cairo studio after he had just returned from a long desert trip, hence the lower half of his face is pale after his beard was removed. His battledress displays the early type New Zealand distinguishing patches and the brass NZ Mounted Rifles shoulder titles (NZ Divisional Cavalry) unofficially worn on his shoulder strap. The picture was taken with two old friends, Private Ashley Garnet (left) and Private Bill Gallagher. Photo: Alf Saunders.

accurately represented, also the LRDG letters were now enclosed within the circle. Most were produced in Egypt, where they were either cast or struck, then hand cut. There was usually no maker's mark, and the quality, finish and design were variable. Some makers displayed slightly different patterns on the back of the scorpion, and the circle varied in form, either being oval or with a single or double raised edge. Private purchase was also obtainable, such as "sweetheart" badges for girlfriends or family. These were brooch-mounted examples that were either plated, or made in solid gold or silver. One New Zealand patrol commander ordered a gold badge inset with diamonds. Furthermore, men could order LRP/ LRDG jewellery such as silver rings featuring gold scorpions, and gold or silver badge tie pins. Brassware items like LRDG engraved shell cases or ashtrays were also available.

In 1945 an English manufacturer, J. R. Gaunt and Son, made 50 pairs of brass LRDG shoulder titles and 50 second pattern LRDG cap badges. The company's name was stamped on the reverse of the insignia. These were especially ordered, to be worn by the LRDG veterans who participated in the Victory Parade in London.

LRDG insignia was at first forbidden for security reasons, but Bagnold later relented in the interest of "esprit de corps". The shoulder titles and badges were mainly worn at base or on leave, but were generally discouraged from being worn in the field. However, photos taken on patrol, notably in the latter part of the desert campaign, often showed the men displaying their LRDG insignia. Due to the general lack of outward identification, especially in summer when the men wore little proper uniform, they all carried paybooks to identify them as soldiers, so if captured they could not be accused of being spies. By the time of the Dodecanese operations in late 1943, LRDG insignia was usually worn in the field.

In the 1970s an English company, Russell King Badges, made reproduction bronze and white alloy LRDG badges for the British LRDG Association. The surface of the wheel is dimpled and the metal is thicker, so they cannot be confused with the originals. The New Zealand LRDG veterans wear a silver scorpion badge stick pin to mark their association, and to commemorate their 50th reunion in 1998 they produced a bronze scorpion lapel badge.

Wedding photo of Staff Sergeant Jack Emslie wearing his late pattern LRDG shoulder titles, while his wife Elise displays an LRDG brooch. Photo: Sharon Palmer.

DESERT LIFE

Life in the Libyan desert sustained many discomforts for the intruder; nature provided extremes of temperature, little water, vast sand seas and salt marshes, sandstorms, flies, scorpions and snakes, which in turn for man, produced the irritations of heat or cold, rain, thirst, fatigue, monotony, and apprehension. There was also the anxiety of operating behind enemy lines for very long periods of time, with little chance of assistance if stranded, sick or wounded, other than that which could be provided from their own resources. Despite these concerns, most men coped with, or overcame the challenges of their environment, and experienced reasonably good health, as Ron Landon-Lane of R Patrol said, "*Most of us enjoyed the desert.*"

Though a place of contrasts, many veterans fondly remember the wonder and beauty of the desert. Derek "Snow" Parker of T1 Patrol described the Great Sand Seas as magnificent clean sand dunes, 80 to 100 metres high, running like huge waves north to south, so clean and quiet. He spoke of the beautiful sunrises and sunsets followed by bright starry nights. Alf Saunders of W Patrol recalls camping with the patrol in a place called Tufawi, where he became in awe of what he saw as the wonderful crystal clear and sparkling sand, which shimmered in the sun like diamonds. He told the rest of his mates that when the war was over he would buy a million acres or so, and ship the sand all over the world to make beautiful concrete! From then on he had earned the nickname "Tufawi".

Probably what best sums up how the men felt about their time in the desert, is the story Derek Parker related about his commander Nick Wilder. One midday, they lay under their truck sheltering from the burning sun, feeling hot and sweaty, enduring the terrible heat, when Wilder said, "*Why the hell did we join such a bloody show as this*". Yet later in the cool of the evening, after dinner and a couple of rums, he laid back looking at the stars, and said to Parker, "*Boy! this is the life, isn't it Snow.*"

The unforgiving desert. The remains of a desert traveller who didn't make it. Often the LRDG came across bones, both human and animal, left by Senussi tribes who were fleeing the Italians in Libya. Photo: Buster Gibb.

R Patrol members Troopers Clarke Waetford (left) and Joe Eyles, patrol navigator, undertake their ablutions. The 4 gallon tins proved very useful when cut to shape to serve purposes such as cooking, carrying and washing containers. Occasionally clothes were washed in petrol, as water was too precious. The Chevrolet WB parked in the background has its Vickers machine-gun ready for action in case of air attack. Photo: Clarke Waetford.

Apart from the discomfort of climatic extremes, the most serious physical complaints endured were desert sores and malaria. The first was like an ulcer, which in severe cases could go through to the bone. It mainly occurred where the skin was broken and exposed to the sun though often irritating and painful, it was not usually bad enough to put a man off duty. Treatment was the application of sulphanilamide ointment and bandaging. But it did not always work, so other methods were experimented with. Buster Gibb tried a remedy he had learned while suffering boils as a youth, which was to bathe them in an Epsom Salt solution and leave them uncovered. This was applied in the desert using ordinary salt, and leaving the sores exposed to form a scab. The dry method proved successful and they healed quite quickly.

Lime juice and ascorbic tablets were also taken to help prevent the condition, which was a type of scurvy. At one time, Ron Tinker of R Patrol had a sore on his calf measuring about 40mm across and 10mm deep. He had to be taken to Cairo for proper hospital care. Some men when they returned to the city, after a diet of fresh vegetables and beer, had their sores heal within a few days.

Malaria was not a problem until the Group established a base at Siwa. Preventive measures included daily doses of atabrine or quinine, while at night the shirt sleeves were rolled down and long trousers worn. When the men wanted to sleep, they would crawl into mosquito nets in the shape of oblong boxes that were pegged out on the ground. On the road to Siwa there was a sign beside a small cemetery that contained the graves of malaria victims, which stated, *"You are entering a malaria area, have you taken your precautions?"* Three men once developed malaria while on a trip a long way out from base, but the patrol had to continue with its mission. By the time the sick had returned and been evacuated to hospital, they had been suffering for 21 days.

One of the worst places for sickness and discomfort was Taiserbo, where T and R Patrols were stationed at different times in 1941. It was an oasis 252 kilometres from Kufra, that consisted of a few scattered palms around brackish salt ponds, though the wells supplied good subterranean water supporting a population of about 700. They experienced very high temperatures and frequent dust storms. The heat was so bad that the men took pills for salt loss, (which were on general issue to desert troops), and spent most of the day lying under the shade of their trucks. Dick Lewis recorded in his diary, "The wind and sun here will dry a washed towel, held up at arms length, before your arms get too tired to hold it." Although they were used to walking about barefooted, by noon they could not stand the heat of the sand on their feet and had to tip-toe from place to place. The area was home to many scorpions and snakes, including the sand viper, the most deadly reptile in North Africa. Also, to quote Dick Lewis, home to "Large hairy spiders the size of the palm of your hand."

Corporal L. H. (Tony) Browne was bitten twice on his back by a snake that had settled in his bed roll. Fortunately it was not poisonous, and with medical assistance Browne recovered after six hours of agony. Gunner C. O. "Bluey" Grimsey was stung three times by a green scorpion. Though he recuperated overnight, the scorpion died. His comrades wondered what "Bluey" had coursing through his veins that would kill a scorpion, and enable him to recover so soon. Normally a sting could incapacitate a person for up to 36 hours or more, as the poison worked its way through the system. From then on most of the men felt safer sleeping in their trucks rather than on the ground.

Grimsey seemed to have a lot to do with scorpions, not only did he design the LRDG badge based on the one that had stung him, he had also on one occasion saved his commander from much suffering. While operating with W Patrol, Captain Mitford was stung in the foot by a scorpion, whereupon Grimsey quickly cut the affected area with a razor blade and sucked out as much poison as he could. Though the sting had given Mitford severe pain, Grimsey's effort prevented the condition from worsening.

Trooper Tom Ritchie of T Patrol gives a comrade a haircut, while in the background a navigational position is being taken with a theodolite.
Photo: Tom Ritchie.

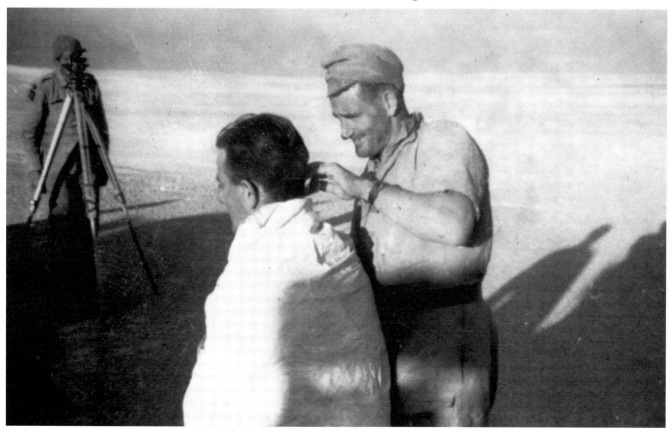

Taiserbo was also notorious for its flies. If a man went about without a shirt, which was usual on hot days, his back would soon be black with flies. At meal times it nearly drove the men crazy, some in sheer desperation threw away their food, plate, and utensils, while others ate their meals with their faces in the smoke of the fire in order to dine with less frustration. Another alternative was to keep walking while eating your food and not giving the flies a chance to settle. At nightfall they disappeared, only to be replaced by mosquitoes that continued the torment. Consequently, these conditions led to an increase in the occurrence of dysentery or malaria.

Because of the shortage of water, some patrol members had gone without a shave and a body or hair wash for up to three months. Yet very rarely did a man suffer adversely, or become lousy or infected with any kind of vermin. In some areas of the Sand Seas the sand was pure enough to "wash" with, use as "toilet paper", and to clean plates and cups. At one time though, several men picked up camel ticks from the site of an abandoned Italian camp. The Italians had very poor sanitation arrangements, such as no organised system of latrines, and refuse left unburied, so their camps usually attracted millions of flies.

The patrol always buried every item of refuse, not only to avoid fouling the area and attracting flies, but to ensure their presence was not given away to the enemy. In order to avoid affecting the subterranean water supply at places like Taiserbo, refuse was buried in drums. When a man wanted to relieve himself, he took a spade and went away from the camp and dug a hole. Due to the heat, much water was lost to the body through sweat. Mick Allen, an English medical orderly attached to R Patrol, wrote that he had seen, "An eighth of an inch of salt caked on a man's spectacles from perspiration."

After several weeks in the desert, urinating sometimes became difficult. Michael Shepherd wrote in his essay of one occasion where his father Mick had to lie on his side in the sand with his feet hard against a truck wheel, so that a "teaspoon" of thick liquid could be made to pass. Constipation was also a concern, though medicine was available to help ease this condition. One veteran recalled, that because of the diet and insufficient liquid intake, it was common for the men to excrete pellets like sheep droppings. Sometimes this problem was aggravated after drinking water from rusty four gallon water tins. This put too much iron in the system that could lead to constipation.

Due to disciplined rationing and good planning, the group rarely suffered serious water shortages while on patrol. Though a notable exception was when R Patrol under Captain Steele was on a trip to Hon, where they had expected to obtain fresh water. Unfortunately, on the way a Ford 15cwt developed a radiator leak. To enable them to reach their destination, most of the patrol's water ration had to be poured into the damaged radiator. On their arrival they found the water in the well had been fouled by goats, and was likened to that of a sheep dip. The men had reached the stage of drinking the cooling water from the Vickers guns, which was better than that in the well. After rearranging the stores, for the return journey the 15cwt was placed on the back of a 30cwt truck, and they were forced to resupply with the brackish water. Before use, Corporal "Curly" Ball strained the foul liquid three times through a sack prior to boiling, but even after generous proportions of tea and sugar, it made the men who tried it vomit immediately. As Ron Landon-Lane recalls, "It made you crook as a ram's horn!". The patrol suffered greatly from thirst until they reached base.

The most unpleasant desert phenomena was the hot dust-laden qibli of Libya or the khamsin wind of Egypt. This was a suffocatingly hot wind that sapped a man's energy, and made him want to lie in a stupor till the sun went down. It was often accompanied by driven dust or sand that stingingly added to his discomfort. The heat of the qibli could be so debilitating, that it sometimes made the men sick after their meals.

Opposite page top shows a pleasant view of Kufra oasis, an LRDG base and a cool place to bath and rest (photo: Ian McCulloch), whilst below Trooper Denis Bassett of T2 Patrol enjoys a bath made from a cut-out 44 gallon drum. Kufra, 1942. Photo: Denis Bassett.

Trooper Alan Nutt of T1 Patrol overlooks the ancient town and now LRDG base at Siwa. This town was said to produce the best dates in Egypt. Photo: Alan Nutt.

The summer heat also brought other irritations, such as causing the tinned food to become runny and sour or to hiss or explode when opened. The medical supplies could spoil and decanted rum soon evaporated if left sitting in the sun. Dick Lewis wrote of the heat in June 1941:

> *Getting very hot now, each day seems to be the hottest we have had, and the next day always manages to be a little hotter. From midday to three is the worst, and then, just as you think you can't stand much more of it, the temperature drops a couple of points.*

The regular cycle of bitterly cold nights, through to the severe heat in the day drained some men both physically and mentally. This along with little water, fatigue and exceptionally hot temperatures could lead to a condition known as cafard or desert madness, where a man's eyes become glazed as he stared with a bewildered vacant look out into the horizon. Shade, rest and plenty of water usually improved this malaise.

On the coast, where the wheels of thousands of vehicles churned up the desert surface, duststorms were common and made life a misery. But in the real desert of the south sandstorms occurred but were less frequent and considered fairly harmless. In 1942 one of the worst duststorms experienced by the Group was at Siwa. It arrived at six in the evening as a solid moving cloudy wall about 2,000 feet high. Stretching across the horizon, it poured down the northern scarp into the depression. A storm of fine dust hit the base at 65 kilometres per hour, blocking out the light, bringing down the temperature, and penetrating everywhere, in a man's eyes, ears, nose and throat. If caught out in the open the only protection was to shelter in the lee of a truck, wear sand-goggles, wrap the keffiyeh around your head and wait. After such an event, many frustrating hours were spent cleaning the dust out of vehicles, equipment, bedding, clothing and weapons. One severe storm was recorded as lasting for two days.

It was not until the Rhodesians, in mid 1941, concocted the *"anti-qibli pick-me-up"* that consisted of equal parts or rum and lime-juice, that the patrols were able to cope better with the extreme conditions. Dick Lewis wrote in his diary:

> *Sunday 11 May 1941: Very hot again today. A lot of chaps are getting sick, some with 'gyppo guts' and others just unable to keep any food down, while any skin abrasions soon turn into desert sores that gradually get bigger and deeper, and hurt quite a lot.*

Cleopatra's pool at Siwa. These cool bubbling springs have brought relief to desert travellers for centuries. Photo: Merlyn Craw.

Buster Gibb recounted his observations of sandstorms:

There were sandstorms that drew blood from exposed skin, burnished the paint off the sides of vehicles, and created static electricity in the trucks powerful enough to knock you over. Also, some that only blew sand about eight feet above ground level. During such a storm it was possible at times, if you stood on top of a loaded truck, to eat your meal in clear air. Usually from the waist up, one was safe.

The undercarriage of a De Havilland DH86 hospital plane, above, collapsed after landing in soft sand at Kufra airfield,1942. Its mission was to evacuate LRDG malaria cases to Cairo for proper care. Photo: Ngaire Lewis.

Kufra airfield. The result of a collision between a Blenheim light bomber and a Bristol Bombay bomber/transport of 216 Squadron, RAF. Kufra airfield was subject to sandstorms and air raids, which often made aircraft movements hazardous. Photo: Shepherd collection.

Derek Parker described the sand-storm he experienced while at Siwa:

We were cooking the midday meal when suddenly it became quiet and fairly dark, then someone shouted, "Good Lord, look at that". In the distance a huge sandstorm was coming in, thousands of feet high, travelling at about 30 kilometres per hour. It was red in colour, but there was no sand that colour for miles around. I couldn't help thinking that if the wind suddenly stopped, and all the sand settled, we would have been buried feet deep. Perhaps that was what had happened to the ancient armies we had read about, that had disappeared in the desert.

In the winter months the weather could produce other extremes such as a hard frost in the morning, where dregs of water left in dixies froze to ice in a few minutes. Frank Jopling of T Patrol wrote in his diary:

11 January 1942: This morning there was the hardest frost I have yet seen in the desert. My water bottle, which was felt covered, was frozen, and if we put a bit of water on a plate, it would freeze straight away.

Such temperatures were intensified ten-fold when travelling at speed in open trucks. As Buster Gibb wrote:

It was like sitting in front of the blast in a freezer, and the person who said, "until the sands of the desert grow cold", never had a clue.

Sudden violent winter storms were also encountered, as Jack Davis of T1 Patrol, recorded in his diary:

11 December 1942: During the night the rain developed into a real storm, and in no time the wadis were filling with raging torrents of water. We were flooded out, so sudden did the rivers form, that it resulted in some gear being lost before we could make higher ground.

Sometimes, in just one night, a variety of climatic conditions could occur, as Dick Lewis wrote in his diary:

27 February 1942: A severe electrical storm last night. The wireless operator had the Wyndom aerial up and it was buzzing and sizzling and charging the whole truck. They managed to pull the aerial wire off and after a bit to let down the aerial. Quite a bit of rain fell, followed by three to four hours of sandstorm.

These conditions left the men cold, wet and miserable. At such times the rum ration was particularly welcome as they rested and looked forward to the other climatic extreme: the heat of the day.

Another desert phenomenon was the mirage, which is an optical illusion caused by refraction of light passing through layers of atmosphere of varying density. Merlyn Craw said he hated them, because they usually occurred on very hot and windless days. Whereas Derek Parker said they were amazing to encounter and recalled one occasion during a journey over the Sand Sea when the patrol saw what appeared to be beautiful lakes stretching into the distance with palm trees growing out of the sky. Another time he saw what looked like a 30 storey building, but upon getting closer it got smaller and smaller, until finally it became a four gallon benzine tin.

One of the drawbacks of long patrols in the inner desert was the lack of assistance for the sick or wounded. On the first two trips of the LRP there were no medical orderlies. When a truck overturned on a razorback dune, Lance-Corporal Fred Kendall split his knee open, so Trooper Dan Ormond stitched it up with a needle and an ordinary piece of string. This accident resulted in the introduction of medical orderlies being assigned to the patrols. They were either recruited

A huge sandstorm approaching Siwa, May 1942.
Photo: Merlyn Craw.

The desert presented some amazing rock formations, as this example, right, known as Mushroom Rock. Driving alongside is a Chevrolet 1311X3 15cwt R2 Patrol vehicle. Photo: Sharon Palmer.

Known as "Penis Rock" to the patrols, the feature far right was the remains of a petrified tree. Standing alongside is Trooper J. T. Bowler, who was later killed in action in October 1943 on the island of Levita, Dodecanese Islands. Photo: Richard Williams.

Pottery Hill, 1940. The patrol occasionally found traces of ancient civilisations in the course of their work. In the top picture, opposite page, R Patrol members (left to right, G. H. Nelson, F. R. Brown, C. G. "Curly" Ball and L. A. "Bill" Willcox) examine some very old pots.

The desert heat meant that the men were often dressed in shorts only, as the R2 Patrol men in the picture at the bottom of the opposite page illustrate. They are, from left to right: H. L. Mallet (later killed on Levita, October 1943), R. R. Williams, J. E. Gill, L. T. Campbell, M. E. Hammond and Lieutenant C. B. H. Croucher. Note the .303 Browning machine-gun mounted on the truck. This was taken from a crashed aircraft and has had a crude shoulder stock fitted. Photo: Richard Williams

from the Royal Army Medical Corps, or were especially trained men. There was no room for passengers, as they also had to be gunners or drivers with a definite job to do. Because this went against the Geneva Convention in regard to medical personnel, they never wore arm bands or displayed the Red Cross. Colonel Bagnold instructed them to leave their paybooks at base, though some still preferred to carry them.

The patrol members knew that even with the orderlies, they could expect only the minimum of medical attention, and they appreciated the difficulties of evacuating seriously wounded or sick cases, and getting expert attention when it was most needed. The orderlies had been taught how to administer a fatal drug, in case it was necessary to resort to such measures. Where there was no hope of recovery it was considered more merciful to release a man from suffering a painful lingering death under the hot desert sun.

Occasionally, especially after shooting up enemy road convoys, severely wounded soldiers were put out of their misery with overdoses of morphine, or by any other means deemed appropriate. For those who

fought in the unforgiving desert, a quick death was thought humane, otherwise it could be slow but certain, tortured by the sun and scavengers.

Some men had difficulty in coming to terms with these mercy killings, being troubled with memories that plagued them long after the war. But because they operated in remote areas, proper medical attention did not exist. So every man knew what had to be done, should he or his enemy become beyond care. Nonetheless, it was hard on those who had to deal with it.

While each patrol carried a medical orderly, the Medical Officer ran a small hospital or receiving station at base HQ for short-term complaints, and for holding serious casualties for evacuation. The MO also had a mobile Medical Inspection Room for treating patients away from base. This was a wooden-bodied canopy mounted on a Chevrolet 1311x3IP 15cwt truck chassis. The LRDG doctor usually only went out with the patrols on major operations, such as the Barce raid. The patrol orderly coped with most injuries and could obtain additional advice by radio. Where possible, the seriously wounded or sick were sometimes able to be evacuated by air, otherwise it meant

a long and tortuous journey in the back of a truck.

One very distracting condition that could turn a long patrol into a nightmare, was toothache. As Trooper Frank Jopling recorded in his diary while out on operations:

3 February 1941: I have been getting a fair bit of toothache lately, I hardly slept at all last night and decided to get the tooth out somehow. I went to the doctor and he wouldn't take it out because it was a back tooth and he had no pincers to get hold of it, but he said he would give me dope. I have had toothache all day today and have been very miserable. If it is going to be like this for ten days until we get to Cairo, I will probably be crazy by then.

Jopling's suffering was suppressed by small doses of morphine, until they finally reached Cairo and the tooth was extracted at Maadi army camp.

As with the fitters, the medical orderlies often had to improvise while in the field. Buster Gibb tells a story of what lengths Bluey Grimsey went to to ensure that he could be among the "first" to enter Kufra. The French had just taken the town from the Italians, and an LRDG party of mostly medical cases was being sent in to rest up. Grimsey professed to be writing a book at that time, so he wanted to be one of the first into Kufra. In order to become a medical case he complained of having bad constipation. The medical orderly recommended an enema, but there was no equipment to perform one. Buster Gibb suggested using a grease gun. Unfortunately the type they carried had a square nozzle on the end of a flexible tube. But Bluey's desire to become one of the first prompted him to agree to it being used. A greased soft cloth was wrapped around the end of the nozzle, and the cylinder filled with a soapy water solution. The procedure was carried out by the medical orderly, and Bluey, being so determined, never complained. His

treatment produced no immediate results. However, he publicly dug holes all round the camp, saying if he had to shoot out in the night there would be no problem finding a hole. The patrol commander, and Gibb the NCO, felt that Bluey might be having them on and was told that he wasn't going to Kufra. That night to great fanfare the patient announced that things were working well again.

Another example of Kiwi ingenuity was when Corporal Rex Beech suffered a bad case of heat stroke. It was considered that ice or cold water would probably revive him, none of which were available. Small quantities of water could be chilled by evaporation, but the necessary amount could not be produced in the time required. Then one of the patrol members had an idea. The trucks carried methylated or white spirits for starting the primus stoves, and it was known that the quick evaporation of the spirit could cause a chill factor. Beech was swabbed down with the liquid and the experiment worked successfully, the cooling effect was sufficient enough to enable him to recover.

In the top picture, opposite page, T Patrol enjoy Christmas dinner in the shade of Zella oasis, 1942. On some occasions meals had to be shared with hundreds of flies, though there tended to be less in the inner desert, as it was cleaner.
Photo: Ngaire Lewis.

Illustrated in the lower picture is a rare sight in the desert. A sudden rainstorm has bogged this R2 Patrol truck which had to be pulled out. Note the pair of inverted Vickers K machine-guns.
Photo: Richard Williams.

Each patrol carried a medical orderly who, when deep behind the lines, was the only medical aid available. Photographed below an R Patrol man receives treatment for an injured finger. 1940.
Photo: Imperial War Museum.

Driving in open top vehicles meant there was no escaping the sun, a keffiyeh or hat being the only protection, and therefore sunstroke and thirst could test a man's sanity at times. An RAF officer attached to W Patrol to plot landing grounds developed sunstroke. He had been left to drive, as the regular crew members were hung-over from a celebration the night before. But as the concentration and heat got to him, his condition grew worse.

When they had stopped he started offering money to others so he could buy their water issue. Nobody accepted, as their limited water ration was considered far too precious. The officer had lost control and drank his own water too quickly without conserving it. The more he drank, the more thirsty he seemed to become.

There was water in the two gallon tins stowed on the running boards, but his discipline was not completely lost. To have taken that would have been a very serious offence and may have put the patrol's strict water rationing in jeopardy. Eventually though, after a rest in the shade and a little water the officer recovered.

Rapid drinking during the heat of the day had to be avoided, as nearly all the water was merely lost again in excessive sweat. The first cravings for water were lessened by just moistening the mouth and throat by taking small sips from the waterbottle.

It was possible for the heat to lead to a "thirst" in a truck, which could bring it to a sudden and untimely halt, as Trooper Frank Jopling explained in his diary:

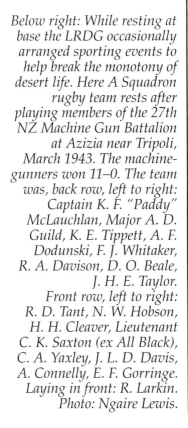

R2 Patrol stopped in the middle of open desert for a radio communication to Cairo. The Chevrolet 1311X3 15cwt on the right is carrying sick or wounded, and has a canopy erected to protect them from the heat.
Photo: Sharon Palmer.

Below right: While resting at base the LRDG occasionally arranged sporting events to help break the monotony of desert life. Here A Squadron rugby team rests after playing members of the 27th NZ Machine Gun Battalion at Azizia near Tripoli, March 1943. The machine-gunners won 11–0. The team was, back row, left to right: Captain K. F. "Paddy" McLauchlan, Major A. D. Guild, K. E. Tippett, A. F. Dodunski, F. J. Whitaker, R. A. Davison, D. O. Beale, J. H. E. Taylor.
Front row, left to right: R. D. Tant, N. W. Hobson, H. H. Cleaver, Lieutenant C. K. Saxton (ex All Black), C. A. Yaxley, J. L. D. Davis, A. Connelly, E. F. Gorringe.
Laying in front: R. Larkin.
Photo: Ngaire Lewis.

16 May 1941: Today I shifted my benzine pipe. Apparently in the hot weather you could be travelling along when suddenly the engine stops. The benzine gets so hot that it turns into gas before it gets to the pump, therefore it doesn't pump. Sometimes you have to wait a long time before you can get it started again, which would be just too bad if a Hun patrol was chasing you. So today I brought the pipe up through the floorboard, and let it through to the engine at the shortest distance from the pump.

To help relieve boredom the LRDG sometimes organised sports days between patrols. Trooper Frank Jopling recorded one occasion:

16 July 1941: Zighen: We took five trucks with us and arrived at Zighen at 1.45pm. Naturally we all made for the swimming pool. At 3.30pm S Patrol put on "Tea and cakes". The cakes were made of oatmeal, cocoa and syrup, they were very good. The sports started at 4pm and the first event was the Bofors shoot. Neither party hit the target so it was a draw. The next was the mortar at 300 to 400 yards range. S Patrol won the 300 yards and we won the other one, so it was a draw again. We then split up into six teams of four for rifle shooting. We won the first, they won the second. We drew the third, won the forth, lost the fifth, and drew the last, so again it was a draw.

Then came the main event of the day, the "All Blacks" verses the "Springboks." When both teams were lined up on the field, our team gave them the Haka (a Maori war dance or challenge). After it was finished, Lieutenant Olivey who was playing for the Springboks, ran to his truck and took his false teeth out saying, "This looks like it is going to be tough." Vic Heard is the best Pakeha (European) I have ever seen doing a Haka. At half time we led 3–0 and never got the ball out of the scrum once. Their backs were good but our backs were good tacklers which saved us the game. The end of the game saw us in the lead 6–0 and only once did

our forwards heel the ball out of the scrum. The first half was 10 minutes, and both sides decided it was too long so the second half was 7 minutes. That put us in the lead.

The next item was tea which consisted of gazelle which S Patrol had shot on recce on the Zella road. It was very good. After tea we had a smoke concert. There was plenty of wine and rum and a very enjoyable evening was spent by all.

The next day, despite nearly everyone suffering a hangover, the patrols continued their sports with a relay race and playing basketball. The total scores were all even, so they tossed for the trophy which T patrol won.

After a long patrol the men looked forward to the pleasures of Cairo: beer, a good meal and women. Below R Patrol members pose for a photo at the NZ Forces Club, 1942. Left to right, standing: R. O. Spotswood, J. H. Jones, F. J. W. McKeown, Sitting: R. A. Tinker, R. J. Landon-Lane, E. F. Gorringe, M. Allen (British medical orderly attached to R Patrol), F. R. Brown. Photo: Erl Gorringe.

AIR ATTACK & DESERT SURVIVAL

The greatest danger to the patrols was air attack, which accounted for most transport losses, with strafing being usually more effective than bombing. The best forms of protection were concealment and wide dispersion if caught in the open. Trooper Frank Jopling of T Patrol wrote in his diary of air attacks:

13 January 1941: In this outfit I don't mind how many machine-guns are firing at us or how many rifles, but one thing we do not like and that is bombers. We seem to be absolutely helpless against them as they are nearly always too high for machine-gun fire and when they pass straight overhead you wonder if they had let go their bombs, if so, will they land anywhere near you. Then you see them pass on and you think, well, if they had let their bombs go they would have dropped them by now, but even then you are not sure. By the time you are sure, the plane is on its way back again, and you go through the same sensation all over again. On the cry of "aircraft", closely followed by "scatter", we didn't need the second invitation, as the drivers started up and got going as fast as possible for cover. The gunners put on a drum or a belt of tracer bullets and as they came fairly close opened up on the planes.

Patrols endeavoured to make the best speed practicable, depending on the terrain, with the pilot car ranging ahead to select the better route. There was always the danger of the tracks being spotted from the air and followed until the patrol was found. At all times, depending on the "going", the formation had to be open and irregular with no two vehicles so close together that one bomb or shell would put them out of action. Straight runs had to be limited to about 10 kilometres separated by right-angled jinks of around 2 kilometres to confuse aerial search. Approaches to dumps or rendezvous were concealed wherever possible by movement over hard ground which left no tracks, or by laying false trails.

Also, both the aero screens and headlights had covers to prevent sun reflection revealing the vehicle's position.

While travelling in open country there was always at least one member of each crew on lookout for aircraft, as their approach could not be heard. Constant watching was the only way to avoid being surprised. The trucks threw up dust plumes that could be easily seen from the air, so the first action on sighting an aircraft was to stop, warn the others by a series of short blasts of the horn and hope that they would be overflown. Long blasts signalled the all clear. It was common procedure not to fire before the enemy, as many aircraft broke off their attacks when the lack of reaction misled them into thinking that they were dealing with Axis personnel equipped with captured Allied vehicles. Because they were usually operating behind the lines they were also in equal danger from their own aircraft.

Where possible, the patrols would travel widely dispersed to help reduce the chances of damage if caught by an air attack.
Photo: Ian McCulloch.

The result of an air attack, a burnt out Ford F30 truck. The extra fuel supplies carried usually meant that if a truck was hit, its destruction was assured.
Photo: Ngaire Lewis.

Trooper Ron Moore on parade (right). After their truck was destroyed at Gebel Sherif in February 1941, he led a three man party on an enduring 10 day, 336 kilometre trek. Consequently he received the New Zealand Division's first DCM of WW2. Other T Patrol members (not part of this trek) shown, left to second right: D. M. Bassett, B. F. Shepherd, E. C. Stutterd and L. A. McIver. Photo: Tom Ritchie.

If an air attack was unavoidable the patrol would widely scatter at speed, with the drivers taking instructions from their spotters who watched the approach of the enemy. If subject to aerial bombing they took evasive action as required, by turning sharp left or right as the bomb loads were released . A classic example of this was in November 1940, when Captain Mitford's W Patrol was travelling over an open plain near Karkur Murr, where they were subject to a bombing attack which lasted for more than an hour. At first the Italian bombers approached at 1,000 feet, but as the trucks returned heavy small arms fire, they circled up to at least 5,000 feet to where they became out of range. The salvos of bombs were easily avoided by wide dispersal and by swerving the vehicles at right angles to the plane's line of flight. Over 300 small bombs were dropped, including 32 directed at just one truck. Luckily the whole patrol escaped without receiving a single hit to vehicles or personnel.

T2 Patrol members who returned to base in the sole surviving truck, T10, after five out of their six vehicles were destroyed by Stukas, January 1942. Left to right: A. H. C. Nutt, ?, Lieutenant C. S. Morris, I. G. McCulloch, J. H. Thompson, C. A. Dornbush. Photo: Ian McCulloch.

The Group were masters in the art of desert camouflage. They utilised their surroundings and hid in the shadows of cliffs or steep dunes, parked amongst large rocks and boulders, and exploited the scant protection of thinly spread bushes and dry wadis. This in conjunction with the concealment of tracks and the effective use of netting, foliage, and vehicle colour schemes, meant patrols were often overflown by Axis aircraft or closely bypassed by ground forces without being seen. At night the trucks positioned themselves facing in different directions so they could get away as quickly as possible in case of emergency. To aid this, every article was packed away in its proper place on the truck after use, and not left laying about till dawn.

Ground strafing was more difficult to deal with. The only defence, apart from manoeuvring, was return fire from the trucks, that if concentrated kept the aircraft high enough to impair aim and prevent the pilots pressing home the attacks. Because the trucks carried a limited supply of ammunition, aircraft were only to be fired at when there was a reasonable chance of inflicting damage. According to Bagnold's 1941 Training Manual, aircraft should not be engaged at over 1,500 to 2,000 feet, and gunners should engage dive-bombers head on at 500 to 600 feet.

One of the first enemy actions that resulted in an epic LRDG survival story was in February 1941, when T Patrol under the command of Major P. A. Clayton was raiding in the Fezzan. Trooper R. J. Moore's truck had been destroyed along with three others after an attack by the Italian Auto-Saharan Company at Gebel Sherif, which was closely followed by aircraft strafing attacks. Moore had received a shell splinter in his foot and one of his crew, Guardsmen J. Easton, had suffered a severe throat wound. His other crew members were Guardsman A. Winchester and RAOC fitter A. Tighe. These men were left behind as the rest of the patrol presumed they had been killed or

captured, but they managed to take cover amongst some large boulders. They also had in their company an Italian prisoner who had been with them in the truck.

After dark the party went back to the vehicles where all they could recover was a three-quarters full two gallon (9 litre) water tin which had a bullet hole near the top. All the rations had been destroyed. The men were dressed in shorts and shirts only, as their headgear and footwear had been lost in the burnt out trucks. Trooper

Some of the T2 survivors who had walked out of the desert after their transport was shot up. Note, Corporal Garven, the leader of the party, still wears the rags that bound his feet on the long trek. January 1942. Left to right: R. A. Ramsay, A. C. Martin, D. M. Bassett, Corporal G. C. Garven, T. E. Walsh. Photo: Denis Bassett.

Moore, using the point of his knife, endeavoured to extract a jagged piece of metal lodged in the back of Easton's throat. He was unsuccessful, as was his attempt to pull shrapnel from his own foot. The men discussed the choice of making for Kufra, about 110 kilometres away, and surrendering to the Italians, or walking out following the tracks of their patrol towards Sarra. They chose the latter, and embarked on what was to become an epic march of desert survival and determination. The Italian pleaded with the group to surrender, kissing the hands and feet of each man in turn, but they ignored him and took him along.

Moore, who became the leader of the party, bandaged his foot with a handkerchief and set out on 1 February for Sarra, 216 kilometres away. During the day the Italian prisoner left them and he was later picked up by his compatriots. The night temperatures were near freezing, which made it difficult to get any sleep or rest. They had to dig a hole in the sand and lay with their arms around each others trying to keep warm.

Trooper D. M. Bassett, T2 navigator, January 1942. This photo was taken soon after he was rescued and returned to base, having successfully guided a 10 man party to safety. In the final stages of the journey, due to exhaustion, his legs gave out and he had to crawl until he was fortunately found by arabs who took care of him. Bassett received the DCM for his skilful navigation. Photo: Dick Lewis.

On 4 February they found a pot of plum jam and some lentils which had been left behind by their patrol on its way north, and scraped out empty milk cans that had been thrown away. The lentils were uneatable as they were too salty and made Winchester ill. Luckily a field dressing was found, so Moore and Tighe were now able to have their wounds properly bound. Moore later wrote that he believed that he could not have continued had he not discovered that field dressing to cover his foot. By the next day Tighe was feeling the effects of an old abdominal operation and could not keep up. He urged the others to go on without him because he felt he was hindering their progress. The men gave him his share of the water, pouring it into a bottle that had been picked up. Sadly, it was not till the others had gone that Tighe discovered that it had contained some salty substance which made the liquid undrinkable.

On the sixth day, despite nearly having lost the tyre tracks they had been following due to a sandstorm, they eventually arrived at Sarra. The place was abandoned and consisted of a few mud huts and a filled-in well, but there was no food. They discovered some waste motor oil and bathed their feet and lit a fire. The next day they moved on.

Tighe, though exhausted, managed to arrive at Sarra the evening of the others' departure. He found a match in the sand, which, along with some oil, enabled him to light a fire. Without this he would have probably died that night from the cold. Three days later a Free French patrol came across him while returning from a reconnaissance of Kufra. Despite his weak state, having had no water for four days, Tighe was able to tell the party about the plight of his comrades.

In the meantime, on the eighth day, Easton became delirious and had dropped behind. Moore and Winchester were seen by two French aeroplanes, and one dropped a canvas

bag containing a bottle of lemonade. When the men recovered the bag they found to their great disappointment that the stopper had come off the bottle, leaving only a mouthful each. The aircraft were unable to land as the ground was strewn with stones, so they flew on to Tekro to organise a rescue party.

On 10 February Easton was picked up 90 kilometres from Sarra, lying in the sand, but alive, and so was taken back to Sarra. He could scarcely swallow owing to the dreadful wound in his throat, from which he had suffered continuously. The medical officer managed to give him a few drops of sweet tea, and with a little smile Easton was heard to say, *"I don't usually take sugar with my tea."* He died shortly afterwards, despite all the doctor's efforts to revive him. Easton was the first Scots Guardsman to die in North Africa and was buried near the well.

A further 16 kilometres on they located a semi-delirious Winchester. Moore had gone on alone, existing solely on sips of water which, in the concluding stages, he returned to the bottle after moistening his mouth. By the time the Free French had overtaken him, 16 kilometres south of where they found Winchester, he was still walking steadily, and while

barefoot had covered 336 kilometres in 10 days. Though close to delirium he felt confident that in three days he could have reached the nearest water at Tekro, 130 kilometres away, and was slightly annoyed that he was prevented from proving this.

Known as "Skin" Moore to his comrades, his trek was remarkable in that although he had nothing to eat for 10 days except a little jam, only four pints of water to drink, and with a shell splinter lodged in his foot, he managed to walk such an incredible distance. Furthermore, he had given support and encouragement to his companions who were physically weaker than himself.

It was considered that such a journey was only humanly possible due to the cold. In hot weather it would have most unlikely that any man could have remained alive in the desert without water for more than three days. Moore's leadership and determination earned him the New Zealand Division's first Distinguished Conduct Medal of World War II. Guardsman Easton received a posthumous Mention in Despatches.

Another example of one of a number of successful enemy strafing actions was in December 1941, when T2 Patrol under Lieutenant C. S. Morris was transporting SAS members after successful raids against Axis airfields. A Me 110 fighter-bomber had followed the tyre tracks from a recently raided landing ground at Nofilia, near Agedabia, and despite intense anti-aircraft fire, strafed the patrol from a height of about 60 feet killing an SAS officer, Lieutenant T. J. Lewes. When the plane had spent its ammunition it returned to base. Soon afterwards Stukas and a spotter plane appeared and began low altitude bombing and strafing attacks which continued for the next six hours. Though T2 was now widely dispersed and its vehicles camouflaged, four out of the five trucks (Ford F30s) were destroyed. The German aircraft continued to attack the men on the ground, machine-gunning every bush that might give cover. The survival of the one vehicle (T10) was due largely to the courage of Private C. A. Dornbush, who although wounded and his truck hit several times, remained behind his machine-gun throughout the battle. He was awarded the Military Medal for this action.

Following the attack Lieutenant Morris could not locate the scattered crews of the destroyed vehicles, so with five T2 and four SAS men he made the 320 kilometre journey back to base at Jalo in the one surviving truck. Dick Lewis recorded in his diary what he had learned about the fate of T2:

2/1/42. The second part of the patrol, T2, which we were to pick up, has had a bit of a knock. Got caught in the open desert by MEs and Stukas just near an enemy aerodrome. Strafed for six hours. One truck, riddled with bullets, came in with survivors. Others may be walking somewhere, but were behind enemy lines.

3/1/42. The other half of T Patrol certainly had a bad spin. They were spotted first by one Me 110, but beat that attack off, whereupon the ME went back to the nearby aerodrome and whistled up some Stukas. There was absolutely no cover to hide in, and when the planes came back the trucks scattered. The crews bailed out and just laid "doggo" on the ground. All the trucks except one were blown up, and every depression and bush in the vicinity raked with machine-gun fire.

The patrol had just picked up some SAS men who had been wrecking enemy planes on the ground, and the Jerries were out to make a clean sweep. They killed the SAS officer who was in T10, and the crews of T6, T7 and T9 haven't been heard of yet, but may be walking the desert, if alive.

6/1/42. Still in Jalo. A hell of a sandstorm raging, one of the worst. No word of missing men from T2 party, but they have a big chance of being alive at least. The percentage casualties from air strafing, of which we have quite a lot, has been remarkably low. Although those planes were out to make a clean sweep of the trucks, the men may have quite possibly lived through six hours of personal strafing in the open desert by lying perfectly still. The position was roughly 250 miles north-west of here, and behind the German lines; quite a long walk.

Amazingly, the remaining men had survived the air attack. The party consisted of Corporal G. C. Garven,

Gunners E. C. Stutterd, E. Sanders and T. E. Walsh; Troopers D. M. Bassett, A. C. Martin, F. S. Brown and R. A. Ramsay. Also two Englishmen, Private White of the SAS, and Private J. Fair, Royal Corps of Signals (radio operator). The navigator, Trooper D. M. Bassett, while still under heavy fire, had managed to recover from his burning vehicle 14 litres of water in a four gallon (18 litre) tin, a packet of nine biscuits, a tin of chocolate and a prismatic compass. This was their entire resources as everything else had been destroyed. They decided to walk to Augila, an oasis 32 kilometres from Jalo and 320 kilometres from where they were stranded—their only other option was to go to the Marada– El Aghelia road and surrender.

To avoid being seen from the air, and as the mid-winter cold was too bitter to allow sleep, the party marched at night, resting during the warmer hours of the day. Most of the men had been wearing sandals which by the second day, because of the stony ground, had fallen to pieces, hence they bound their feet with cloth from their jackets and greatcoats. On the third day, White the SAS man, who had already walked many miles in the raid on Nofilia and whose feet were almost raw, left the party at the Marada road. He said he would try to seize a truck and get home that way. White was given his share of the water and never seen again. The next day the group met four Arabs who directed them to a spring and provided some dates, which were more palatable than the desert snails the men had been sampling. That night they sat around a fire, and the next morning set off with their water tin refilled. However, in their weakened state it wasn't long before it became necessary for the men to form teams of four to carry the water in short relays.

At the end of the fifth day they boiled some water and made a chocolate drink which renewed their strength, for the following night they marched an estimated distance of 65 kilometres. By the sixth day they were very tired and foot sore, but the cold weather kept them moving. When they stopped to rest they dug holes in the sand to shelter from the wind, and at night the cold forced them to huddle together for warmth. As Denis Bassett recalled,

We were like a mass of worms, intertwined together desperately trying to keep warm.

Thinking they were only 40 kilometres from Augila, they drank as much water as they could and abandoned most of what was left. On the sixth night, after a long walk, the men dug a hole to rest in, though because of the cold, Brown and Martin decided to keep going on their own. It was not long after the party had set out again that Bassett said he needed to rest, as the heavy boots he was wearing had caused his legs to ache. He told the others to press on without him and gave the compass with a heading to Corporal Garven who continued to lead the party.

On the seventh day, in the final stages of exhaustion, the men staggered through a violent duststorm which got so bad that they had to lay down and take turns at sheltering each other. Two hours later they pushed on into a very strong headwind, and by the afternoon they had arrived at the Italian track from Agedabia to

Private M. F. Fogden was wounded in the air attack, and had to suffer a three day journey in the back of the Breda gun truck before his mid desert evacuation. He is being prepared for transfer to the RAF Blenheim bomber which took him to Kufra. Photo. Merle Fogden.

Jalo. That night it was freezing cold, so once again they were compelled to dig a large hole where the men stayed till morning trying to keep warm.

In low spirits they set out on their eight day with terribly sore feet and little water. After a while they sighted a wadi and as the sun was warm, settled down for a two hour sleep. When the party moved off again Stutterd saw what he thought were palm trees, but kept this to himself, for fear that he too like the others might be seeing things because of sore eyes. Nonetheless, the image became so clear that he mentioned it to the men who all agreed it must be an oasis. It was Augila, about 8 kilometres away, but they could only walk in short stages before resting, though Sanders decided to head straight for it, non-stop. The party reached the place at dusk where they found water, an empty hut, and a garden which provided some onions and turnips. They lit a fire and settled down for their most comfortable night since 30 December (it was now 8 January). The next morning they were found by two Arab policemen who took them to their barracks, where Brown, Martin and Sanders were already recovering.

Meanwhile, Bassett, whose legs were giving out, continued his journey slowly limping and near exhaustion. Fortunately he found an opened-up 44 gallon drum in which he sheltered for the night. This lucky find probably saved his life, as it provided protection from the wind and cold. The next day he saw the glow of an Arab fire which he was forced to approach on his hands and knees because he was so weak. The Arabs took care of him, refreshing him with a welcome meal of mashed dates and camel's milk. On 9 January the men's arrival was reported to the LRDG base at Jalo and Captain Steele the CO set out to pick them up. Bassett's navigation earned him the DCM.

Another action where an air attack brought casualties and loss of transport was on 18 November 1942 at Wadi Tamet, near Tripoli. R1 Patrol under Captain L. H. "Tony" Browne had the previous day exchanged fire with an enemy column, destroying two of their vehicles without loss to themselves. Consequently, the next day R1 came under attack from seven Italian CR42 fighters and a number of bombers. The six trucks dispersed, taking cover in the wadi banks, and fought back with all their weapons. While manning the guns, the navigator, Lance-Corporal N. O'Malley, received a fatal wound in the stomach, and Captain M. Pilkington, an officer of the Arab Legion attached to the patrol, was killed. Also the driver of O'Malley's truck, Private M. F. Fogden, was hit by an exploding bullet and suffered splinter wounds to both thighs.

That day Captain Tony Browne had a lucky escape. He was firing a Vickers K, and as the ammunition was running short he handed the gun over to Pilkington so he could get more pans. Meanwhile the CR42s had swept round for another attack, coming in low, and as Browne was bending over an ammunition box a bullet grazed his buttocks. Pilkington however, was killed. Private Fogden's wireless truck, R2, *Rotowhero*, was damaged, as was Lance-Corporal M. D. Richardson's *Rotoma*. There was no time to repair these vehicles in case the enemy returned, so they were stripped and abandoned.

The dead were buried nearby. Private Fogden was given morphine to ease his pain, and two trucks were assigned to take him on a three day journey to Landing Ground 165. From there he was evacuated by an RAF Blenheim to Kufra, then after a few days was flown to a hospital in Cairo. Tony Browne, though slightly wounded and unable to sit comfortably, continued his mission in the remaining two vehicles. The next day a sandstorm blew up, which enabled the men to get away without further incident.

Two months later, while operating with his troops in the Wadi Tamet area, Lieutenant Duncan McRea, a Transport Officer with the 28th Maori Battalion, came across the abandoned *Rotowhero*. They saw that it had been strafed and nearby lay a couple of graves, but they were puzzled as to how the vehicle came to be there and what had happened to its crew. The men soon got the Chevrolet running and adopted it for the rest of the desert campaign. It was used to transport wounded and as a hearse to carry those killed in action to a Tunisian burial ground.

Long after the war Duncan McRea had always wondered about the fate of *Rotowhero*'s crew, so in 1992 he wrote to the Returned Services' Association newspaper, the *RSA Review*, who published his story about finding the truck and asked whether anyone knew its history. The resulting correspondence brought Merle Fogden and Duncan together and Merle, who thought his vehicle had been left to rust, was pleased to learn that it had been recovered and had continued in good service.

An Me 110 fighter-bomber shot down by T1 Patrol in December 1941.
Photo: Merlyn Craw.

A number of LRDG vehicles were destroyed by Stuka attacks. On this occasion T Patrol views a downed Italian Ju87 Stuka.
Photo: Ngaire Lewis.

WITH THE EIGHTH ARMY

To take part in the British offensive in Cyrenaica in November 1941, the LRDG was placed under the command of the newly formed Eighth Army, and the whole Group was moved from Kufra to Siwa. The patrols were to watch the desert tracks to the south of Gebel Akhdar and to report on the movements of enemy reinforcements and withdrawals. However, on 24 November when the battle in the Tobruk-Bardia area had reached a critical stage, the role of the LRDG was suddenly changed. They were issued orders for the patrols to *"Act with utmost vigour offensively against any targets or communications within your reach."*

Consequently, Y1 and Y2 Patrols were ordered to patrol and ambush on roads in the Melchili–Derna–Gazala area; G1 and G2 the main road near Agedabia; and the combined Rhodesian and New Zealand patrols, S2 and R2, the Benghazi–Barce–Maraua road. Y1 damaged 15 vehicles in a transport park, Y2 captured a small fort and about 20 Italians, and S2 and R2 ambushed nine vehicles and killed and wounded a number of the enemy. Mechanical breakdowns prevented G1 and G2 from joining forces, so G1 made two independent attacks on road traffic and shot up a few vehicles.

The Rhodesians under Second-Lieutenant J. R. Olivey, accompanied by the New Zealanders led by Second-Lieutenant L. H. Browne, destroyed the telephone wires in their area on the night of 29 November, then turned eastwards towards Maraua and laid an ambush near a cutting in the road. A vehicle approached from the east and as it drew level the LRDG racked it with machine-gun fire. To his dismay Olivey saw that the truck was marked with a red cross. However, as he shouted at his men to stop firing, enemy troops armed with rifles and sub-machine-guns clambered out over the tailboard. After about a minute of sustained shooting on both sides several of the enemy were killed and wounded, and the rest ran off.

The patrols then moved towards a vehicle approaching from the opposite direction and fired upon it. The truck halted and a red liquid, presumed to be wine, gushed from its load.

Further along the road R2 and S2 patrols attacked four lorries with trailers, killing the crews and destroying the vehicles along with their cargo. From there they took up positions in a deep cutting where they overlooked the road in both directions, and attacked two more lorries with trailers, and an oil tanker. The patrols wrecked the vehicles and

T1 Patrol, December 1941. Left to right; Trooper Frank White, Trooper Gerry Gerrard and Second-Lieutenant Paul Freyberg, the General's son. He was attached to the patrol to gain more field experience, until he was hit by shrapnel during an air attack and had to be evacuated.
Photo: Merlyn Craw.

killed all the enemy except one badly wounded man. After the telephone wires were cut the force retired south, having completed their task without casualty to themselves. For their role in these actions, Second-Lieutenant Olivey was awarded the MC, and Lance-Corporal C. Waetford of R2 Patrol, along with a Rhodesian, received the MM.

Rommel disengaged his forces from the battle in Cyrenaica in mid December and began to withdraw towards Agedabia. In an attempt to prevent the enemy's escape from Benghazi the Eighth Army despatched columns, including the 22nd Guards Brigade, across the desert to the south of Gebel Akhdar to the Benghazi–Agedabia road. The navigation during this move was in the hands of Trooper Frank Jopling, under the command of Major Bruce Ballantyne, T1 Patrol, while R1 and R2 Patrols provided flanking scouts for the Guards Brigade.

T1 waited two weeks at a place near Bir Hacheim for the Guards to disengage from the battle west of Tobruk. During this time they were busy trying to survive the Luftwaffe's repeated Stuka dive bombing and fighter strafing attacks. The patrol sergeant, Dick Lewis, recorded in his diary:

December 7, 1941. Air activity is intense, and not all our own. An hour ago we had 15 German dive bombers over, but luckily they had another target and dropped all their stuff a little way off. As many as up to a 100 British aircraft appear in the air at once, and we have seen three spectacular air battles with losses on both sides. Strangely enough, you feel a lot more secure up here near the front, than away out on patrol. There were hundreds of other vehicles round us all the time and we would get due warning of anything that is going to happen. Out on patrol you are strangers in an enemy land, and keyed up the whole time.

During these attacks the only LRDG casualty was a passenger, Second-Lieutenant Paul Freyberg, the General's son. He had just come out of OTCU, and though he had seen action in the Greek campaign he was with the patrols to gain more experience. Dick Lewis wrote:

December 12. Aircraft of one side or the other are overhead most incessantly. Just had a visitation from three bombers that singled us out for attention, and dropped five bombs within a radius of a chain or two, but only scored one hit. Young Freyberg collected a bit of shrapnel in his back and was evacuated. A couple of British chaps were killed on an AA gun.

The advance began on 20 December with R1 and R2 patrolling the country to the north, while T1 guided the main column of the Guards Brigade westwards towards Antelat. As Dick Lewis recorded:

December 18, R Patrol turned up yesterday, been up on the coast. They are to patrol far out on the northern side of the column. The idea is to get the column near Benghazi without it being discovered, and make a surprise attack. To take 6,000 men and vehicles across 250 miles of desert without being seen is a pretty tall order.

Corporal R. A. Tinker, with two trucks, was responsible for the navigation of the Scots Guards through Msus towards Sceleidima, 50 kilometres to the north of Antelat. On the way they were subject to a strafing attack by two ME 109 fighters. An LRDG truck had a tyre punctured and Corporal R. J. Moore, DCM, was hit in the leg. The medical orderlies took him away in a following ambulance. The wheel was changed and the truck soon caught up with the rest of the patrol.

The operation with the Guards ended in failure. An enemy covering force including 30 tanks held up the

*R1 Patrol having a lunch
break between raids.
Photo: Merle Fogden.*

outflanking columns in the Sceleidima–Antelat area on 22 December, which enabled the Axis troops to complete their withdrawal from Benghazi. Rommel's forces retired from Cyrenaica to strong defence positions among the salt marshes between Agedabia and El Agheila. From a base at Jalo, an oasis about 225 kilometres to the south-south-east of Agedabia, the LRDG continued to harass the enemy's communications farther to the west.

While supporting the Guards, Merlyn Craw of T1 Patrol recounted an amusing story about his driver Trooper Gerry Gerrard. Craw had received orders from Major Ballantyne to report to the Colonel of the Guards for the password of the day. Instead he sent his driver Gerry, who according to Craw should never have been in the LRDG in the first place. He was "an old chap" with false teeth, which were always breaking on their ration of hard biscuit.

He had a cigarette holder with a home made cigarette in it most of the time. His scruffy beard was stained and dirty like most of us, and at that time we had sheepskins for coats. We all looked unkempt, but Gerry was by far the worst. He went to the Colonel's tent, strolled

past the sentries to be met by an immaculately dressed Colonel who yelled at him to take that cigarette out of his mouth, don't you chaps know how to salute etc., anyway what did he want. Gerry looked at him for a second, and said, "Never mind, if that's how you feel," and walked out. I had to go and get the password myself, as I should have done in the first place.

In mid-1942 when the Road Watch was under way, the Eighth Army HQ wanted the LRDG to interrupt enemy supply columns on the Tripoli–Benghazi road. Avoiding the sections of the road where raids could have compromised the watchers, T1 Patrol under Lieutenant N. P. Wilder operated between Agedabia and Benghazi, and G1 Patrol led by Captain J. A. L. Timpson, worked between Nofilia and Sirte. Colonel G. Prendergast, Officer Commanding LRDG, had received orders from Eighth Army HQ that they wanted explosions to happen in Benghazi town and harbour. To achieve this the plan was to place time bombs on passing enemy vehicles as they headed for the port.

T1 patrol left their base at Siwa and went to a point on the Benghazi road where it was estimated that a truck would take two hours to reach the town. In an effort to slow the convoys down, drums were put in place to indicate road works. Corporal Merlyn Craw, the T1 explosives expert, made up the bombs which were concealed in Italian haversacks along with beer cans of petrol. These were set with a two hour time pencil. It was a night time operation and two of the patrol's fastest runners, Private Jack Davis and Trooper Keith Tippett were selected for the job.

They were to lie on the side of the road and listen out for the sound of approaching transport. Further down the road another man was positioned where a truck would make its first approach. He had a length of string that was connected to the bombing party. When the observer tugged on the string it meant that the truck was to pass unmolested as there were troops visible in the back. No tug indicated it appeared safe to give chase. When the signal was positive Craw would press the time pencil and give the pack to one of the men, who in turn would run after the vehicle and attempt to throw the device into the back. The plan wasn't very successful as the trucks were nearly always too fast. Even with the drums to slow them down the trucks just swerved round them at speed. Sometimes in desperation the packs were thrown from a distance in the hope that they would land in or on the target.

Trooper Frank Jopling explained in his diary the frustrations of this exercise:

15 May 1942: We decided to try the first truck that came along without any road block at all. Three men went out and laid down at the edge of the road. The first truck that arrived turned out to be a large tanker and trailer. What a beautiful target for a spot of gun play. But that is not our job, our job was to put bombs on them. So as the tanker was passing, one man got up and tried to put a bomb on it, but couldn't catch it as it was going too fast. After that two trucks passed going west, but we were not allowed to touch them as G Patrol are doing all west-bound traffic near Sirte.

The night was passing with little result and the men soon became discouraged with the idea, as bombs that were due to explode in an hour or two were now being strewn all over the road. Craw managed to persuade Wilder to abandon this approach and revert to the simpler method of shooting up transport. Thereby it was decided to attack the next vehicle that came along and then withdraw.

1942. Mid-desert meeting. R Patrol alongside Y Patrol to exchange information on enemy movements. Note the heavily laden truck carrying an assortment of stores and equipment necessary for a long operation.
Photo: Imperial War Museum.

At 2.30 am, as a 10 ton Lancia truck and trailer approached, three T Patrol trucks lined up beside the road and fired their machine-guns into the vehicle. Its lights were quickly extinguished and the terrified driver ran off into the desert. When the patrol examined the truck it was found to be empty of supplies. However, before they left the area three time bombs were set and the Lancia was destroyed.

The Guards' patrol, having tried Wilder's method against the Benghazi transport, experimented with a different plan. They chose a site where they could erect a high wire between telephone poles, and attempted to release time bombs onto the trucks as they passed underneath. But this also proved ineffective. The Guards withdrew to the hills, during which they were attacked by enemy ground forces and Guardsman G. Matthews was killed. A few days later though, they made a successful raid shooting up transport parked at a road house near Sultan.

With T1 and T2 Patrols now under his command, Wilder later returned to the Agedabia–Benghazi road and divided his force to lay ambush at different localities. At midnight on 7 June four trucks of T1 Patrol, impatient after waiting in the desert trying to spot convoys, decided to drive along the road to see what they could find. They travelled with their headlights on, and as they turned a corner they encountered the enemy checkpoint and staging area at Magrun. There were a number of trucks parked and men moving about; despite this Wilder decided to try to bluff his way through. His driver, Trooper Derek "Snow" Parker, remembers seeing a soldier behind a big gun as they entered the camp. He considered that the sentry must have known that it was the enemy approaching, but allowed them to pass probably thinking that he would be the first to die if the LRDG was challenged. The column slipped through unimpeded.

A further 8 kilometres on Gunner E. Sanders climbed a telephone pole and cut the wires. Not long after Corporal Craw saw moving lights in the distance, so they decided to pull off the road and conceal themselves behind a sand dune. As soon as their pursuers drew level, Gunner Sanders opened fire on the first truck with his 20mm Breda gun, then all the patrol's weapons opened up. The second vehicle was a large half-track mounting a heavy gun and carrying a number of men. It tried to escape by turning off the road into the desert, but Corporal Craw's truck with Trooper Tom Milburn at the wheel chased them. Craw manned the twin .303 Brownings alongside Trooper Euan Hay with the .5 Browning, and managed to pick up the vehicle by firing around the ground with tracer. After a long burst it caught fire and exploded.

Wilder's men destroyed the half-track and a truck loaded with troops and ammunition, which also caught on

1942. Captain D. Lloyd Owen (in the sheepskin coat) and his men of Y Patrol rest up during the day, as most convoy attacks took place at night. The truck is a Ford F30.
Photo: Ngaire Lewis.

The aftermath of an LRDG raid on an Italian convoy, 1941.
Photo: Buster Gibb.

fire and blew up. At least twenty of the enemy were killed before T1 escaped into the night. Trooper Keith Tippett recalled the action:

It was absolutely horrifying the way we shot at them, but it had to be done to cause havoc. In the light of the flames of burning trucks you would see jokers trying to get out of their vehicles, it was quite sickening. Normally we would just hit and run, and didn't linger to view the carnage. We weren't supposed to bring any wounded back, though occasionally some of us did.

Two kilometres further on some heavily laden trucks were seen parked on the side of the road. The patrol formed a semi-circle round them and then opened up. After receiving no return fire they approached the vehicles to find that they had been abandoned, apart from one Italian who had received splinter wounds to his arm. He said his comrades had run off when they had heard the sound of gunfire coming from up the road. They had left three lorries complete with a trailer, carrying timber and supplies. The prisoner's wound was dressed and he was set free. Time bombs were placed on the vehicles which exploded about an hour later, long after the patrol had left the area.

Due to the LRDG attacks, the enemy started putting out their own patrols about 30 kilometres from the Benghazi road. On 11 June T1 Patrol encountered a party which consisted of a half-track carrying a gun and two machine-guns, and two motorcycle sidecar combinations also mounting machine-guns. The force put up a fight, but the devastating firepower from T1's guns proved too much with only one motorcycle escaping. Two Italians were killed, two wounded, and five prisoners taken, including an officer.

One of these men had been very badly wounded and nothing could be done for him. Although they were near the main road, it was a remote area, and the man would have probably died in the sun by the next day if not sooner. The patrol decided to take the humane course of action and gave the soldier a fatal overdose of morphine to put him out of his misery.

Another prisoner had a bullet pass right through him and out the other side. So Corporal Craw, who was also trained as a medical orderly, attempted to save the Italian's life by using the relatively new drug sulphanilamide for the first time. An ointment was made out of crushed sulpha tablets with petroleum jelly mixed with cotton wool. This was then plugged into both the entry and exit wounds after another four tablets had been inserted. Further pills were given by mouth. Five or six days later the patrol had returned to base, where to everyone's surprise, the Italian had survived the discomfort and suffering of the 1280 kilometre journey in the back of a truck.

During these operations the LRDG also laid mines on the road, and wrecked telephone lines. Overhead wires were cut, underground cables were torn up then tied to the rear of a vehicle and ripped out of the earth over a great distance, which made repairs much more difficult. To enable the patrols to escape without being observed, most of the hit and run convoy attacks took place at night. Great apprehension grew in the minds of the Italian drivers, many of whom were semi-civilian contractors, as they feared when their turn would be next.

Tractor-drawn trailers intercepted by the LRDG, 1941. Loaded with stores for Italian outposts, anything useful that could be carried was taken and the balance destroyed. Photo: Buster Gibb.

T1 Patrol, Siwa, 1942.
Back row, left to right:
T. Scriven (British radio
operator attached to patrol),
R. E. Hay, K. Kelly,
S. D. Parker, H. D. Mackay,
K. E. Tippett.
Centre row: B. F. Shepherd,
A. H. C. Nutt, R. W. N.
Lewis, Captain N. P. Wilder,
M. H. Craw, T. E. Ritchie,
F. W. Jopling.
Front: E. Sanders,
T. B. Dobson, T. A. Milburn,
J. L. D. Davis, P. V. Mitford.
T1 Patrol took part in a
number of successful actions
on the Agedabia–Benghazi
road, shooting up enemy
convoys.
Photo: Merlyn Craw.

Trooper Derek Parker recalled the horror of shooting up convoys:

The poor beggars didn't have much of a show at all, we cut them to pieces. It was a pretty cruel sort of fighting, but when you were way behind the lines it was either them or us. We always made sure, where we possibly could, that it was them. I always felt a bit guilty and ashamed about some of these raids, the one-sided ambushes seemed a bit unfair.

Sometimes the attacks got so bad that all traffic after dark was stopped. Furthermore, convoys had to endure being regularly strafed or bombed by the RAF during the day. The best result from these raids was not only the destruction of enemy transport and supplies, but it also meant that Axis troops, armoured cars and aircraft had to be diverted from the front to perform convoy protection work from within their own lines.

The fall of Tobruk on 21 June 1942 and the Eighth Army's retreat to Alamein made it necessary for the LRDG to leave their base at Siwa. The evacuation was completed on 28 June, a few days before the Italians occupied the oasis. Major C. S. Morris took A Squadron to Cairo for supplies

and then on to Kufra, a base from which patrols continued to operate in northern Libya. The rest of the unit withdrew to the coast between Alamein and Alexandria and then to Faiyum, about 80 kilometres to the south-west of Cairo.

The Alamein Line extended from the coast southwards to the cliffs of the Qattara Depression, a huge basin 240 kilometres in length, 156 metres below sea level at its deepest point, and passable to vehicles only where narrow ribbons of firm sand wind across its salt marshes. To penetrate behind the Axis positions at Alamein, the patrols based at Faiyum had to go through the Depression. Renewing their partnership with Major Stirling's SAS they continued to attack the enemy from the rear.

After the Allied victory at Alamein in October 1942, the Eighth Army drove its forces into Tripolitania from the east. Meanwhile, General Leclerc's Fighting French Forces of Chad Province moved into the Fezzan from the south.

This Anglo-French co-operation had been set in place a year earlier when R2 Patrol, led by Second-Lieutenant C. H. B.Croucher, had been sent to a French outpost in the Tibesti

Mountains to act as a wireless link between the Allies. Rommel's counter-offensive in Cyrenaica, however, had necessitated the postponement of the French advance and the recall of R2 Patrol.

Leclerc lacked the support of fighter aircraft for his operations, so LRDG patrols including R2 were sent to the Fezzan to destroy enemy aircraft on the landing grounds at Hon and Sebha, but their attempts failed due to heavy rain and very difficult "going". Although the French were exposed to air attack they succeeded in capturing one outpost after another while the LRDG blocked the enemy's

line of retreat to the north. T1 under Captain Wilder, Y2 and an Indian Long Range Squadron patrol mined the roads, destroyed transport, killed a number of Italians and took prisoners.

The Eighth Army entered Tripoli on 23 January 1943. This rapid advance of 2,250 kilometres in three months had made it necessary for the LRDG to move its base from Kufra 965 kilometres north-westwards to Zella, and later another 240 kilometres to Hon. These moves from one place to the next were successfully completed by the trucks of the Heavy Section in a single journey.

The face of the enemy. Apparently relaxed, Italians and Germans pose for the camera. The LRDG hit-and-run attacks on Axis convoys put much apprehension in the minds of the drivers. This photo was taken from the wallet of a dead German soldier. Photo: Ernest McGonagle.

WITH THE SAS

In July 1941, Lieutenant (Later Colonel) David Stirling of the Scots Guards and Commandos, and Lieutenant J. S. "Jock" Lewes, an Australian born Welsh Guardsman and Commando, created L Detachment, Special Air Service Brigade. An actual brigade did not exist, it was so titled to mislead the enemy into thinking that paratroops had arrived in Egypt in brigade strength. The theory behind the unit was that a small group of specialists could parachute undetected behind enemy lines, and operate with great effect against Axis airfields.

A school was established at Kabrit, about 160 kilometres from Cairo, called "Stirling's Rest Camp". The first 73 volunteers from the 8th and 11th Commandos were put through a rigorous training course which applied to both officers and men alike. Each recruit had to be a parachutist and an expert in the use of small arms, explosives and close combat. He also had to be tough enough to endure a 160 kilometre march with a heavy pack. The LRDG called them "parashots". By the end of 1941 a detachment of Free French parachutists had also supplemented the Brigade.

Their first "sortie" was interestingly enough, against a 2nd NZ Division base camp not far from Stirling's position at Kabrit. At that time, the SAS being only a "detachment", meant they had difficulties obtaining the necessary equipment to set up a comfortable camp, so they took matters into their own hands. While the New Zealand troops were away on manoeuvres their base was being guarded by Indian sentries. One night L Detachment's only 3 ton truck with a dozen men on board approached the camp gate, declared themselves as "Kiwi" officers and successfully drove in. They then spread out in search for their "requirements".

Throughout the night the truck had made four trips back to Kabrit, loaded with tables, chairs, lamps, crockery, glasses, kitchen utensils, 15 small tents, and even a piano and bar.

The New Zealand Division never appreciated what a contribution it had made in the establishment of the SAS, as the pillaging was put down to the many Arab thefts in the area.

L Detachment's first operation was carried out on the night of 16–17 November 1941, in the Gazala–Tmimi area, Cyrenaica. Targeting five German airfields, they parachuted in strong winds and torrential rain. The men and equipment were widely scattered with only two out of their 10 supply canisters being recovered. Of the seven officers and 50 men who were dropped, only four officers and 18 men reached the appointed LRDG escape rendezvous. It was a disaster with nothing achieved, as the fuses for the bombs could not be found, and all those highly trained men tragically perishing in the desert.

Captain J. R. Easonsmith's R Patrol carried the survivors over 400 kilometres back to Siwa. During the trip Stirling realised that if the LRDG could find its way hundreds of kilometres across "impassable" desert and arrive at a patch of sand that was only identifiable from any other by sun compass, theodolite and mathematics, then this unit was the one to get his force into action.

Lieutenant-Colonel David Stirling, founder of the SAS, standing alongside Major Don Steele, Commanding Officer A Squadron, LRDG. These two men organized many successful operations together.
Photo: Richard Williams.

Men of T2 Patrol, December 1941. Note the variety of dress in one patrol. Lieutenant C. S. Morris in centre back with cap. Photo: Ian McCulloch.

For future operations it was decided that it was more practical to use the expertise of the Group to deliver the SAS to within walking distance of their objectives, as well as bring them home again.

The next mission was launched from A Squadron's (Major Don Steele, CO) new base at Jalo, and proved the success of this marriage of "special forces". On the night of 14 December 1941, ten "parashots" were transported by the Rhodesian S2 Patrol under Captain C. A. Holliman, to Tamet, in the Sirte area, where they crept on to an Axis airfield, wrecked 24 aircraft with time bombs and blew up a bomb dump. The same men returned about a week later and destroyed another 27 brand new aircraft that had only arrived the day before. On 18 December four SAS men travelling with S2 Patrol under Captain J. R. Olivey accounted for 37 Italian CR42 fighter-bombers on a landing ground near Agedabia.

The main weapon used against these aircraft was the Lewes Bomb. Invented by "Jock" Lewes it consisted of plastic explosive and thermite. Designed to start a fire, it was set off by means of a time pencil and detonator which gave a time delay of anything from ten minutes to two hours or longer. This enabled the SAS to put several kilometres of desert between themselves and the enemy before the devices went off and the alarm was raised. The bombs were usually placed where the wing joined the fuselage, or on the aircraft's tail. This was done because a wrecked airframe ruined the plane, whereas a damaged engine could be replaced. It proved an effective way of destroying aircraft on the ground.

In the meantime, on 10 December, Lieutenant C. S. Morris set out with 14 men of T2 Patrol and 12 SAS to raid the landing ground of El Ageila, and then on to the anchorage at Marsa Brega. The airfield was found to be empty, so the patrol continued on to their next objective. They travelled at night, eastwards along the main road led by an Italian Lancia lorry, captured by the "parashots", that displayed no lights. Though so as to blind any approaching traffic, the following five patrol trucks had removed their headlight dimming masks and put the lights on full. Undetected, they passed 47 vehicles, giving the occasional wave as they went by, until they reached the turn-off at Marsa Brega.

At the cross-roads they encountered 20 enemy lorries parked by a road house (Casa Cantieri), where troops could halt and get some refreshment on their journey to or from the front. About 60 men were having an evening meal when the LRDG opened fire at a range of 20 metres into the building, then the "parashots" followed up and ran from truck to truck tossing in grenades or placing sticky bombs on the vehicles. They dispatched anyone who stood in their way. After attacking for a quarter of an hour at very close range Axis reinforcements appeared to be arriving, so the raiders withdrew at speed. Morris's men put most of the vehicles out of action, killed at least 15 of the enemy and wounded many others without casualty to themselves.

The patrol could not disperse into the desert because the road on which they were travelling was flanked by salt marshes. In order to obstruct pursuit Corporal G. C. Garven, who was in the last truck, hurriedly laid mines which destroyed at least seven of the following enemy vehicles.

Before turning off to the south, the men wrecked the telephone poles to slow down pursuing traffic and disrupt communications. Enemy planes searched all the next day and passed twice overhead without seeing the patrol hidden in well camouflaged positions. This action resulted in Lieutenant C. S. "Bing" Morris earning the MC and Corporal George Garven the MM.

T2 Patrol next took two SAS groups led by Lieutenants Jock Lewes and Bill Fraser to raid the airfields at Nofila and Marble Arch, west of El Agheila. After the raid on Nofila Morris picked up Lewes and his men and set out together for Marble Arch to collect Lieutenant Fraser.

Studio photo taken in Cairo, December 1941. Left: Lance-Corporal A. H. C. Nutt, Lieutenant C. S. Morris, (patrol commander) and Trooper I. G. McCulloch. What they are wearing is all that was left after five out of their six truck patrol was shot up by German aircraft. They were on their way back after picking up several SAS men who had raided an enemy airfield near Agedabia.
Photo: Ian McCulloch.

Studio photo taken in Cairo early 1942. T2 Patrol members with the L Detachment SAS men whom they had recently completed a mission with.
Back row, left to right: Lance-Corporal A. H. C. Nutt, Trooper F. S. Brown, Trooper I. G. McCulloch. Front: Sergeant Jim Almonds, Sergeant-Major Bob Lilley. They are wearing the first pattern white SAS beret, the colour was later changed to beige.
Photo: Ian McCulloch.

On the way a Messerschmitt 110 fighter-bomber spotted the wheel tracks and caught up with the patrol. Despite intense anti-aircraft fire, it came in very low and shot up the trucks, hitting the co-founder of the SAS, Lieutenant T. J. Lewes, who died shortly after from severe leg wounds. Later, further air attacks were mounted resulting in Stukas progressively destroying four out of five trucks. The events which followed this action are recounted in the chapter *Air Attack and Desert Survival*.

Meanwhile at Marble Arch Fraser and his four men had been waiting three days to be picked up and were becoming short of water and rations. Deciding they could wait no longer they set off on foot, east towards their own lines. The men travelled by night, often up to their knees in salt marsh, and hid during the day. Soon thirst became a problem as they had little water to start with, and the pools were too salty to drink. The party grew tired of walking and headed for the road and started to hold up cars. They managed to hijack two Italian trucks which provided some food and rusty water from the radiators. Later they seized a German staff car which carried them for 40 kilometres before it became bogged in the sand beyond extraction. It was only after an enduring eight day 320 kilometre trek that Fraser and his men finally reached safety.

Co-operation with the SAS meant the Group was exposed to greater risks that their work normally encountered. Even so, this did not deter the patrols from taking the "parashots" behind the lines anywhere and at any time if asked of them. The impact of this successful partnership was reflected in an enemy intelligence report, written in April 1942, which stated:

The LRDG plays an extremely important part in the enemy sabotage organisation. The selection and training of the men, the strength, speed and camouflage of the vehicles for the country in which they have to operate have enabled the Group to carry out very effective work, particularly in the destruction of Axis aircraft on the landing grounds at Agedabia and Tamet.

The SAS had developed a fresh technique for attacking enemy aircraft which was first tested on the night of 7 July 1942, at Bagoush airfield. Using a captured German staff car and two jeeps, all mounting Vickers K machine-guns, they drove down the middle of the runway with weapons blazing and within five minutes had destroyed 37 aircraft without loss to themselves. Inspired by this success Stirling requested HQ Middle East to supply his unit with 20 Willys jeeps, fully armed and equipped for desert work, along with several Ford 30cwts as support vehicles. He had also seen Captain Nick Wilder's new LRDG jeep armed with twin Vickers Ks. This impressed him, along with the formidable armament on the T1 Patrol trucks. Stirling wanted his force to become mechanised and thereby independent of the Group. His request was granted and the jeeps eventually supplied. The SAS was now also responsible for its own navigation, hence Sergeant Mike Sadler of S Patrol transferred from the LRDG to become the unit's chief navigator.

The new jeeps proved their worth on the night of 26-27 July 1942, at Sidi Haneish airfield in the Fuka area. This was one of Rommel's main staging areas for all aircraft movements and operations. The raiding party consisted of 18 jeeps, each of which carried a driver and two gunners with twin-mounted Vickers K machine-guns. Led by Stirling they drove down the centre of the runway in a hollow two sided arrowhead formation. It was designed to move between two rows of planes, with the weapons of the three leading jeeps firing ahead at the defences, while all the other guns fired outwards at the parked aircraft. The firepower was devastating as 68 guns poured volumes of tracer, explosive and incendiary ammunition into the targets as they passed.

Consequently 40 aircraft were destroyed, which included Heinkels, Messerschmitts, Stukas, and a large proportion of Junker 52 transports, vital for supplying the Afrika Korps. Two jeeps were put out of action including Stirling's, with the crews being picked up by following vehicles, though one SAS gunner, Rowlands, was shot through the head and died instabntly. After the raid the men successfully escaped to their desert rendezvous.

Prior to this action T1 Patrol under Captain Nick Wilder had been operating with the SAS in a support role. With one jeep and five trucks carrying a month's supply of water and rations, they had established a hideout shared with the French and English members of the SAS and G2 Patrol. It was located at Bir el Quseir, a place of high escarpments and caves, between Qattara Springs and Alamein. They did not mix much with the SAS as they were camped 3 kilometres from their position and due to the amount of enemy air traffic, movement was kept to a minimum.

G2 Patrol was out on a raid when they were caught out in the open and shot up by three Italian Macchi C200 fighters. Their commander, Lieutenant R. B. Gurdon, was mortally wounded after being hit by two cannon-shells and bullet. His driver, Guardsman Murray, was wounded in the arm and their truck set on fire.

While at the hideout Stirling left for Egypt to arrange for the new jeeps, along with additional men, supplies and equipment. The remaining SAS and LRDG patrols rested and kept watch. Corporal Merlyn Craw was ordered to take a truck and make a reconnaissance back towards the coast, travelling by night to avoid being seen from the air. He was accompanied by his gunner, Trooper Wally Rail. When they arrived in the area they saw a lot of wrecked and abandoned transport from recent battles, including a Honey light tank and a Bren Carrier. The men considered recovering the tank, but there were three bodies inside and as they had no shovel they were not keen on removing them. Craw decided to

T1 Patrol pose in the desert. Back row, left to right: W. G. Gerrard, ?, A. H. C. Nutt, Captain N. P. Wilder (patrol commander), J. L. D. Davis, B. F. Shepherd, F. W. Jopling. Front: M. H. Craw, R. W. N. Lewis, T. A. Milburn, ?, ?. Note the twin aircraft .303 Brownings mounted on Merlyn Craw's truck, Te Paki. Photo: Shepherd collection .

leave the tank and move on to the carrier which he found had belonged to the Maori Battalion, as the maintenance manual was still in place. That evening Rail caused some panic as he drove the tracked vehicle back to the hideout, because it was thought an enemy tank was approaching.

Just as the food and water situation was becoming serious, Stirling returned to camp with his 20 brand-new jeeps, along with more men, equipment and supplies. Very soon plans were being laid for the raid on Sidi Haneish. The night before the attack a briefing was held, and a practice run undertaken in the desert using live ammunition. The role of T1 was to drive to the north side of the airfield to deal with any defence positions in the area. The SAS would approach from the south. The next night the raiders set out for their target, 64 kilometres away.

Included in this column was the carrier, which was to be used to create a diversion on the escarpment. It was driven by Trooper Keith Tippett and mounted a machine-gun manned by Wally Rail. But along the way the vehicle developed mechanical problems that could not be fixed in the dark, so it was abandoned. Later one of the patrol trucks hit a land mine

causing the men to walk as the drivers negotiated their way out of the minefield. Further on a halt was made as it was suggested a rum would be in order. While it was being poured, Gunner "Sandy" Sanders went off to relieve himself. When he returned he told Wilder that he had seen four Germans, so it was decided that they had better be taken. Sanders set off with his revolver drawn and after a short while came back with four prisoners. They were from a recovery unit camped nearby whose job had been to lift the mines. But this was not considered a good time to be looking after POWs so Wilder told Craw to "get rid of them". Uncertain as to what that order really meant, Craw and Trooper Keith Yealands decided to drive the prisoners out into the desert and drop them off, far enough so the mission would not be compromised.

When T1 arrived at their position north of the landing ground at about one o'clock in the morning, they encountered a large tank trap which they were unable to cross to reach their objective. While they waited a bomber circled overhead and when it came in to land the whole runway was lit up. When the plane touched down Stirling fired a Very light and led his 18 jeeps on to the airfield with all guns blazing. Instantly the lights

Unnamed SAS men being transported by R2 Patrol members, 1942. The LRDG sometimes referred to the SAS as the "Parashots" or "Gabriels Angels." In front are Trooper Sam Lucas (left) and Trooper Bill Hammond. Sam Lucas is wearing a captured German cap displaying a NZ Onward badge. Photo: Richard Williams.

were switched off, yet the glow of tracer and burning aircraft soon illuminated the scene. Craw recalled:

We fired a few rounds, but were too far away to be effective, so we could only watch. It was up till then the best sight I had seen in the war.

After the raid the SAS and T1 made their way back to the hideout. However, Craw's truck received a puncture, delaying the patrol. By daylight they were only half way back, so they stopped and camouflaged their vehicles. There were many wadis in this area and the trucks of Sanders and Wilder were parked in one, while 180 metres away those of Lance Corporal Alan Nutt and Craw were in another. It was not long before two Fiesler Storch spotter planes were seen circling overhead, and they would land occasionally to confer with ground troops. Craw was surprised to see Wilder leave his truck and walk towards a low hill where one plane seemed to go. He set off on foot to intercept him, but had second thoughts and went back to his vehicle. It was at that point that a Storch landed between Craw's truck and that of Trooper K. E. Tippett accompanied by Trooper T. B. Dobson.

Wilder had been seen and was being shot at from a German half-track coming over the hill. Craw and his crew (Troopers R. E. Hay, T. A. Milburn and K. Yealands) pulled the camouflage net from their truck and took off to rescue him. On the way Craw fired a couple of bursts at the plane, but could not prolong it as his driver was on his right and in line with the aircraft. Three enemy half-tracks mounting 47mm anti-tank guns fired at the truck. Craw and Trooper Euan Hay returned fire with *Te Paki's* twin .303 Brownings and .50 Browning, suppressing the German gunners whose fire became erratic. Wilder was picked up on the run, but as he jumped into the truck his knee knocked the engine switch, stalling the vehicle.

This proved fortunate as an enemy shell had just exploded right in front of them. Craw handed over the guns to Yealands who along with Hay kept up the rate of fire. Apart from a few shell splinters to the truck they had escaped unhurt.

Meanwhile Tippett and Dobson had been resting in a wadi when they spotted a Fiesler Storch on the ground not far from their position. Keith Tippett recounted the action that followed:

When the plane was sighted we were trying to get some kip, as we had been up all night. I was only carrying a captured German Luger, so I yelled out to Dobby to grab the Tommy gun from the truck. The Storch was just about airborne when Dobby fired the first burst. Something vital must have been hit, as the plane stalled and came to a halt. It was a shame it wasn't airborne as if we had shot it down we would have earned the LRDG prize of a case of whiskey for shooting down an aircraft.

We approached the plane and the occupants came out without a fight. It had been flown by a sergeant pilot, who it transpired was one of Rommel's personal pilots. The passenger was an English speaking German doctor, Baron Von Lutteroti, who while waving a Red Cross arm band over his head shouted, "You can't shoot me I am a doctor". He had only been up for the ride and later complained, "I went up for pleasure, and it ended unhappily".

Just as we were taking the crew away a German half-track came into view. Leaving the prisoners with Dobby, I rushed to the truck where I dismounted the twin Vickers K machine-guns, and set them up on a nearby mound. I blazed away at the enemy, and they started throwing shells at us.

Fortunately their shooting was inaccurate, the morning haze may have made it difficult for them to see us. But the shells were getting closer and closer, and I wasn't in

Trooper Keith Tippett, T1 Patrol, 1942. He wears his favourite desert hat, a floppy German officer's cap. While operating with the SAS Tippett won the MM for his part in capturing a Fiesler Storch reconnaissance aircraft along with its crew in July 1942. Two months later he saw distinguished service on the Barce Raid. Photo: Keith Tippett.

the mood to be captured, so I yelled out to Dobby, "Get those jokers and stand them up behind me!" It seemed to work, as the half-track immediately ceased firing and withdrew.

We then screamed at Gunner Sanders truck, who were not far away, to get on the job with their Breda gun. At first they were reluctant to start shooting, Dobby and I had to be a bit firm on them and threatened to shoot them if they didn't get on with it. Apart from Sanders, it was their first time in close combat so they needed to be shocked into action. We were facing a full German unit who had thought they had come across a fixed position. They didn't know that we were only a couple of rag-tag trucks.

As the rest of the Germans came over a hill Gunner E. Sanders manned the 20mm Breda mounted on the back of his truck and coolly targeted the enemy. His steady and accurate shooting knocked out two 50 mm Flak half-tracks and two troop carrying trucks. The rest of the Germans withdrew. Before the New Zealanders escaped they set fire to the Fiesler Storch after soaking it with a can of petrol. Tippett, Dobson and Sanders all earned the MM for this action.

After they were safely away, Craw and Alan Nutt stopped their trucks and looked back. There was a cloud of black smoke and Wilder was convinced it was Sanders' truck and thought that Germans must have got Tippett also. Then he saw eight more vehicles with infantry over the hill, so he decided to return to base as they were nearly out of ammunition, rations, and water. Sanders and Tippett travelled to the hideout to resupply and then went on to base. The prisoners were left with the SAS from whom they escaped a few days later. Amazingly T1 survived this action without a scratch, whereas the Germans lost one plane with its crew, four vehicles and an unknown number of dead and wounded.

During these actions the New Zealanders and SAS formed a special bond, as Malcom James the SAS Medical Officer wrote in his book *Born of the Desert* in 1945.

It would be impossible to praise the New Zealanders too highly; their rough friendliness, their generosity; and their reliability was beyond that. You could not have wished for better company, and soon we became very intimate.

Several other SAS/LRDG operations enjoyed varying success. In the 15 months of desert operations the SAS, either with the support of the Group or on their own, had destroyed over 250 aircraft, wrecked dozens of supply dumps, put hundreds of enemy vehicles out of action, and disrupted road and railway communications. All this had been accomplished at a relatively small cost to the LRDG and SAS. Lieutenant Colonel David Stirling once made the comment that in his view the LRDG was the finest of all the units serving in the desert.

In early 1943, Stirling was captured after being betrayed by Arabs near Gabes in Tunisia. His replacement was Lieutenant Colonel Paddy Mayne, one of the original members of L Detachment and an SAS legend. He had participated in many raids against enemy airfields, and had personally accounted for over 100 Axis aircraft. Mayne was a brave and outstanding leader. He encouraged Stirling to adopt their own transport to reach targets, as opposed to relying on the LRDG, hence the SAS jeep was born. By 1945 he had been awarded the DSO and three bars, and was one of the most decorated soldiers in the British Army.

The final tribute came on the 13 May 1943, the day the Axis forces surrendered in North Africa, when as part of a message sent by General Alexander to Winston Churchill, the following was stated:

The victory had taken three years, many battles, and much sacrifice; of the formations engaged, the desert raiders of the LRDG and SAS formed numerically a minute part. But it is true to say that without their efforts victory would had come later at a far greater cost. Their role in the history of warfare remains unique.

Some 57 years later in June 2000, this bond between the SAS and the New Zealand LRDG members was commemorated by way of a permanent tribute to this wartime partnership being established. The 1st NZ Special Air Service Group's base at Hobsonville, Auckland, has opened an LRDG Lecture Room which honours the link between the SAS and the LRDG. The room features a Roll of Honour, a list of gallantry awards, photographs, and a small museum display of LRDG artifacts. Not only does it recall the fascinating history of this unit, but acts as a source of inspiration for members of today's special forces.

Lieutenant-Colonel David Stirling alongside his men and jeeps of the SAS, 1942. On his left is Lieutenant Edward McDonald who also led many patrol missions. By July 1942 the SAS were equipped with their own transport, though the LRDG continued to assist when required. The jeeps mount .303 Vickers K machine-guns and a .50 cal Air Pattern Browning. LRDG vehicles carried similar weapons. Photo: Imperial War Museum.

THE TAXI SERVICE

The LRDG operated a service which became known amongst the patrols as *Libyan Taxis Ltd*. This involved carrying observers, and the inserting, supplying and collecting of British and Arab undercover agents. They also rescued Allied prisoners of war and downed airmen, and brought in enemy captives. In addition they delivered or guided the Special Air Service, Popski's Private Army (until they got their own transport), and detachments of the Free French, Middle East Commandos and the Sudan Defence Force to their targets.

In their courier role, as experts in the field of desert survival, geography and navigation, they were able to drop off or pick up men from far behind the lines, which for the most part was done without being detected by the enemy. Insertion by air or sea would have provided a greater risk for these parties. Over 80 men from various organisations were carried from 1941 to the end of the desert campaign. During these runs only four passengers are recorded as having been killed while operating with the patrols.

In August 1941 Major Don Steele was appointed Commanding Officer A (NZ) Squadron. He was awarded the OBE in recognition of his services while in command at Siwa and later at Jalo. Steele had planned operations which included successful attacks on enemy communications and airfields, reconnaissance as far as Tripolitania, and the carrying of demolition parties, secret agents and search parties to various points behind the lines.

To enable them to discover all they could about the enemy, and to enlist the support of the friendly natives, British agents lived as Arabs among the tribesmen of Gebel Akhdar, transmitting information by wireless. The LRDG took the agents to where they needed to go, delivered their wireless batteries, ammunition and explosives, and distributed food among the natives. Also later the Intelligence branch of GHQ had agents operating in Tripolitania. The Group carried these men, along with their stores and wireless equipment, to a place where they could complete their journey more discreetly by camel or on foot.

In August 1942 R1 Patrol under Captain A. I. Guild took a party of three agents from Kufra to Bir Tala, about 190 kilometres to the south-east of Tripoli. Three months later the same patrol now led by Captain L. H. "Tony" Browne, repeated the 3200 kilometre return trip to deliver fresh stores and to relieve the wireless operator, who had become ill, suffering sores all over his body.

Captain J. R. Easonsmith, early 1942. A highly respected and brave British officer who led R1 Patrol in many close encounters against the enemy. In September 1942 he commanded the force that undertook the very successful Barce Raid. He became Officer Commanding LRDG in October 1943, but was killed in action a month later while on operations in the Aegean island of Leros. Photo: Richard Williams.

Major John Haselden, a British agent who worked amongst the Arabs. He was a typical passenger in the LRDG "Taxi Service", often being carried to and from his missions far behind the lines. He was later killed in action leading a Commando raid on Tobruk in September 1942. Behind him is an LRDG Ford 15cwt with a Westland Lysander reconnaissance aircraft in the foreground. Photo: Ngaire Lewis.

In November 1941 T2 Patrol commanded by Captain A. D. N. Hunter took four British officers and two Arabs to a rendezvous at Wadi Heleighima, in the southern hills of Gebel Akhdar to the west of Mechili. They were to collect them three weeks later. After delivering their passengers the patrol divided into three parties to spend the time watching the roads leading to Mechili.

A truck of R1 Patrol has its wheel changed, while a British agent (Flower) on the right looks on. He was being transported to a secret rendezvous, 1942. Photo: Merle Fogden.

While on picket duty with the party on the Mechili–Derna road, Lance-Corporal R. T. Porter was captured by an Italian patrol. Hunter took two trucks to the area where Porter disappeared but was attacked at close range by about 20 Italians in two vehicles, one armed with a Breda gun. Hunter's vehicle was put out of action and though he managed to escape, his crew, Corporal F. Kendall and Trooper L. A. McIver, were both captured. The other truck survived the engagement and slipped away to warn the rest of the patrol. They reported their situation to HQ and were told to withdraw to Siwa. Second-Lieutenant C. H. B. Croucher was ordered to set out with three trucks to uplift the passengers previously delivered. Not only were they successfully recovered but in their company they had found Hunter who had evaded capture and made his way to the rendezvous.

Often the "Taxi Service" provided much more excitement than was expected. Such as the time when R1 Patrol under Captain J. R. Easonsmith was to pick up Captain J. Haselden, a British agent who had been working in the Gebel with friendly Arabs. But he could not be found at the appointed rendezvous so Easonsmith went off to search for him on foot. While doing so he discovered an Italian camp in which he counted four light tanks and about 40 trucks. He wanted to seize a prisoner for interrogation, so he decided to lay an ambush on the route leading to the position.

Protected by two patrol trucks hidden behind a rise, Easonsmith pretended his own vehicle had broken down on the track, while his gunner Corporal R. O. Spotswood lay concealed under a tarpaulin in the back.

Soon a convoy of 20 lorries came along, which was much larger than expected. Undaunted, Easonsmith emerged from under the bonnet and held up his hand for assistance. He then approached the two occupants of the leading truck while trying to conceal a Thompson sub-machine gun behind his back. But the driver suddenly realised the trick, threw open the door and grappled with him onto the ground. The passenger, an officer, drew his pistol and fired at Easonsmith, but missed. He then ran off, only to be brought down by machine-gun fire from the R1 trucks. The driver broke free and fled, but was felled by a burst from Easonsmith's Tommy gun.

All this commotion caused armed soldiers to leap from their trucks and cautiously advance up beside the column. Corporal Spotswood had only just managed to fire a few rounds from the back of Easonsmith's truck when his machine-gun jammed. Fortunately, by this time the rest of the patrol had joined in the fray. Shouting, *"I must get a prisoner,"* Easonsmith ran down the column and threw grenades among the Italians who sought cover under their transport. He captured two men, but one was badly wounded and later died. The other later revealed that the Trieste Motorised Division was on its way to Mechili. Having killed six or seven of the enemy and wounding a dozen the patrol escaped unscathed. To add to the success Haselden was found and returned to base.

Rescuing downed pilots or escaped POWs was a rewarding job for the "Taxi Service". One typical story took place between 12 and 21 July 1943. A USAAF B24 Liberator of the 9th Air Force based at Benghazi had become lost over Libya after returning from a raid in Italy. It had ran out of fuel and

the crew bailed out over the desert about 320 kilometres south of the Gulf of Sirte. The 9th Air Force conducted its own search for the men, but was unsuccessful.

The desert in the area was rock covered, with the metal in the terrain affecting compass readings, which complicated the search.

Air/sea rescue, 294 Squadron RAF, based at Benghazi, operating Wellington and Blenheim aircraft, was called in to assist. The Flight Commander, Flying Officer Gray Thorp, a New Zealander, first spotted four of the crew while piloting his Wellington on 14 July. Another two were found the next day. All were dropped rescue kits. Three others were still missing and one of those sighted had been injured in the parachute landing. Because the aircraft were unable to land close by, getting the men out was a problem, so the help of the LRDG and the Sudan Defence Force was requested. While on their way the LRDG patrol required some urgent vehicle spares. A radio message to 294 Squadron resulted in a Blenheim successfully delivering a low altitude drop of truck springs.

To enable Flying Officer Thorp to safely land his Wellington a desert airstrip was established as near as possible to the downed airmen.

The LRDG were often called upon to rescue downed airmen from the desert wilderness. Here an USAAF B24 Liberator crew have been located after they were forced to bail out when their aircraft got lost and ran out of fuel.

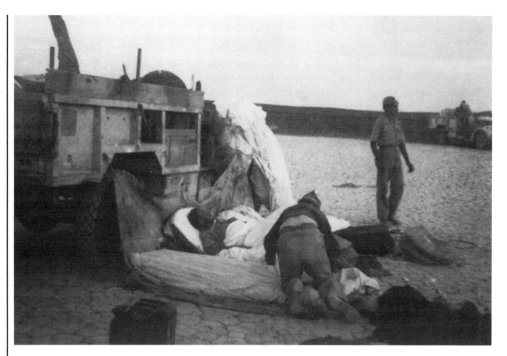

On 19 July he guided the ground forces from the air to the rescue sight. An RAF doctor, Flight Lieutenant Jim Lowe, also a New Zealander, went with the trucks to assist the injured. He took his camera and recorded the event. The six aircrew were picked up and transported to the landing ground. On 21 July they were flown out to their own unit hospital in Benghazi. Unfortunately no trace of the three missing Americans was ever found.

There was almost another serious incident when the 294 Squadron commander decided to fly in to inspect the rescue mission operation. As he approached the desert landing ground in his Miles Magister the aircraft lost its propeller, but he managed to land, folding up his undercarriage. Fortunately no one was hurt and the liaison aircraft was able to be repaired. Eventually the commander flew home without further incident.

Though the patrols tried to avoid it, prisoners sometimes had to be carried, which if deep behind the lines put a strain on resources. If there were a number of them they could be driven some distance away from where they were captured, given a supply of food and water and set a compass direction to the nearest enemy position or oasis. This provided plenty of time for the patrol to escape the area before the alarm was raised.

Captain Bruce Ballantyne was operating with T Patrol near Benghazi when they came across a detachment of Germans driving English Bedford trucks accompanied by two BMW motorcycles. They were from a recovery party who were out collecting spare parts from derelict British vehicles. As Dick Lewis recorded in his diary:

24 October 1941: One of the patrols arrived last night bringing in two captured lorries, five Germans and two Libyans. They surprised them when the patrol was near Benghazi, and made a quick capture. The Jerries never expected to see British troops so far behind the lines.

Ballantyne had given chase in his lighter Ford 15 cwt, racing ahead of the rest of the patrol. Mounted on his vehicle was one of the first Vickers K machine-guns carried by the LRDG. It had been brought along by Pilot Officer Rawnsley of the RAF who was travelling as an observer. He had fired only a few rounds in front of the trucks, which were running on synthetic fuel and not performing well, before they pulled up and surrendered. The motorcycles were put in the back of a truck and were later used as base transport. The Germans couldn't believe that while out on a peaceful mission behind their own lines they had encountered the enemy and were now captured. They became the LRDG's first Afrika Korps prisoners.

When the patrol continued, Ballantyne, still accompanied by Rawnsley, carried the captured German officer with them because he wanted to interrogate him at a later stage. After a time the column came to a halt and Ballantyne told the rest of the patrol to go on ahead, because he wanted to have a rest stop and talk to the prisoner. They had also decided to have a "sponge off", the desert equivalent of a wash using a damp cloth.

As the men undressed, Ballantyne, without thinking, left his revolver in its holster on the running board. The German remained in the vehicle as both men carried out their ablutions. The prisoner seized the opportunity and quickly grabbed the gun from the truck step. When Ballantyne raised his hands his shorts fell to the ground. He later said that there was nothing more demoralising than standing in your birthday suit looking down the barrel of one's own revolver.

The German started up the truck and drove off into the desert. Luckily there were some tyres strewn about which the men used to light a signal fire. The rest of the patrol, who had been waiting for their commander to catch up, saw the black smoke and returned to rescue the embarrassed and stranded officers. The German travelled nearly 100 kilometres before the 15 cwt's radiator failed. He was later picked up by a South African armoured car patrol.

Prisoners, sometimes wounded, had to be carried in the cramped confines of a LRDG truck. Shown here are the first Afrika Korps POWs taken by the Group. The German officer in the centre (with his head bowed), while later being transported by Captain Ballantyne of T Patrol, overcame his captors and raced off in the commander's Ford 15cwt. He was later recaptured when the vehicle broke down. Photo: Merlyn Craw.

THE ROAD WATCH

In 1942 Rommel's Afrika Korps had broken out of El Agheila on the Gulf of Sirte in Libya, and the Allies were desperately in need of reliable intelligence for their planned counter-offensive in Cyrenaica. To help gather this information the LRDG established the "Road Watch". The Tripoli–Benghazi road *("Via Balbia")* which was 643 kilometres behind enemy lines, was kept under constant observation, day and night, from 2 March until 21 July 1942. It was along this road that the Axis brought nearly all their armour, supplies and troop reinforcements.

The patrol would take up position 8 kilometres east of Mussolini's "Areo Philaenorum", a grandiose stone archway straddling the highway which marked the demarcation point between Cyrenaica and Tripolitania. Known as the "Marble Arch" to the Allies, it was built by the Italians as a monument to their colonisation of Libya.

The men first sought cover in shallow wadis in order to make camp and camouflage vehicles. Then before dawn each day two observers would select a hiding place 270 to 370 metres from the road and conceal themselves in a fold in the ground, or amongst the small scattered camel-thorn scrub. Equipped with notebooks, binoculars, a vehicle silhouette reference, and rations which included a waterbottle that was buried in the sand to keep cool, they lay all day watching the traffic.

One man would be responsible for taking notes, while the other looked through his binoculars describing all transport going to or from the front. Personal weapons were not always carried, the idea being that if surprised, scruffy and unarmed they could pass themselves off as evaders from an overrun unit. The rest of the patrol would then have a chance of moving the watch elsewhere without interference.

1942. T1 patrol Chevrolet 1533X2 30cwt trucks lined up about to set out to take their turn on the Road Watch. On the left is J. L. D. Davis, behind Te Aroha is R. W. N. Lewis, in the middle with goggles is F. W. Jopling, sitting in Tutira is Captain N. P. Wilder, patrol commander. Photo: Shepherd collection.

As stillness was the best camouflage, the observers could not move during the day except to roll on their backs. When night fell they were able to move about, not only to keep warm but to get closer to the road where they could judge the vehicles by their sound and outline. Just before dawn, having been replaced by two others, the men would return to camp for breakfast and rest. It was a wearisome task, bitterly cold in winter, blowing dust in spring, and blistering heat in summer; from dawn to dusk it was a very long day. As one watcher put it: *"You look at your watch at 11, and look again about four hours later and it's 11.15".*

The classification, markings, loads and other details of all troop and supply transport, armoured vehicles and artillery, were recorded as they passed. They even observed Allied POWs being trucked to the rear. Yet rescue was out of the question, as the Road Watch could not be compromised. If the information was considered vital it was immediately transmitted to LRDG HQ at Siwa, otherwise it was sent when the patrol was relieved and clear of enemy territory. This intelligence proved invaluable to GHQ in Cairo in assessing the enemy's strength in Cyrenaica.

There was always the risk of discovery. One night an enemy convoy of some 200 men in 27 vehicles left the road and camped in the desert close to two R1 Patrol observers (Private F. R. Brown and Trooper G. C. Parkes). Fortunately in the darkness they were not discovered, as they spent the hours prostrate and warm under their sheepskin coats. Throughout the whole operation, despite some close calls, the enemy never detected the LRDG presence. Occasionally members of Italian road gangs worked or wandered about without noticing them, and Arabs who did see the men did not betray them to the enemy. One time the watchers thought the game was up when two German officers from a passing convoy fired shots in their direction. They kept their heads down, but there was no cause for concern as a couple of desert hares foraging in the vicinity were being used for target practice.

It took three patrols to do this work, while one was watching the road for a week or ten days the other was going out from the base at Siwa to relieve it, and the third was making the 965 kilometre journey back. Both squadrons shared in this important, though sometimes tedious job. As Ron Landon-Lane of R Patrol recalled, *"Of all the patrol duties this was the most hated".*

The result of one particular watch proved the importance of accurate intelligence gathering. Two T1 Patrol observers, Trooper J.L.P. Macassey and Private R.A. Simpson, were watching the road near Marble Arch when they counted 120 Axis tanks heading for the front. The information was considered so vital that it had to be reported immediately to HQ, because at that time, prior to Alamein, the Eighth Army had only about 400 tanks. Captain N. P. Wilder the patrol commander risked leaving the watch hideout in daylight and took the wireless truck into the desert to transmit the observations. After the message was sent, a repeat was requested, which was given. When Maccassey and Simpson returned from their 24 hour watch, they had compiled a complete report listing all the different tank types. That night this detailed account was sent as part of the usual communication. However, panic soon developed at HQ as the operators had inadvertently logged the three transmissions separately, resulting in sightings of 360 tanks heading for the front in one day! When the patrol returned to base shortly afterwards, Macassey and Simpson were flown to HQ to give personal reports of their observations.

Dick Lewis of T Patrol recorded in his diary a good account of his experiences while on the Road Watch:

09/03/1942: A beautiful day. We have taken over from S Patrol, and we are now in a very good concealed wadi three miles from the road. The first two are on the watch now. I went down with them when they took over just before dawn this morning, to get the lay of the land, as Peter M. and I are on tomorrow. It's all pretty flat with little cover except a scattering of low camel thorn, but the secret would be to keep absolutely still during all the daylight hours. There's an aerodrome a couple of miles up the road, and at intervals planes sweep overhead, seemingly only a few feet up. Further in the wadi we have the camouflage nets over the trucks,

with bushes sticking out here and there, until it is nearly impossible to pick them out from more than a hundred yards or so.

Peter and I spent all yesterday and last night watching the road. Our picquet changes every 24 hours just before dawn. We got there in the dark of the pre-dawn, and took up a fairly good position a couple of hundred yards from the road, lying down among a few low bushes where we hoped to be inconspicuous. The big sheepskin coats we wore blended in well with the surrounding desert, but again, stillness was the best camouflage.

There was a good deal of traffic, mostly covered lorries, most of them towing trailers, big ten ton affairs that on a flat road such as this could cut the petrol consumption in half. There wasn't much risk in us being seen if one kept still, except by a gang of Italian workmen on the road nearby. They came along in the morning from a blockhouse about half a mile away, talking and singing out, and returned in the evening after a day's work. Aircraft zoomed close overhead at intervals, but they were on their own missions, not looking out for "oddbods" lying about in the desert. Altogether it wasn't a bad day.

R Patrol break for a mid-desert meal on the way to the Watch. The trucks are camouflaged, but it can seen as to how exposed the men were in the open desert. Photo: Merle Fogden.

The night was worse. A cold wind came up, and though we huddled in an old stone dugout and pulled our sheepskin coats around us, it wasn't the best. We took a stroll on the road after dark, it was bitumen with a good surface, and watched a big truck and trailer go by from the roadside. We had to take a note of everything that went past: its size, classification, load and so on. The number of wheels, kind of guns on the tanks, uniforms of any soldiers travelling, and any other details we could distinguish.

A noticeable thing about this part of the world is that any road is very hard to approach unseen in daylight. They either go along big flats, the tops of rolling hills, or big valleys. They must have been made that way in the first place to avoid the risk of ambush. They made a good job of it, because they are all damned difficult to spy from close quarters.

Trooper Peter Mitford, T1 Patrol, concealed by a small scrub, records the passing traffic as he endures his exhausting 24-hour stint observing the road. The intelligence gained from the Road Watch proved invaluable in assessing Rommel's dispositions in the Western Desert. Photo: Ngaire Lewis.

At three o'clock next morning, we took a bearing on another star and thankfully started trudging back, arriving at the camp in the wadi soon after noon, tired and hungry, but with the satisfying sense of something unpleasant done.

The more unpleasant side of the activity was explained by Trooper Frank Jopling who kept a diary while on the same watch, though on a different shift from Dick Lewis:

12 March 1942: 4pm. Gosh! We are looking forward to the sun to go down so we can get up and stretch our legs. To make matters worse, the wind is blowing and the sand is flying, so you can hardly keep your eyes open. There are only about two more hours of daylight to go, but every hour seems like a year.

As each truck goes past we have to put down the time in our notebook and since 6am this morning I have had my watch out in front of me watching each minute go past. If you can imagine lying on your stomach without hardly moving and watching the minute hand of your watch take twelve complete circles you may be able to imagine something of what we had to go through.

An R Patrol vehicle expertly concealed while based at a Road Watch camp site. This was necessary because they were deep behind enemy lines, with much road and air traffic activity close by. Photo: Richard Williams.

6pm. Well, the sun has now gone behind the hill, but it is still too light to get up and walk around, but it won't be long now. I have never longed for the sun to go down as much as I have today. I am aching all over and if I stay in this position much longer I think I will die. So far 274 trucks have passed.

The following morning Jopling continued his diary relating what took place during the night:

13 March, 7am. We had a cup of tea yesterday morning and from the time we left to go to the road until 6.30pm we never had a bite to eat or a drink of water. So believe me, we felt like a bit to eat. So the first thing we did when it got dark was to stand up and walk around, and then sit down to a tin of bully and some shortbread. We also opened a tin of apple juice that I had in my pack. After that we didn't feel so bad except that it started to get very cold after a while.

Only an hour ago we had been longing for the sun to go down, now we were longing for it to come up again so that our watch would be finished. We nearly froze during the night and there was a very heavy dew. We counted 38 trucks during the night which brought our grand total to 336. We set off on our walk back at 4am, and believe me it seemed an awful long three miles, but we eventually arrived at the camp at 6am and set about getting some breakfast in.

After the Allied victory at Alamein in late October 1942, the Middle East Intelligence requested the watch on the Tripoli–Benghazi road to be reactivated. During the first spell of watching carried out by Y1 Patrol from 30 October to 8 November, less than 100 vehicles passed both ways daily. By 10 November, when they were relieved by Y1, the results of the Eighth Army's victory were apparent. Enemy traffic streamed westwards at the rate of 3,500 vehicles a day, carrying many thousands of troops, and the evacuation of Italian civilians

with their furniture confirmed that Rommel did not plan to return.

When it was evident that the enemy intended to withdraw from El Agheila, the watch was transferred farther westwards to the Gheddahia–Tauorga section of the road. S1 Patrol began the first to spell on 13 December, and T2 took over a week later. Its commander, Second-Lieutenant R. A. Tinker, leaving a rear camp about 48 kilometres to the south-west of Gheddahia, took nine men in two vehicles to the vicinity of Seddada. The watchers, who had great difficulty in passing on foot through enemy camps near the road, were soon discovered by the Germans. Three armoured cars attacked T2s forward camp on 22 December. The men who had evaded capture began to walk back to the rear camp, which Tinker and three others managed to reach safely.

The next day, as eight German vehicles were seen approaching from the north, Tinker successfully withdrew his patrol. However, six men were missing: Troopers E. Ellis, L. R. B. Johnstone and J. L. Reid, and Privates C. A. Dornbush and J. M. Simonsen, along with Private E. C. Sturrock, an English radio operator.

Ellis and Sturrock had escaped the enemy and set out eastwards towards their own lines, then separated in search of water. The men walked for days with no food and little to drink. They rested by day and moved at night when the cold made sleep almost impossible. Eventually they reached the British lines independently. Both were awarded the MM. The others had been captured, though Trooper Reid was able to evade the Germans for a week before being caught. He later escaped from a POW camp in Italy.

In late 1942, Director of Military Intelligence at GHQ in Cairo recorded the following analysis of the Road Watch:

The LRDG Road Watch provided the only trained traffic observers.

Not only is the standard of accuracy and observation exceptionally high, but the Patrols are familiar with the most recent illustrations of enemy vehicles and weapons. During periods of withdrawal of reinforcement of the enemy, the LRDG has provided an indispensable basis of certain facts on which calculations of enemy strength can be based. Without their reports we should frequently have been in doubt as to the enemy's intentions, when knowledge of them was all important; and our estimate of enemy strength would have been far less accurate and accepted with less confidence.

The Road Watch immediately in the rear of the El Aghelia position has been of quite exceptional importance, and the information which it has provided, in spite of interruptions due to a difficult and dangerous situation, has been invaluable. From the point of view of military intelligence the risks and casualties which the Patrols have accepted, and are accepting, have been more than justified.

The success of the LRDG's behind the lines intelligence-gathering role, compared against the risk, did not go without comment from one of its members, as Trooper Frank Jopling wrote in his diary:

I can truly say that it is a miracle the LRDG gets away with it the way they have done up till now. If GHQ want information, they tell us off to do the job, whereupon we set out in unarmoured and practically unarmed trucks, against armoured cars or planes, which are the two most likely things we would strike, and bring back the information required or prisoners who can give it, and generally a lot more besides. It seems to me the LRDG is doing the impossible and getting away with it.

The final word goes to Kennedy Shaw, from his book on the LRDG, where at the end of the chapter on the Road Watch, he says:

Considering all things, it was perhaps the most useful job the LRDG ever did. I wish Rommel could have read this chapter.

December 1942. Trooper Eric Ellis of T2 Patrol rests besides a Marmon Herrington armoured car of the King's Dragoon Guards. After being cut off by the enemy while on Road Watch, he was on his fifth day of a desert trek before he was rescued. He had to rest by day and walk at night, becoming very footsore until he stumbled across an action between German armoured cars and those of the KDGs. Fortunately the latter won the skirmish, leaving the enemy with two burning vehicles before they withdrew. The New Zealander was picked up and was later awarded the MM. Photo: David Ellis.

THE BARCE RAID

The raid on the Axis held airfield and town of Barce (present day Al Marj) in Cyrenaica, though chaotic with loss of men and vehicles, was considered one of the most successful "beat ups" ever undertaken by the Group. For the purposes of this publication it is worth recounting in detail, as it encompasses all the elements of procedure, direct action, incidents and desert survival—factors common in many of the other LRDG's operations.

September 1942, a month before the battle of Alamein, a force under the command of Major J. R. Easonsmith left their base at Faiyum, with orders to, *"Cause the maximum amount of damage and disturbance to the enemy"*. The code name was Operation "Hyacinth". This was the most successful of the four operations the unit was involved with at that time.

The others were code named, *Daffodil*– a Commando land (guided by Y1 Patrol) and sea attack on harbour installations and the coastal defence guns at Tobruk: *Snowdrop*– an SAS attack against shipping at Benghazi, with S1 and S2 Patrols in support; and *Tulip*– an assault to take Jalo, to provide the SAS with a forward base. This involved the Sudan Defence Force along with Lieutenant R. J. Talbot's R2 and Captain A. D. Hunter's Y2 Patrol. This series of operations were to take place simultaneously in preparation for the attack on El Alamein. They were designed to divert attention and disrupt Rommel's communication and supply lines.

Easonsmith led two patrols: T1, the New Zealanders under Captain N. P. Wilder, and G1, the Guards under Captain J. A. L. Timpson, a total of 47 men in 12 trucks and five jeeps. For security reasons the planned objective was given out as Derna. It was only when the column was in mid-desert that they were told that Barce was the target. The outward 13 day journey, a distance of 1860 kilometres, involved the difficult crossing of the Egyptian and Kalansho Sand Seas, resupplying at dumps on the way. Also

for part of the trip they were supported by Heavy Section carrying rations and fuel.

During the first crossing Timpson's jeep capsized over the edge of a razor-backed dune, throwing the occupants out and rolling over them. He suffered a skull fracture and lost some teeth, while his gunner, Guardsman T. Wann injured his spine, paralysing him from the waist down. Fortunately, in response to a radio message, they were able to be airlifted out to Cairo, by way of an RAF Hudson guided by Captain Tony Browne of R Patrol.

Captain D. Lloyd Owen, Y Patrol (left), Major J. R. Easonsmith (centre) and Captain C. A. Holliman, S Patrol. The vehicles are R Patrol which Easonsmith commanded when this photo was taken. He later led T1 and G1 Patrols in their successful action against the Barce airfield and town in September 1942.
Photo: Sharon Palmer.

Lieutenant N. P. Wilder. Later prompted to captain, he led T1 Patrol on to the Barce airfield destroying 35 aircraft. On the way out he had to crash his truck through two light tanks to enable his escape, and was later wounded in both legs during a strafing attack. He received the DSO for his role in this operation.
Photo: Warner Wilder.

T1 Patrol lined up at the edge of the Sand Sea. Te Anau II, T6, the fitter's truck on the right (note the spare springs hooked on the front) was the only vehicle to return out of the 17 that set out. All the weapons have been covered in shrouds to protect them from the dust. Photo: Merlyn Craw.

Easonsmith took a British agent, Major Vladimir Peniakoff (of Popski's Private Army fame), and two Libyan Arabs to within a few kilometres of Barce. The Arabs were to walk into the town, contact fellow tribesmen and establish the enemy dispositions before rejoining the column. In the meantime, 24 kilometres from Barce, the patrols were hidden amongst an olive grove, busy cleaning their guns, priming grenades, preparing time bombs, tidying the loads, and receiving final orders for the raid. The main intention was for T1 to destroy the aircraft on the landing ground, while as a diversion the Guards would attack the Italian HQ in the main street, the railway station and the barracks just outside the town. The men were made aware of the light AA defences at the airfield and the possibility of encountering enemy armour.

On the evening of 13 September, Corporal Merlyn Craw was handing out some of the meal, when Trooper Derek "Snow" Parker commented to his heavily bearded NCO, *"You know Merlyn, you look just like Moses standing there"*, to which came the reply with a grin, *"And this could well be your last supper."* Soon after the patrols set out in the darkness on the road to Barce.

The first enemy contact was made when they were challenged at a police checkpoint at Sidi Raui on the outskirts of the town. The Tripolitanian sentry was disarmed and captured, and an Italian officer who arrived on the scene was shot and killed. After several hand grenades were thrown into the building the rest of the guard ran off leaving a dozen horses. The telephone lines were cut to ensure Barce was not warned of the approaching danger.

The sudden halt of the column had caused T1 Patrol's Breda gun truck to run into the back of the wireless vehicle. Put out of action due to a smashed radiator, the gun truck had to be stripped and abandoned. Its occupants, Gunner E. Sanders and Troopers A. Vincent and K. Yealands joined other crews. The wireless truck was able to continue. However, a short distance down the road a G Patrol truck hit a rock and broke its sump. That also had to be stripped and left.

Peniakoff rejoined the Group at Sidi Selim without his two Arab spies, who had not returned. To act as a rallying point after the raid, the T1 wireless truck with its driver, Trooper P. V. Mitford the medical officer, Captain R. P. Lawson (RAMC), an English radio operator, Private A. Biddle and Gunner E. Sanders remained at this rendezvous. They were also to listen out for Lieutenant-Colonel Stirling of the SAS who was raiding Benghazi. The rest of the patrol then proceeded with their lights on full, pretending to be an Axis convoy.

Not far from Barce, at the top of an escarpment, there were two Italian light tanks parked on either side of the road. The crews were relaxing outside their vehicles and presumed the approaching traffic was Italian. This proved fatal to them because as they closed, the LRDG opened fire with all weapons and raced through un-scathed.

By midnight the force had arrived at the cross-roads outside the town where the men split up. Peniakoff stayed behind with a Guards' truck to deal with any pursuers, T1 set off to attack the airfield and G1 the barracks. Wilder wanted to get behind the wheel of his Chevrolet, therefore he took over from his driver Trooper Derek Parker who manned the twin Vickers K machine-guns, alongside Trooper H. R. T. "Mick" Holland operating the .50 Browning.

With their lights switched off Wilder led the Kiwis in their four trucks and a jeep to the airfield entrance where he found the gate shut. He simply dismounted his vehicle and opened the iron gate then drove in, while doing so the gunners shot some Italians who had come to investigate. Soon afterward a burst of fire exploded a petrol tanker with its trailer which lit up the whole scene and made it easier for the drivers to see their way around.

As the men approached the airfield they destroyed a petrol dump and threw grenades through the windows of the mess and station buildings. Then in single file they drove round with the gunners firing mixed tracer, incendiary and explosive ammunition at each bomber in turn. This took some time as the landing ground covered a large area and the planes were widely dispersed. The day after

the event, Trooper Frank Jopling commented in his diary:

> 14 September 1942: My one ambition in this war has been to set a plane on fire because then you know you have done some damage. Well, I certainly achieved my ambition last night, as I know for certain I set five planes on fire and possibly several more.

The patrol also had to defend itself against the enemy. Some gunners were told their sole job was to knock out the opposition not the planes. For example, the trucks were receiving fire from the top of the hanger, whereupon Trooper Wally Rail using his twin .303 Brownings destroyed that gun emplacement. Also Trooper Euan Hay was responsible for quelling much of the enemy fire with his .50 Browning. Against the light of the burning aircraft the trucks should have been easy targets, but the steady and accurate firepower generated by the gunners helped suppress the Italian defences.

G1 Patrol Guardsman T. Wann sits in a patrol jeep mounting a .303 Vickers K machine-gun. On the outward journey he and the patrol commander Captain J. A. L. Timpson were injured when their jeep capsized over a razor-back dune. They were evacuated back to Cairo by air. Photo: Merlyn Craw.

Medical orderly Guardsman Astell, talks with Guardsman T. Wann who lies on a stretcher awaiting evacuation by air. When his jeep had overturned he received spinal injuries that paralyzed him from the waist down. Photo: Merlyn Craw.

Trooper Keith Tippett recounted the action when he entered the aerodrome:

I was driving the navigator's truck "Te Aroha III", right behind Wilder in "Tutira III", it was quite scary going in, as there was a machine-gun on top of a building which was firing directly down on us, but a few bursts from our Vickers and their tracer started going straight up into the air. The same applied to the other emplacements around the aerodrome, as soon as we saw their tracer coming down from going skywards we would give them a burst, and up they would go again. I had a bit of a shoot myself, there was no time for fear, with the noise, tracer and confusion, it was really exciting against the light of the moon and blazing aircraft.

Corporal Craw, who was in the last vehicle, methodically stopped at each plane that was not burning and took one of his home-made time bombs from a box mounted on the running board. He lept from his truck and ran to an aircraft where he placed the device on top of the wing above the fuel tanks and pulled the switch. The timer was set to explode shortly afterwards. Though it was dangerous work with the planes on fire and blowing up all round him, he managed to destroy 10 aircraft in that manner.

Despite the men spending an hour on the airfield subject to wild, inaccurate enemy fire, including light anti-aircraft guns and mortars, a total of 35 planes had been destroyed or damaged, without casualty to themselves. As they were leaving Wilder's truck went off the track and got stuck on a soft mound beside a ditch. The column stopped and while still under fire extracted the truck. Amazingly no one was hit.

Expecting the road by which they reached the airfield to be blocked, T1 Patrol drove out through the narrow main street of Barce. Then in his headlights Wilder picked out three light tanks staggered across the road. The two rear tanks, in their eagerness to come forward, crashed into each other and went dead. The other one dazzled by the lights started firing high. Trooper Keith Tippett, who was driving the second vehicle in the column, remembered the moment as,

Heart stopping stuff, seeing this tracer coming boom, boom, boom off the road, but we had no option but to charge at pace and hope for the best.

In the narrow street there was no room to turn, and the trucks were without weapons capable of knocking out armour. Parker's guns had overheated and jammed, so he fired a Very pistol at the tanks, doing no harm apart from blinding them. Wilder, seeing no other way out, shouted, *"Get out of the way you bastards!"*, and with his gunners holding on tight, pressed his foot down on the accelerator and rammed his Chevrolet, *Tutira III*, at full speed into the side of the tank, skidding it into another. The truck was wrecked, but they had managed to clear a passage.

Unhurt, they abandoned their vehicle. While doing so Wilder and Parker attempted to immobilise the tanks by tossing grenades under them. At this point Parker was hit in the stomach by a bullet that passed through his left side and out the right, leaving him

The journey to Barce—note the spread-out vehicles and the exposed landscape. If aircraft were sighted the column would disperse. Photo: Merlyn Craw.

unconscious for a short time. He recovered just in time to hear a jeep arriving. As Wilder jumped on board Parker called out, *"Wait for me, wait for me!"*, and despite his painful condition managed to throw himself into the back. Meanwhile, Holland, along with Lance Corporal Alan Nutt who left the jeep to assist, were both captured.

The driver of the jeep, Trooper Peter Burke, dazzled by the tracer fired by Wilder's twin Vickers Ks, steered into the kerb near the Barce railway station, overturned the vehicle and threw the occupants out, apart from Wilder who was pinned underneath. Though Burke was injured he asked Parker to give him a hand to try to lift the jeep. But the agony proved too much for Parker, who in great pain collapsed onto the road. He was resigned to being captured and thought it would be wise to get rid of a Luger pistol he was carrying, so he threw it away as far as he could.

Before long Private Jack Davis's truck, *Te Anau II*, arrived on the scene, and Burke ran out onto the road to try to stop it. He was lucky that in the darkness he was not mistaken for the enemy and shot. As the gunner, Trooper Wally Rail, who was noted for being quick on the trigger recalled: *"To this day, I don't know why I didn't*

shoot him." Four men righted the jeep, extracting Wilder who was unconscious and soaked in petrol from ruptured jerrycans. Parker who was now also unconscious was picked up along with Burke. They were taken to the rendezvous at Sidi Selim where they recovered, and Parker was given morphia to ease his pain, which he said, *"Felt like white hot agony, as if I had been kicked in the stomach by a pretty frisky mule."*

Just before *Te Anau II* had arrived, Troopers Keith Tippett and Bruce Dobson had put the tank Wilder had rammed completely out of action by boarding it and placing bombs and grenades on the vehicle. Keith Tippett recalled the action:

We left our navigator, Frank Jopling, to man our guns as Dobbie and I endeavoured to put the tank out of action. I threw one of our home-made bombs under the tank and put grenades on the track, then we climbed onto the tank and tried to open the turret hatch but couldn't, so I left a grenade on the lid. Unfortunately Dobbie climbed down the side where I had left a grenade on the track, and he got quite a few splinters in his back and hand.

Meanwhile Jopling was getting pretty unsettled exposed in the truck with all this action going on, and he was shouting, "Hurry, hurry!" So we got under way again, but now I had to try to find my way out, trying to remember the way I came in. We reached the town square where we saw armoured cars milling around, so we gave them a burst as we passed which caused great confusion. This amused Dobbie, but didn't help Frank's nerves at all. I reckoned the next turn must be the way out, but I was wrong. Having a general idea of where the main road we came in was, I continued on regardless. We went through a rubbish dump, a bit of scrub, and over the side of a hill, eventually getting back on the right road only to be confronted by another two light tanks.

We gave them a burst, but they didn't reply, I think they was more scared of us than we were of them. Maybe they had taken off, or were hiding inside. When we reached the rendezvous Dobbie was bleeding down his back, he had not been aware in the excitement that he had copped

shrapnel in his back. However, at this point he was able to have his wounds dressed.

Tippett had come out on the main Tobruk road and had gone several kilometres when they encountered two light tanks that didn't fire on them, but were blocking most of the road. The truck just managed to squeeze through, though in doing so it scraped heavily alongside a tank, losing their left mudguard, a spare tyre and a sand tray. They carried on regardless and were the first T Patrol men to arrive at the rendezvous and report to Easonsmith. As Trooper Frank Jopling wrote in his diary:

I told him the position, and that some probably wouldn't get away, and he said, "You seem to have done a good job anyhow." From here we could get a great view of the fires and it looked wonderful, the whole place seemed to be burning.

Corporal Craw's truck, *Te Paki III*, at the rear of the patrol, stopped at

Captain N. P. Wilder, sheltered by trees at Gebel Akhdar, reads orders to his patrol in preparation for the attack on Barce. Photo: Merlyn Craw.

Wilder's abandoned vehicle, saw nobody there so continued along the narrow street till they came to a roundabout and stopped.

Craw, accompanied by Trooper Keith Yealands, left the vehicle and explored the area on foot. On their return they told the driver Trooper Tom Milburn that there was no way out and they would have to go back in the direction they had come. The men had just boarded their transport again when they were fired upon by an armoured car. As the truck raced off it was hit and set alight in the rear. To avoid the enemy fire Milburn turned sharply to the right, in doing so the front wheel got caught in the entrance of an air-raid shelter next to a building. Consequently the truck overturned and landed on its side.

Craw was standing up behind his guns when he was thrown head first into the entrance where he lay knocked out for several minutes. The shelter was dark and full of Italian officers and men, so the New Zealander was not noticed at first. The truck was burning, and occasionally a jerrycan would explode sending flames right down into the shelter. It was getting hotter and hotter, therefore Craw decided to remove his battledress. As the heat intensified he edged in further, where the men were becoming fearful and crushed in together. Craw thought he was going to be burnt to death, and everytime there was an explosion the Italians frantically prayed.

After about half an hour he was eventually discovered, whereupon he instinctively drew his revolver only to see the barrels of four Berettas pointing at him. The gun was struck from his hand and he was grabbed by the braces, then dragged through the mob to some steps on the other side of the shelter. Craw later said that had he known there was another exit in the chaos he could had easily passed through the Italians and escaped into the darkness.

The driver Trooper Tom Milburn had been thrown into the street, but he

quickly recovered, grabbed his "bail-out" kit and shouted to the others to follow him behind a brick wall. For several minutes he waited for them to appear, but soon found enemy soldiers on the scene. Milburn managed to escape the town, only to be captured by an Italian sentry who struck him across the forehead with a rifle butt. Dazed, he was dragged into a building where he was propped upon a benzine tin. His captors then grabbed him by the hair and proceeded to knock his head against the wall, all the time asking him where he had come from. The only answer they got was that they could all go to hell!

Craw's truck had been shot up the rear and was on fire underneath the engine and driving seat. Trooper Euan Hay, the gunner, by the light of the flames saw a pair of heels sticking out the back of the vehicle. It was Trooper Keith Yealands, who had been badly wounded in the head. Though before Hay could extract him he was grabbed from behind and a pistol was poked in his back. An excited voice shouted *"Me shoot! Me shoot!"*. Hay surrendered, but with the help of the Italians he didn't hesitate in continuing to remove his comrade from the burning truck. Yealands had suffered a severe head wound, yet despite the enemy waiting five days for him to die, he later recovered in hospital. To this day he still carries bullet fragments lodged in his brain.

Cleaning and checking weapons prior to the raid. Major Vladimir "Popski" Peniakoff uses the jeep bonnet as a table. Photo: Ngaire Lewis.

Captain N. P. Wilder (with map) gives final briefings as the evening meal is being consumed. When this photo was taken an enemy aircraft was flying overhead, which for that moment has made the men look a little apprehensive.
Photo: Merlyn Craw.

The six New Zealanders spent their time in Barce chained together in pairs. The manacles bit into their ankles and allowed little freedom, which made sleep almost impossible. Craw had been captured without a battledress, and at some time during the action Wilder had left his in the town. The Italians had found it and presumed Craw was the officer. It took many hours of interrogation to convince the enemy that he was only a corporal. At one stage an Italian general arrived and Craw was expected to stand up and salute him,

but he didn't, and was bashed over the head with a rifle butt to remind him.

While the men were chained up their greatest fear were the Tripolitanian guards, who constantly threatened to torture them, cut their throats, shoot them and similar taunts. It was only the intervention of the Italian soldiers that kept the men safe. Following three days of interrogation the New Zealanders were taken to Benghazi and spent time in a civilian jail near the port. There Merlyn Craw recalled his most disturbing memory of that time, which was the screaming that took place during the night. The Italians were torturing people, probably Arabs, by leaving them hanging all night with meat hooks under their jaws. The men's other concern was that the port was subject to regular air raids by the RAF, therefore it was with some relief that after 10 days they were shipped to Italy.

Whilst T1 Patrol raided the airfield, Sergeant Jack Dennis, who had taken over command from the injured Captain Timpson, attacked the town barracks to create a diversion. Using their Vickers K guns, rifle grenade discharger cups and the Guards' 20mm truck-mounted Breda gun, they created havoc firing into buildings and along the streets, killing and wounding a number of the enemy. Consequently they were successful in keeping the troops away from the main battle on the landing ground. In two jeeps Major Eason-smith, now joined by Peniakoff, attacked the Italian HQ and other buildings, shot up and threw grenades among Italians in the street, then wrecked a dozen vehicles in a transport park. After which the LRDG withdrew and reassembled at the rallying point to prepare to retire south. T1 had lost six men, two trucks and a jeep in Barce, and G1 had lost four men (two of whom later escaped and rejoined the patrol) and one truck.

Sergeant Merlyn Craw, 1944. As a corporal during the Barce raid in September 1942 he won the Military Medal for destroying 10 enemy aircraft by placing time bombs on them. After which he was captured when his truck crashed in the town. A year later he escaped from an Italian POW camp and eventually rejoined the LRDG, He remained with the unit until it was disbanded in 1945.
Photo: Merlyn Craw.

On a hill track heading for Sidi Selim the top-heavy Guards' Breda gun truck suddenly tipped over sideways down a bank. Fortunately the high mounting of the weapon saved the crew from being crushed. Easonsmith and a G Patrol truck went back and successfully recovered the vehicle. But vital time had been lost, and it was nearly daylight by the time they returned to the rendezvous.

Shortly before dawn on 14 September, as the column approached the police post to the south of Sidi Selim, they found the G Patrol truck that had been previously left and took it in tow. Shortly afterwards they came under fire from both sides of the road where Tripolitanian troops under Italian officers were waiting.

At speed they ran the gauntlet and successfully broke through, though a truck was damaged and three men were wounded. This included Trooper Frank Jopling, who was hit in the legs and Major Peniakoff had lost part of a finger. In the pre-dawn darkness they had been subject to rifle and machine-gun fire from a well concealed enemy, and it was only the sustained return fire targeting the gun flashes that prevented the patrol from being totally decimated. Trooper Wally Rail recalled that as he operated his twin Brownings he was hampered by trying to avoid stepping on Trooper Parker who was laying badly wounded on the truck floor.

Private Davis's truck had received a puncture. His driver, Private David Warbrick, brought the vehicle to a halt and in record time changed the wheel, during which his back was exposed to the enemy machine-gun position. Warbrick later said that he could feel the shivers running up and down his spine, expecting at any moment bullets to rip into his back. Meanwhile Tripolitanian cavalry were seen approaching, but a burst of fire from Rail's Brownings soon scared them off. In his haste to depart the scene after changing the wheel Warbrick drove off the jack, leaving it behind.

The damaged truck had to be towed, and further down the road they also recovered the T Patrol Breda truck which had been left near the police post the previous evening. An attempt was made to repair these vehicles, but the attack was renewed before the fitters could complete their work. Trooper Tippett was on sentry duty among some trees when a Tripolitanian Arab wearing long white robes appeared before him. As the New Zealander challenged him the Arab produced from under his clothing a rifle which he fired, but missed. Tippett returned fire with his captured Luger, whereupon the Arab ran off. The close presence of the enemy was reported to Easonsmith,

G1 on the way to Barce. Guardsman Duncalfe behind the twin Vickers K machine-guns with Sergeant Jack Dennis at the wheel. He took over the command of G1 when Captain Timpson was injured. Behind him is a .303 EY rifle fitted with a grenade discharger cup which was later used with great effect in Barce town. Sergeant Dennis won the Military Medal for his role in this action. To avoid capture after the raid, Duncalfe and a fellow Guardsman spent three months hiding out with Arabs before advancing Allied forces picked them up. Photo: Merlyn Craw.

Trooper Tom Milburn, T1 Patrol. He drove Corporal Craw's truck Te Paki III that overturned and crashed in Barce. He was captured while trying to escape the town on foot. Photo: Merlyn Craw.

who along with Guardsman Duncalfe behind the guns, climbed into a jeep and chased them back 3 kilometres. During this time the petrol and stores were removed and time bombs placed in the crippled trucks. The column then continued its withdrawal until the Guards' wireless truck broke down with a stripped rear axle pinion.

Captain R. P. Lawson, LRDG Medical Officer. After the Barce Raid he was kept busy looking after the wounded, including exposing himself to great danger from air attacks while doing so. His bravery and devotion to duty earned him the Military Cross. Photo: Richard Williams.

Unfortunately it had stopped on an exposed hilltop and when daylight came it was seen by an enemy reconnaissance plane. The other vehicles were in camouflaged positions scattered along a valley, but their general location had now been revealed. Thereby from mid morning until dusk, six Italian CR 42 Falco biplane fighters strafed the vehicles and men inadequately hidden in the low scrub. They would attack for about 50 minutes then return to base to re-fuel and re-arm. After a 20-minute lull the planes would be over the valley once again. This cycle went on for the rest of the day.

Trooper Tippett hid behind the back axle of his vehicle and decided to give them a burst next time they came round. But the truck crew, in their hurry to get out of Barce, had failed to cover the guns which had since gathered dust causing them to jam. The course of events had denied the men any opportunity to clean them. Nevertheless, it was not too long before Tippett's truck was hit and set on fire.

As the strafing continued a Guardsman was wounded, and Wilder, in addition to a slight face wound, was shot through both legs. Progressively most transport was put out of action, with the men saving what they could from the burning trucks. Wilder and "Popski" disagreed with Easonsmith about hiding the vehicles during the attacks. They suggested the men should run the gauntlet, as the Vickers K and twin Brownings would be more than a match for the slow outdated biplanes. However, Easonsmith felt that exposing themselves would only lead to further casualties.

During the attacks Dr Lawson managed to get all the wounded away to a safe spot, apart from one. He remained on the surviving truck with Trooper Parker who had been difficult to move, as a bullet had severely lacerated his stomach. They were hidden under a large olive tree with their truck further obscured by a camouflage net. Parker, who was conscious throughout the attacks, said the planes were coming in so low that he could see the pilot's faces in the open cockpits. Luckily they never spotted his vehicle. As the aircraft swooped down Dr. Lawson bravely shifted from side to side sheltering Parker with his own body.

By the evening all the vehicles that remained were one truck and two jeeps to take 33 men back to Kufra, a journey of 1,126 kilometres. In order to make them into a smaller target for enemy aircraft, Easonsmith split his force into driving and walking parties.

Despite suffering a leg wound, T1's navigator Trooper Frank Jopling, without a compass and only an inadequate silk "escape map", took nine Guardsmen and began the 96-kilometre walk to Bir el Gerrari, where G1 patrol had left a vehicle on their way northwards to Barce. The truck, complete with stores of water, petrol and rations, had been put in place in case of an emergency such as this. Jopling had to navigate from memory having seen the position marked on a larger map in his truck.

Lawson set off in T1's truck and a jeep with six wounded men (Wilder, Peniakoff, Parker, Dobson, Burke and a Guardsman). Private Jack Davis acted as navigator, and Private David Warbrick was the driver/fitter. Easonsmith organised the remaining 14 men into a walking party accompanied by the other jeep carrying supplies. Though not long after, due to a bullet hole in the fuel tank, the doctor's jeep had to be abandoned. It was wrecked and two wheels were removed as spares for the walking party's jeep. The men from Lawson's jeep had transferred to the sole surviving truck, T6, *Te Anau II*, T1's fitter's vehicle, which now carried some 4 tonnes of stores and personnel—2 tonnes over its normal load.

On 15 September the party reached Bir el Gerrari and located the well-concealed truck. They took on supplies and a spare tyre and left a note for the walking party. The next day they set out for Landing Ground 125 by the Kalansho Sand Sea, where they found Captain Lloyd Owen's Y1 Patrol.

In response to a radio message, an RAF Bombay transport aircraft flown by the commander of 216 Squadron, Bill Coles, and skilfully guided over the featureless desert by his New Zealand navigator, landed at LG125. Before the wounded could be taken on board the plane had to be refuelled by hand from 4 gallon tins that the aircrew had brought with them. Mindful of the dangers of being behind the lines and exposed in open desert, the job was completed with some urgency. The men were successfully evacuated to Kufra and before long transferred to Cairo.

Prior to this mission Bill Coles had sent a message to his HQ to gain permission to depart on the rescue call. After a long wait he still had not received any response so he decided to take off regardless. While they were airborne his base received a signal stating that on no account were they to leave Kufra because enemy fighters had been spotted over Jalo Oasis. Yet Coles, in his slow and vulnerable Bombay, continued on with his mercy flight. Parker, after six days of discomfort in the back of a truck, without food, surviving only on morphine and a little rum and water, was certainly pleased to see him. Three months later Parker had fully recovered and rejoined the patrol. He went on to become one of the first members of the Eighth Army to enter Tunisia, when T1 found "Wilder's Gap" in January 1943.

The success of the difficult overland journey was largely due to Davis' skilful navigation, as the theodolite had been lost and there was no radio, hence he could not check his position from the stars by astrofix. Fortunately he had managed to save his log book and maps, and with the aid of a magnetic and sun compass was able to navigate the truck by dead reckoning over 1,100 kilometres to Kufra. This included making landfalls at Bir el Gerrari, and at LG125 to drop off the wounded on the way. Warbrick, who was half Maori, skilfully drove the overloaded vehicle over the steep terrain, day and night, with an indomitable cheerfulness which encouraged the others. When "Popski" suggested that he nearly overturned the truck twice during the night drive, he said, *"I know exactly what I am doing, and where I am going, and all Maoris can see in the dark anyway."* "Snow" Parker said it must have been true, because his expert driving over the rough terrain at night, without headlights on, was amazing.

Keith Tippett walked with Easonsmith's party and he recalled that when spotter planes flew over, the men would just crouch down and keep still. Easonsmith was better prepared as he carried a blanket which he put round him whenever a plane was sighted. On the morning of the 15th the group came across a Bedouin camp where they bartered to have a sheep killed. The Arabs could spare no water but offered a little milk.

This welcome meal helped to revitalize the exhausted men. Prior to this Tippett had been lagging behind the main party as he was accompanying Gunner Sanders who was slowed by a sore ankle. By the time they had arrived at the camp all the boiled lamb had been eaten, leaving only the greasy mess at the bottom of the pot. The men were so hungry they ate it regardless.

When Easonsmith's party was approaching Bir el Gerrari on 17 September, having walked about 130 kilometres, they unexpectedly met with S2 Patrol. The other walking party had unfortunately not reached the rendezvous, so Easonsmith and the Rhodesians combed the area for three days but found only eight men. Jopling and Guardsman Gutheridge (Easonsmith's driver) were missing. They had also met the other Rhodesian patrol (S1), who had picked up the two escaped Guardsmen from Barce.

The patrols then withdrew to Kufra. Not long after they had arrived the town was subject to an air raid. Remarkably, the combined firepower of the vehicle-mounted weapons of the LRDG and SAS units based in the area at that time, managed to shoot down five out of the eight raiding Heinkel bombers. This was some achievement, considering the biggest calibre guns were only 20mm Bredas. Even so, the enemy were able to destroy two Bombay aircraft on the ground, and while strafing killed four Arabs in Kufra fort and wounded Guardsman Harkness. In addition, Captain David Lloyd Owen of Y Patrol was badly wounded when a cannon shell passed through his back and left arm.

Meanwhile Jopling was leading his party of nine Guardsmen in the direction of the hidden truck at Bir el Gerrari. His leg wound had been giving him trouble, though it was tolerable when walking level it was painful travelling downhill. Also after resting up for a while it became very sore when he started to walk again.

The newly-issued 1942 Chevrolet 1533X2 Te Aroha III, T9, prior to setting out on patrol. The driver is Private Tom Ritchie, alongside is Trooper Frank Jopling the navigator. Standing in the back is Signalman Tommy Scriven the British radio operator attached to the patrol. This vehicle was later lost on the Barce Raid and Trooper Jopling along with a companion went on to endure a 12 day trek ending in captivity. (The other original crew members did not participate in the raid.) Photo: Imperial War Museum.

The nights were bitterly cold and the men suffered badly, as they had no blankets or greatcoats to keep them warm. Fortunately for part of the trek they were aided by friendly Arabs who supplied water and occasionally some food. By the middle of the day it was too hot to walk, so the group would have to seek shelter in any scattered bushes they could find. Added to their concerns at all times they had to remain vigilant and mindful of searching enemy aircraft overhead.

By September 17 the party had only two gallons of water to last 10 men at least another three or four days—when they thought they could reach their destination. They came across a derelict Italian truck and attempted to drink the liquid from the radiator, but it was unpalatable and seemed to dry out the mouth. It was thought it may have contained anti-freeze. Looking at the landscape, one of the Guardsmen believed the location of the truck was only 12 kilometres from their position, but Jopling disagreed, reckoning it was at least another 48 kilometres away. He kept his diary throughout the trek and wrote:

17 September. They are travelling too fast for me now that they think they are getting close. They are also going too fast for another man. One of the first rules of travelling in the desert is never try to hurry. My mouth is dry and the saliva dries in my mouth and I have to scratch my lips, tongue and the roof of my mouth with my fingernails to scrape it off.

On the 18th the group came across jeep tracks which they followed for a distance. At one point they found two LRDG keffiyehs and a web pack containing food that must have fallen from the jeep. But it wasn't much good to the men because their mouths were so dry they couldn't eat. Jopling wrote:

18 September; My throat is dry and I have been doing a lot of retching, but nothing comes up. We now

have less than a gallon of water between 10 of us, and only have a spoonful every two hours. We are now resting near a road which is about 15 miles from where we left the truck. We are all getting very thin and weak, and being so dry makes things almost unbearable.

8pm. We set off this evening before the heat had gone out of the sun, not only that, they went far too fast for another man and myself. We hadn't been going long before we had to sit down. Rather to my surprise the others carried on. We hadn't been resting long when my mate said to me, " You go on Jop and leave me here." That will give you some idea of the condition we were in, and we are still along way from water. I wouldn't leave him, and we had a bit of a sleep. However, I am weighing the chances of finding the truck, maybe someone had got to it first and taken it away. I also thought of the other eight men who now had no navigator, but if they didn't want to wait for a wounded navigator, they must reckon they can manage O.K.

The next day Jopling, with Guardsman Gutheridge who was suffering exhaustion, set out with no water, but nonetheless had made good progress. On the 20th they spotted an Arab on a camel.

Te Anau III, the sole surviving truck. It is festooned with weapons taken from wrecked trucks. Major "Popski" Peniakoff (right) lost part of his finger during an enemy ambush. Sitting in the shade of the truck is the driver Private David Warbrick who skilfully drove the overloaded truck to safety.
Photo: Ngaire Lewis.

Excited, they eventually caught his attention, but were sorely disappointed when the Arab told them that he had no water and there was none nearby. He then rode off, and the men with their hopes dashed sought rest in the shade of a bush. Not long after the Arab returned and said he could take them to water, 12 kilometres away. By then it was 11am and very hot, so the fatigued men needed to rest at regular intervals. Gutheridge again asked Jopling to go on without him, but he was encouraged to continue with the thought of reaching water. However, when the rest stops became more frequent the Arab grew annoyed and asked them if they had any money. When they said they no he went off and left them. The disheartened men found a bush and rested for the rest of the day. Their desperation was reflected in what Jopling recorded at that time:

How we have been getting on for water for the last couple of days I leave to the reader's imagination, but whatever we did, it saved our lives.

That night the two men continued their walk and had not been travelling long when they heard the sound of a dog barking in the distance. They knew that where there was a dog there was an Arab camp and water. With renewed energy the men travelled for four hours in the direction of the barking, as sound carries a long way in the desert night, and eventually arrived on the top of a rise where they saw the glow of an Arab fire. Jopling described the moment in his diary.

No one can ever realise how we felt as we made our way to that glow, and I'm afraid I couldn't describe it. When we arrived there we asked an old man for some water which he immediately gave us. We had very little to start with and gradually took more, and we asked the Arab if it would be alright to sleep under some bushes not far away. We made ourselves more comfortable than we had felt for a long time.

After a while they were awoken by an Arab offering bread and tea. The tea was welcome but despite having eaten practically nothing for the last five days, the men didn't feel like eating much food. After their meal they slept till midday. Jopling's leg was now very sore, it was poisoned and he had a lump in his groin. He knew he was still a long way from any proper medical treatment. Using boiling water and a field dressing from his kit he cleaned and bandaged the wound. An Arab told Jopling there was a doctor in his village 20 kilometres away. The men travelled with the Arab who fortunately was very attentive, as the painful journey proved to be closer to 50 kilometres. Jopling wrote:

23 September: We are now sheltering in a cave. I'm afraid I can't walk much further. Every time we set off after sitting down, I tell the others not to watch me start, but to keep going. I am certain that if we didn't have the Arab with us I would have failed to start before now. My leg is now swollen very big, and it stinks.

4pm. After another hour of travel we were climbing a hill, I was about 100 yards behind the other two, and was just about to shout out that I couldn't possibly go any further, when my mate shouted back that he could see the Arab tents about 100 yards away. I gritted my teeth and carried on, but had it been another 100 yards I am sure I would have never made it.

By the next morning Jopling was unable to walk as his leg had turned gangrenous. He was put on a donkey and the Arab took him to a doctor, arriving about midday. His wound was cleaned and dressed and he was told he would have to see another doctor the next day. On the 25th Jopling was placed on a white horse while the Arab and Gutheridge walked. After about two hours an Italian truck intercepted them. Jopling noted:

They were obviously expecting us. It was then that the Arab told me that the doctor had told him that he couldn't do anything for me, and if I didn't get to a proper doctor quickly I would lose my leg, if not my life, so he thought this was the best way out.

They were taken by truck to an Italian outpost where they were questioned about how long they had been walking and where had they come from. From there they were returned to Barce, 12 days after they had left. Jopling recorded:

I wondered what sort of reception we would get. However, when I told them we had been on the raid there, they seemed glad to meet us. It was seven hours after I was captured that they took me to a first aid post, which was just across the road. There was an Itie medical orderly there, and he made a good job of cleaning and bandaging my leg, although it was very painful. When he had finished he gave me some brandy, which was very welcome. When I asked how many planes we destroyed, they said 27.

Later that day the two prisoners were taken to Benghazi. Gutheridge was sent to a POW camp, and Jopling to hospital where he wrote:

An Italian and a German doctor examined my leg and asked me how long since I had received this wound, and how long since it had any medical attention. They shook their heads and said it would have to come off. I asked them to have another look and if there was any show to try and save it. So they looked at it again and talked to each other for a while and then said, Alright, we will give it a go, but one more day and it would have to come off.

Jopling kept his leg. Despite his condition and Gutheridge's exhaustion the two men had walked a remarkable 240 kilometres, mostly at night, navigating by the stars.

Barce is the Italian word for "kiss", but on this occasion it was a kiss of death delivered by the LRDG. Many of the enemy were killed and wounded and over 30 aircraft were damaged or destroyed, along with a number of vehicles. The cost to the Group was six men wounded, all of whom recovered, 10 captured (seven from T1 Patrol, and three from G1), several of whom were wounded, and 14 vehicles lost. Four of those captured, Corporal Craw, Lance Corporal Nutt and Troopers Milburn and Hay, escaped a year later. Two Guardsmen, Duncalfe and McNobola, who became separated from the rest of the patrol during the raid, stayed for three months in the Gebel, fed and sheltered by Arabs till they were able to rejoin the Eighth Army as it swept through Cyrenaica in November. It was miraculous that during this operation none were killed, considering the mayhem and the firepower directed at them. Also, their desert navigational and survival skills enabled those on foot to be eventually rescued.

The losses to the LRDG were more than balanced in comparison to the damage this small force had inflicted on the enemy. The raid had played a part in relieving the Eighth Army of some of the pressure in its preparation for the Alamein offensive. Due to poor security though, the other three operations mounted at the same time all proved costly failures.

On this mission the New Zealand/Guards partnership worked well. As Derek Parker put it, " *Most of the Guardsmen were good fellows, and we got on well with them, they were very fine soldiers to have on our side.*" It was rare for the New Zealand patrols to work together. Combined operations were invariably with the British or Rhodesians.

For their role in the operation, Major Easonsmith and Captain Wilder were awarded the DSO; Captain Lawson received the MC; Sergeant Dennis of the Guards and Corporal Craw the MM, as did Troopers Tippett and Dobson, whose citations also refer to their capture of the Fiesler Storch spotter plane after the Sidi Haneish raid. Jake Easonsmith became Officer

T1 Patrol revisits Barce airfield in April 1943, where the burnt out aircraft still remain from the year before. Photo: Ngaire Lewis.

T1 Patrol men Trooper W. H. Rail (left) and Trooper S. D. Parker stand in front of a well-concealed truck. Trooper Parker was badly wounded while fighting in the town after the Barce airfield attack. This photo was taken three months later when he was fully recovered and the patrol had become the first members of the Eighth Army to enter Tunisia in January 1943. Photo: Wally Rail.

Commanding LRDG in October 1943, but was killed in action a month later while on operations on the island of Leros, in the Aegean Sea. W. B. Kennedy Shaw described him as:

Brave, wise, with an uprightness that shamed lesser men, he was, I think, the finest man we ever had in the LRDG. The northern Arabs knew him as "Batl es Sahra" (the Hero of the Desert).

An interesting postscript to this story was in 1974, when Derek Parker was invited to England by Thames Television to appear on the show *This is Your Life*. The subject was Sir William Coles, who, at great personal risk, flew the Bombay that rescued Parker and his wounded comrades. He was also reunited with Dr. Dick Lawson, who had taken such good care of him, and probably saved his life. Sir William was highly decorated during World War II, and was one of the first to fly the Meteor jets. After a long Air Force career he became an Air Marshall in 1966, and was later knighted.

See Appendix VIII for the list of New Zealanders who participated in the Barce raid.

SCORPION TALES

The purpose of this chapter is to recount a few of the personal stories as told to the author by several "Kiwi Scorpions", or from other sources. They are included here because the tales may not have had any particular relavance to the previous headings but they reflect an interesting and sometimes amusing insight to LRDG life.

Buster Gibb, of W and R Patrols, related much information and wrote many anecdotes about his time with the unit. The following are as told in his own words. His first episode tells about the time he found the "bomb".

While on a trip from Kufra to Siwa we stopped for lunch, so I took the opportunity to test my guns. As the rest of the patrol took off, I was delayed cleaning my weapons. I followed on and eventually saw them lined up on a ridge. It was then that I spotted a bomb ahead of me. Evidently the patrol had given it a wide berth and the formation on the ridge told its tale.

Having a curious nature I decided to have a closer look, so I left the vehicle at a reasonable distance and approach-ed the bomb on foot. It turned out to be a parachute flare. The tail plate had lifted off and silk material was peeping out. Realizing what it was, I rushed in and hauled out the parachute and carefully cut the linen ropes, then bundled the silk into the truck.

When I rejoined the rest of the patrol, I was well and truly in the "dog box". They thought it was a bomb, and were waiting for me to clear the area as they were going to blast it "to hell". Nobody likes to be made to look foolish.

The sequel to this story is that I carefully unplucked the linen bands holding the ropes to the silk. I then posted it home to my fiancee. Three years later I returned to New Zealand on furlough and we were married. The wedding dress was made from the silk of the parachute flare that had been recovered from the middle of nowhere!

Buster was not alone in recounting his next tale, many other veterans have told similar stories about their antics with revolvers in the open top tanker's pattern holsters.

I had a .38 revolver, preferring it to a .45. I became quite good in the use of it, and decided to try the old cowboy quick draw. The holster was tied down and I practised for days with an unloaded gun, drawing and firing. After a time I considered I was becoming very proficient, so decided to have a go with the gun loaded. I tried the quick draw and came within a half an inch of blowing off my foot, because I was pulling on the trigger while still drawing. Needless to say I gave that pastime away.

Snakes were always a concern in the desert, as the following accounts describe. First, Buster wrote about the time Trooper Ron "Skin" Moore nearly stood on one and produced a "world record".

Skin was walking across the sand with an Italian ammo box across his shoulder. The box was about a three feet long, 10 inches wide and about 12 inches deep. He had a bandage round his ankle and the end of it was trailing behind by six or eight inches. Suddenly he noticed a deadly Hammer Headed Viper right where he was going to place his foot. With an almighty yell he took off from one foot and landed several feet away. When he landed, the trailing bandage flipped up and slapped the calf of his leg. About six feet in front of him was the stump of a date palm that we had cut down some days before. Skin thought that when the bandage slapped him it was the snake having a go. Then with another mighty yell, he took off and landed on top of that stump. All this was done while still carrying the heavy ammo box. All the world records are not performed at the

Olympics or on the playing fields. This magnificent leap I am sure could never be equalled.

Some encounters with snakes were a bit too close for comfort, as Buster explains in the next two stories.

One chap was enjoying a piddle into a camel thorn bush, when suddenly he noticed a snake wriggling about three inches away from his penis. Cutting short his relief the trooper quickly withdrew in case the serpent had intentions of mating, or worse!

I carried in my truck an Italian wire wove bed which I managed to fit in just behind the gun mount. When we stopped somewhere for the night, I would take it out and placed it on four benzine boxes to make a comfortable bed. While based at Siwa I had the locals make me a palm hut, where I set up my bed and used other boxes for beer and books, etc. One night we had a party to celebrate my birthday as we were able to obtain a supply of Australian beer. When I woke up in the morning Clarke Waetford came into the hut looking through the empty discarded bottles hoping to find an overlooked full one. He was successful, and sat there enjoying a beer for breakfast. Then suddenly he changed hands and reached down beside him, grabbed a large knife and threw it right next to me, giving me a hell of a fright. He said a snake had just come out from under my pillow. Soon after giving his knife back he did it again, as another snake appeared. I was more frightened of the knife than the snakes. Then finally a third snake wriggled out. That night I had shared my bed with three snakes!

The desert often played tricks, with its strange atmospherics. As Buster recorded:

Bob Rawson was "allergic" to snakes. Though he feared them, he would attack them vigorously and with much profanity. The episode in question happened one day when we had a sandstorm. Bob had left his blankets on the ground where he slept the night before. Evening came, and Bob decided to rescue them from the sand and shake them clear. When he reached down to grasp the blankets he heard a loud hissing. But didn't see what I saw, blue sparks from his finger tips. He just heard the hiss. Jumping back with much profanity, including the word snakes, he rushed to the truck to grab a shovel and started to beat hell out of his blankets. After a long period of bashing and rolling the blankets about, Bob reckoned that no snake would survive that performance. Reaching down once more, he again got the loud hissing and so repeated the pantomime. When he had finished the second time, Bob saw that I was bottling up laughter so much that tears were streaming down my legs. Naturally I came in for much abuse. Static electricity had built up in the wool, and when it was touched, it shorted. He didn't see the resulting blue sparks, but only heard the hissing. I'd already had a shock from the vehicle.

Reliable equipment was essential for desert survival, and the men were not hesitant in bringing it to the attention of their officers if they felt they were being issued with an inferior product.

All our original vehicles had Firestone tyres. It was estimated we did a million and a half truck miles on these tyres, with only one puncture. Suddenly just before our next trip, we were ordered to remove all Firestones and replace them with Dunlops.

With Firestones each vehicle carried one spare with an extra one on every second vehicle. When transversing the Sand Sea the tyre pressures had to be lowered to give a broader tyre base on the sand which reduced the breaking of the surface crust. We had no trouble with the Firestones. With Dunlops each vehicle carried two spares, with two more on each second vehicle. It was obviously considered that we might have trouble with Dunlops. I accused the bosses who prevailed at the time of accepting a bribe to put on Dunlops, and demanded a cut for the patrol members. They in turn threatened me with a court-martial. But the charge was eventually dropped. To this day I'm still convinced I was right. At the end of the trip we had one spare between the eleven vehicles. We were ordered to remove all Dunlops and replace them with the original Firestones.

Alf Saunders of W and R Patrols wrote a series of stories about his time in the unit. His first account recalls the challenges of the early days of desert training.

We went out for a practice patrol about a hundred miles from Cairo, on the way back, a few miles from the Pyramids, we came across some large sand dunes. Our commander at that time was Captain Mitford, he decided that this was a good opportunity to give the drivers some training in the crossing of sand dunes. These were large dunes similar to the ones of the Great Sand Sea, and rose from a broad valley to a height of about sixty feet. The drivers with their crews went to the other side of the valley and awaited the signal to advance up the dune in front of us. It looked very high, so there was much apprehension and chain smoking as we waited.

I was the first to get the signal to proceed, so we motored up the rise. Captain Mitford was standing on the top by the outer edge to signal the drivers whether to speed up or slow down as the case may be. When I was three-quarters of the way up and going well, I could see him signalling frantically by waving his arms up and down. In the Divisional Cavalry this signal meant speed up. We were doing about 60 mph at this stage, so I assumed the dune must have been very soft at the top. Slamming the truck into third gear, I floored the throttle, which must have increased our speed by another 15 mph. I caught a glimpse of the Captain covering his face with his hands as we went past, then suddenly I saw nothing except sky. We must have been doing close to 80 mph when we took off from the top of what turned out to be a razor-back dune. It had a steep side and at the bottom was a large area of liquid sand, very much like thick muddy water. We flew over 50 feet (15 metres) and landed with a colossal "Squish," and stopped very smoothly with the sand coming up over the floor boards.

Captain Mitford and the patrol Second in Command, Lieutenant Jim Sutherland, peered from the top of the dune calling out if anybody was hurt. We replied no, but the truck's front wheels had splayed out at right angles and the tie rods were bent. The officers then came down, so we prepared for the blast that was coming. Captain Mitford said, "Why did you not stop when you saw my signals to do so?" I replied, "The signal you gave me, in the Div. Cav. meant speed up, so that is what I did." Lieutenant Sutherland backed me up. I then had to put in my two pence worth of conversation, and I said, " Sirs, that flight was the most exhilarating thrill of my young life, try it yourself sirs". Mitford stated though it looked spectacular, it did nothing for the well-being of the vehicles. Next time they trained on the dunes they were to go over the razor-backs very gently, because the following week the patrol was to cross the Great Sand Sea where there were dozens of that type of dune.

Bill Willcox then came along looking very worried, as he had "pranged" his truck in a similar manner. He looked relieved that I had done the same, because if any rockets were coming over the damage to the trucks, there were now two of us to bear the brunt of any reprimands.

I personally didn't care less, because in my opinion it was the fault of Captain Mitford for giving me the wrong signals. We dug the vehicles out of the sand, removed the tie rods , and straightened them out best we could. To enable the damaged trucks to return to Cairo in good time our loads were transferred to the other vehicles. The LRP had priority for spare parts and workshop time, so when we arrived at the Citadel in Cairo the repairs were completed by the time the rest of the patrol had returned to the city.

In the following two stories, Alf Saunders tells about the occasions where the locals were particularly pleased to see the LRDG.

In the early days when a patrol would depart Cairo, they would first have to wind their way through all the city traffic. We played a game with the barrow boys selling fruit, sometimes a barrow was side-swiped and the fruit would spill over the road. We would then leap off our trucks and throw as much fruit as possible into the back.

Usually there were apples, oranges, grapes, pome-granates and pineapples. This was all done in about 15 seconds, then we would catch up with the truck in front. Before moving off we always threw a handful of small change at the boys. This had become a ritual, and even if we did not tip over their barrows they would do it themselves screaming blue murder. Then we would do our stuff, and chuck what we could in the trucks, throw them some money and move off.

One thing that always puzzled me was the fact that it did not matter if we changed our route, the barrow boys were always waiting in ambush for us. Their Intelligence Section was certainly on the ball and they never missed our departure from Cairo. After a while we got to know them by name and enjoyed yelling at each other in the street. For the first few days in the desert the patrol gorged themselves on fruit .

When I think of the manner in which the fruit seeds were scattered over the desert wastes, I often speculate on the possibility that in the future if those areas ever received a regular rainfall, what would the historians think. They would ponder on how fruit trees came to be there, and talk of lost civilizations, ancient cities or a dried up oasis. No one would consider it to be New Zealanders travelling in a foreign land, spreading a few seeds in nature's way.

One day we captured an Italian convoy bound for Ethiopia. On one of the huge diesel trucks we found a few cases of what we called "Wog silver jewellery rubbish". Some of us filled a couple of sandbags with this jewellery and threw them in the back of the trucks and forgot about it. When we had finished our patrol we came back to Cairo, following the Nile river. We passed through a number of villages, and when we saw a group of women and kids we would throw them handfuls of the jewellery. This was received with great joy and amazement.

When we got back to Cairo we had a few pieces left, so had them valued. As it turned out the joke was on us. The patrol had apparently tossed away an average of £200-worth of jewellery per two sandbags. We had a good laugh at ourselves and forgot it. No wonder those women and kids were overjoyed, in the general scramble some of them would have received a very nice nest egg indeed.

The ingenuity of the LRDG fitters was legendary. This next story appeared in the magazine *New Zealand Free Lance*, in 8 July 1942, and tells about the time Trooper I. G. McCulloch lost his dentures whilst swimming in a pool at Siwa.

While T2 was camped at Siwa Oasis, several men cooled off with a swim. One bather, Trooper "Snowie" McCulloch, found to his dismay that he had lost his upper dental plate in the pool's 7 metres of water. Frantic efforts were made to recover the teeth, but all to no avail. Private C. A. "Dorny" Dornbush, the patrol's fitter, had an idea and went to his truck where he obtained an Army respirator (gas mask).

He removed the metal filter, and fitted a tyre-tube valve to the unattached end of the corrugated intake pipe. With the use of two long leads of air-line joined together he connected the respirator to the air pump. The engine of the truck was set running and the pump was operated. Dorny put the mask's rubber face-piece on, and after the engine was regulated to a certain speed, was satisfied that sufficient air was being produced. He entered the pool to try it and found his unique diving-helmet worked.

Then came the real test. He stuffed his ears with wadding to combat the water pressure and descended to the bottom of the oasis. After a short time he successfully recovered the dentures, which gave Snowie and Dorny much pleasure. Snowie—to have his teeth back, and Dorny—because with his experiment went the knowledge of probably being the Group's only unofficial diver.

One of the many problems of desert life was disorientation. In his diary, **Dick Lewis** of T Patrol described such an occasion when he decided to have a night time stroll:

20/01/42; Last night after tea, when darkness had fallen, Jerry Gerrard and I went for a bit of a walk heading out into the desert. We strolled in one direction for about a quarter of an hour, taking of this and that, when we were pulled up suddenly by the sight of a dim light ahead of us. Thinking an enemy party had camped somewhere near, we turned to go back to get our rifles. Then we thought it was strange that they should have a wireless set up and going. We crept back a bit and listened and found it was tuned into an English programme. Then it tumbled, in a quarter of an hour we had walked in a complete circle and had come upon our own camp again.

Peter Garland of T Patrol told the story about how sometimes the desert created illusions of speed and dimension:

The sun gleaming and shimmering on the sand makes things so deceptive that the hills appear flat and small stones like high mounds. Even the vehicles appear still at a speed of about 40 miles per hour. I had an unusual experience on the Sand Sea when my driver saw a hat drop from the truck ahead. I decided to pick it up and stepped out, but to my surprise I hit the sand with a thud and did a few flips. Luckily I was not injured, my driver said he was still doing 25 miles per hour when I stepped off. I thought it was only about 5 mph.

Fellow T Patrol member **Frank Jopling** wrote of similar experiences:

7 September 1940. We have been crossing sand dunes ever since we left at 12 noon. Talk about thrills, it was great! Travelling at 80 kph up and down smooth dunes. I had to keep looking at the speedo to see if we were moving, to look in the sand in front of me you would think we were standing still.

Peter Garland also spoke of sounds of the desert that could deceive the mind, such as that which occurred after the battle of Ain Dua in November 1940:

After the fight was over everyone was a little nervy and a funny incident happened that evening. All the boys were sitting about the fire, relating incidents of the day, when suddenly we heard what sounded like the roar of an engine. Someone put the fire out, others ran about to their guns and waited. As the sound did not increase investigations were made. It was found that the wind blowing over the top of the rum jars had caused a few quick heart beats.

In April 1941 T Patrol's Chevrolet WB 30s were replaced with Ford V8 4x4 F30s. **Dick Lewis** noted in his diary the problems they had with their new trucks while on their first trip to Kufra, along with his impressions of that town:

16/04/1941. The V8 Fords are giving a lot of trouble. By the second day four of the batteries had gone flat and there was trouble with some of the gearboxes. The trucks are sticking a lot and having various mechanical problems. Besides the batteries, tie-rods are bending and one steering box has broken. But they certainly get a thrashing, loaded to top capacity, and driven over all different types of going.

19/04/1941. Last night, after a good crossing of the Sand Sea we camped about 30 miles outside Kufra, and now, 8.30am, we are waiting outside the oasis. The Free French, who came up from Central Africa with their black troops, captured it from the Italians a couple of weeks ago. You can see the fort on a central hill and through the glasses it looks pretty substantial. Kufra is a series of oases which used to be an important slave trading station, as it stands on one of the routes from Central Africa to the top end. Being just north of the Tropic of Cancer it gets pretty hot and never rains.

We have now gone into the oasis and are pulled up in what shade we can find under the date palms. Some chaps have had a wander round already and report the place lousy with scorpions. Later, we moved in a bit further and bedded down amongst the palms. Very picturesque, but the flies are bloody terrible.

20/04/1941. While on picquet last night I struck a squall the like of which I have never imagined. At first it was windy and very warm, and about midnight a terrific burning hot sand squall swooped down and just blotted out the world for five minutes, and then passed on. It was impossible to do any-thing except crouch down on the ground.

By noon it was still blowing a sand storm. Here in the oasis it's pretty bad, but the desert looks just one murky haze 100 yards from the edge of the palms. In all the daylight hours the flies are terrible. The natives here are a much more Negroid looking lot, very black, with squashed in faces, and short curly hair.

21/04/1941. We camped amongst the palms with only a tarpaulin for three men to put beside the truck and act as shade, shelter, and sleeping accommodation. Our right to the ground is keenly contested by various vermin who consider themselves the original inhabitants, the "tangata whenua" as it were. Scorpions abound, as well as tremendous bloody great black spiders, and the odd snake or two. Mosquito nets have been issued in the shape of oblong boxes that you peg into the ground and crawl into. Very awkward things, but they do give some relief from the flies by day, and the mosquitoes at night, as well as some slight protection from scorpions and spiders.

Long after the war, Dick Lewis explained further his relationship with the creatures of the desert:

They didn't molest us on purpose, and we left them strictly alone. It's strange when there's a human enemy, animals and insects seem almost to be blood brothers, and you understand a bit more their point of view. I actually wasn't stung by a scorpion till much later, lying in

low scrub alongside a road one night, when we were trying some harebrained scheme of placing time bombs on passing enemy vehicles.

As I put my hand down on the sand beside me, I felt a needle sting in my thumb. For the next six hours I was only interested in the most excruciating pain I have ever felt. We ended up having a bit of a battle that night, but faded away into the desert before first light, and by mid-morning the pain had gone. To add insult to injury, there wasn't the slightest mark anywhere on my hand.

Frank White of T Patrol, described one of the more spectacular pastimes while he was based at Kufra:

The South Africans had an air base at Kufra. The Germans sometimes raided the oasis and dropped bombs. One of our jobs was to blow up any unexploded bombs if they were in a position where this could be done. After one particular raid we listened to a German broadcast in English and it said that of all those planes in the raid it was reported

that only four had failed to return. It was propaganda. To our know-ledge there had only been four planes, and we had shot them all down. I don't think they did any damage that I can remember. Some of the unexploded bombs contained messages from German forced labour; little notes inside that said so and so had made the bomb and it wouldn't go off—that sort of thing. One of our joys was blowing them up!

Sandstorms were a regular part of desert life, Trooper **Frank Jopling** of T Patrol wrote of two occasions in his diary, where these had made a particular impression on him:

28 January 1941. The wind has become very strong and we experienced our first real sandstorm and believe me it was very unpleasant. The wind was travelling across the road and the sand beat straight at us from the side. I can quite understand why the Arabs have the headdress they do, because I happened to have a scarf and it didn't take me long to wrap it around my head the way the Arabs do, and practically all the other drivers found something to wrap round their face so that only their goggles could be seen. We had to keep very close to the truck in front of us or else lose sight of it

altogether, and twice the sand was so thick that the Skipper got off the road and then had to look for it again.

Siwa, 5 May 1942. Well, today we saw the most wonderful sight I have ever seen in the desert. We had just had tea and gone outside in the cool when we saw a long thick cloud on the horizon. It reminded me straight away of the sight we just saw as we were leaving Murzuk 36 months ago. So I said, "Look at this dust storm coming". But no one would believe me, they all thought it was just an ordinary cloud. At the time there wasn't a breath of wind blowing. Half an hour later the cloud was a lot closer and one or two distant hills vanished, and I said, "Do you believe me when I say it is a dust storm coming now?" And one or two started to become a bit suspicious. After a while we could see what looked like thick clouds of smoke pushing through each other in the cloud. Again, after a while some of the nearer hills vanished in the cloud. But the best sight of all was as it came across the oasis. It looked as though an enormous dam had broken through and was crashing down on us. As it came across the palms and over the hill of ruins, we could hear the wind, and just before

it came upon us, the wind got up. Well, I have never seen a dust storm like it. It was far thicker than the Murzuk dust storm and everything went dark and a dull orange colour, and we couldn't see more than 10 yards ahead of us. Sand and dust got everywhere; but in spite of the discomfort, it was a sight I would very much like to see again, and words certainly cannot describe it. It has to be seen to be believed.

The following story reflects the priority HQ placed on the intelligence gathered by the LRDG. Corporal Frank White accompanied Lieutenant Ron Tinker on a long journey from Tunisia, via Algeria, to Eighth Army HQ in Tripoli, then on to Cairo. They had to personally deliver vital maps, compiled as a result a reconnaissance made by T2 Patrol and the PPA, of the enemy held Mareth Line (*see the chapter on Reconnaissance and Survey*). **Frank White** describes the course of events:

When we arrived in Constantine, Algeria, Ron Tinker and I had to try to get back to Tripoli with our maps. We were sitting on the aerodrome, discussing what we were going to do, when an Aussie pilot came along and said, "I'll guess you're two bloody Kiwis!" How or why he thought that, one wouldn't know. He told us that he was grounded for being drunk in charge of a plane, and was now in charge of all the landings at Constantine.

He then took us to his control tower. We still had our beards on, and hadn't had a wash for three or four weeks, so looked generally pretty rough. The different people around the place who saw us seemed horrified by our appearance, as they had seen nothing like it before. Then someone said, " They are from the Eighth Army!" That sort of hushed everything. As if being from the Eighth Army we were somebody— the top! The Aussie then set out with Ron to try to arrange for a flight to get us back.

As I was waiting there talking, in came some British Fleet Air Arm staff wearing beards. They were sort of in the same spot, and wanted to know where we had come from. One of the officers said, "Oh, we will have to celebrate this!" So away he went and got some drink . While we drank in the control tower the Australian officer told somebody off for doing a bad landing, and dressed him down a treat. A little while later a squadron leader came in and said "Who's in charge?" With a smart salute the Australian said he was the squadron leader, then said, "You told somebody off for a bad landing. You were quite correct, it was an appalling landing." He then spotted me in the corner, and demanded to know who I was. He was told I was sort of from the Eighth Army, and he didn't appear to be too concerned about our drinking. All sorts of funny people came in and out on different missions while we were there, so I just sat there and talked to them.

When Ron Tinker returned after trying to arrange things, he said, "Inter-Allied Headquarters, I've never seen anybody having so many rounds. There's majors telling off colonels, colonels telling off majors." The Americans and English were supposed to be co-operating , but were having trouble. Ron went on to say, "Oh, I think we can get back, some generals and brigadiers are going through to Tripoli and if their pilot says you can go on the plane (being only a corporal), that will be all right."

But we wouldn't know till later that night. So they took us to the officer's mess, but of course as a corporal, I had to go to the cook's and batmen's mess. For every drink they had in the officer's mess, one was sent down for me. I couldn't drink them all, so I gave it to the men. As the evening wore on, Ron and his party came down to the cook's office and we all celebrated there.

Eventually it was decided that if the pilot wasn't willing to take the extra men, two of the brigadiers would have to stay behind. Well, we had the vital maps, so we got on the plane. Feeling half under the weather, we flew over the desert and had to go right down to the south so that we would not be over enemy territory, then came round. When we landed I dashed off to some bushes, and as I returned one of the brigadiers kindly asked if I was alright, to which I replied, "I am now".

After we landed I heard a general tell the officers at Tripoli airport that we were to be taken to Eighth Army HQ. About an hour later we were still waiting, as there was no transport. There were a lot of Tommy officers in their "giggle" suits, that is brass buttons and everything, waiting to go on leave. Ron Tinker had been away trying to arrange a lift, when he returned I said, "Look, there is a truck over there that has bought all those officers in, couldn't we take that. So Ron walked over to the fellow and said, "You had better take all those things out, we have got to go to the Eighth Army HQ." The wretched Tommy driver didn't know what to do. There was nothing he could do. We just dumped the officers gear off and he took us to where we wanted to go.

When we arrived we were taken to the New Zealand section of Eighth Army HQ. Being still dirty and bearded I was given a map and had to explain the information we had gained, and mark out a route where transport could cross. After that we were sent to where the LRDG was

camped, which was alongside Freyberg's office.

I was going to OCTU (Officer Cadet Training Unit) in Cairo for officer training, so that night we had a great party, with fires and everything. But nobody seemed to stop us, I mean we were really undisciplined. Right alongside the general's camp there was a big fire going, it was not exactly security.

I was told to call into the office the first thing the next morning to find out about transport, but when I arrived the officer and clerk didn't know anything about it. Freyberg must have heard the conversation from the other side, as he came through and said, "What's this all about?" (he was always a man of few words). I told him what was happening and he told me to go and get my gear. I only possessed what I was standing up in, and a blanket or two. Then I had to get into the car with Freyberg and all these officers, and on the way to the aerodrome I was asked to tell them something about what I had been doing. When we arrived, Freyberg told the officers arranging the flights that I had to have a berth back to Cairo. They got in the plane and away they went. I thought, having experienced this sort of thing before, that I would be forgotten about. But a little while later, a lot of officers arrived waiting to go on leave. They called out for Corporal White, so still unwashed and unshaved, I got on the plane.

After arriving in Cairo I went straight to the LRDG base, had a wash and a shave, and finally I got into some clean clothes. The next day I was interviewed by a brigadier. When I went to his office he looked at me and said, "Corporal White, you haven't got your stripes on," I replied, "No sir, I wasn't a corporal when I was last in this uniform." He then said, "I know it's a tradition in your unit that you don't wear badges of rank." It was left at that. There was a big map on the wall, I had to show him where we had been and what we'd done.

DODECANESE OPERATIONS

In mid-1943 the New Zealand Government repatriated members of the 1st, 2nd and 3rd Echelons of 2 NZEF. Thereby having "run out of desert", many LRDG veterans returned home on furlough, though quite a number chose to stay on. This meant recruiting more men for the Group. But they were never short of volunteers, Private Ian Judge of R1 Patrol who joined at that time said with that his intake he was one of only a dozen selected out of a total 240 applicants.

From June 1943 A Squadron spent nearly three and a half months training at the picturesque Cedars of Lebanon, a peacetime ski resort 6,000 feet above Beirut, where the mountains rose a further 3,000 feet above that. The patrols were reorganised into small self-contained units, varying from eight to fourteen men, capable of maintaining communications over distances of around 160 kilometres while operating behind the enemy lines on foot. This was a radical departure from nearly three years of relying on transport to now walking to complete their mission. The fitness level had to be high, so some of the desert veterans who were unable to make the transition returned to their original units.

Their beloved trucks, apart from those used by HQ, were gone, but a proportion of jeeps mounting .50 Brownings were still retained, being used only where the "going" was good and the operation appropriate. Though the Group now essentially worked as foot patrols, they continued in their intelligence gathering and reconnaissance role.

The men were trained in mountain warfare, demolitions, skiing and the handling of pack mules. They were also taught German and Greek, so they could seek the assistance of the local people when needed. Because they were independent units they had to carry all their own supplies. Due to the altitude of the Cedars the ability to carry heavy loads had to be attained slowly, and sometimes the

difficult alpine treks resulted in men sufering from altitude sickness. On one exercise Ian Judge remembered becoming very short of breath and feeling ill while loaded down on a steep climb. He had to return to base where he became greatly concerned that he might be dismissed from the LRDG, thinking that his fitness level may not have met the criteria. After being sick for two days the doctor reassured Judge that he had only been overcome by the lack of oxygen, not fitness.

At eight weeks training the men could do a climbing trek of 27 kilometres with 14 kilogram packs, while after three months they were achieving 100 to 160 kilometres with 30 to 36 kilogram packs. Sufficient food was carried for 10 days, should it be that long before they could be resupplied. The rations were made up packs for so many men per day, and had to be chosen for the highest food value in the smallest volume and weight. Everest-type packs were used to carry the loads, and some were adapted with frames made to support wireless sets or batteries. This meant that those men's gear and rations had to be shared amongst the others.

While at the Cedars A Squadron was issued with a quantity of New Zealand manufactured dehydrated food to be assessed in the field. The use of this product would reduce the weight carried in the packs

The Cedars of Lebanon, a picturesque ski resort high in the mountains 6,000ft above Beirut. It was used by the LRDG in 1943 for training in new skills such as mountain warfare and skiing.
Photo: Charles McConachie.

LRDG jeeps mounting .50 cal. Brownings parked at the Cedars. These replaced the faithful 30cwt trucks, though operationally the jeeps were rarely used with foot patrols becoming the mainstay. Photo: Richard Williams.

considerably, as most rations were normally tinned. Ian Judge recounted the result of that trial:

At that time we were carrying about 25 to 30 kilograms in our packs, and so that we could carry some more useful gear, other that rations in tins, we were issued with this dehydrated food. As a training exercise the patrol set out from the Cedars on a trek, and at about 8,000 feet we stopped for the night. Tried and hungry, we took out our dixies and examined our dried food, which consisted of cabbage, onions, carrots, potatoes and mince that looked like rat's droppings. We added water to this mixture, brewed it up, and had a great feed. Soon after we crawled into our heavy warm sleeping bags and looked forward to a good night's sleep.

But then about half an hour later our stomachs began to swell, as the food was still working inside, like yeast. We all felt bloated, and the bags began to stink a bit as the men began breaking wind excessively. Not before long we had to get out of our sleeping bags to air them, and have a stretch to overcome our discomfort. The next morning someone semaphored to the Cedars,

as we were in line of sight, and asked them to send up some tinned bully beef and meat and veg stew, and to take away that explosive dried stuff!

Several weeks later R Patrol members read an article in the magazine *New Zealand Weekly News* which described the production of dried food at Pukekohe (a vegetable-growing region), and what a great boon it could be for the troops in the Middle East. Amused, Ian Judge and his comrades felt it would be more likely to cause a "boom", rather than anything else.

The LRDG received orders for their next operation in September 1943. The New Zealanders travelled to the port of Haifa to board the Greek destroyer *Queen Olga*, and on the 21st sailed to Portolago, Leros, in the Dodecanese Islands. They were stationed in the Italian military barracks which Ian Judge described as, *"The most filthy place I have ever been in my life!"* A few days later after an air raid, the *Queen Olga* was sunk while in dock with the loss of 6 officers and 54 ratings.

The HMS *Intrepid* was also sunk in the raid and the naval barracks were damaged. Judge had lost his pack and his sniper's rifle when the Stukas bombed the wharf. He later managed to acquire a Thompson sub-machine gun, but unfortunately he had no spare magazines.

In September 1943 British forces from the Middle East began to occupy the Dodecanese Islands in the Aegean Sea between Greece and Turkey. Despite there being actually 14 major islands, the name comes from the Greek word for "twelve". They had been occupied by the Italians since 1912, who called them "The Italian Islands of the Aegean", though the population was mainly Greek. Code-named "Operation Accolade", the objective was to tie down the German forces in the eastern Mediterranean while the invasions of Sicily and Italy got under way. They were also to take advantage of any weaknesses in the enemy defences that might follow the Italian surrender. It was hoped that the Italian troops who garrisoned the islands would join the Allies against the Germans.

The day after Italy capitulated, on 6 September, the Germans began to occupy all the main Italian-held islands. Because Rhodes was the key to the Dodecanese group, Major the Earl of Jellicoe of the Special Boat Squadron, supported by two of his men, arrived on the island by parachute. Their mission was to try to persuade the Italian commander, Admiral Campioni, to co-operate and hold Rhodes for the British. But it was all to no avail, because the following day the Germans attacked, which resulted in the garrison of 40,000 troops surrendering. On Hitler's special order, any Italian officers offering resistance were to be shot. The SBS successfully escaped.

The British landed on the island of Leros where there was a good natural harbour, complete with a naval and seaplane base; and at Cos, which was important because of its airfield. They also landed at Samos, Simi and Castelrosso, as well as other smaller islands. Where the British had

Dressed in floppy caps and heavy packs, R1 Patrol poses before setting out on a mountain trek exercise. Cedars, July 1943. Photo: Merle Fogden.

established their forces the Italians offered no resistance and aligned themselves against the Germans. This unfortunately later proved to be at their great cost.

The Group became part of the Raiding Forces, Middle East, which was made up of close to 200 men of the LRDG, 150 men of the SBS, and 30 commandos. Colonel Guy Prendergast was appointed as second in command of the Raiding Forces, and Lieutenant-Colonel J. R. Easonsmith was promoted to Officer Commanding, LRDG.

The New Zealand A Squadron of about 110 men was commanded by Major A. J. Guild; and B Squadron, the British and Rhodesians, were led by Major D. L. Lloyd Owen. They were to be used to support the nearly 4,000 regular British troops of 234 Brigade holding the islands. Also on Leros there were 5,000 Italians, though only half of them were armed. They manned the big 6-inch guns on the heights as well as the smaller emplacements guarding the bays and harbours. Five LRDG patrols were located at these positions to stiffen the morale of their new allies, and to ensure the guns would not be turned against the British. They also acted

Trooper D. Munro displays the amount of equipment the patrol members were expected to carry on their backs, thereby a high level of fitness was essential. Some desert veterans who were unable to meet the required standard, had to return to their original units.
Photo: Ken Johnson.

as observers in the outlying islands astride the sea and air routes to the Dodecanese to report the movements of enemy shipping and aircraft. Many of these islands were occupied by the Germans, so the patrols had to keep well concealed.

Concerning their Italian allies, Ian Judge recounted a story about the time his patrol was undertaking a reconnaissance of a small island. They came upon a group of six Germans whom they took prisoner. In a very serious tone, a big fair headed German officer who spoke good English gave the following advice to the New Zealanders: *"Don't trust the Italians, we did!"*

For transport around the islands 18-tonne caiques were used. These were small local craft fitted with tank engines, giving them a speed of six knots, and manned by the Royal Navy with a crew of three. They were known as the "Levant Schooner Flotilla". When lying close inshore these vessels were able to be camouflaged with their masts down to avoid easy detection.

The Group had set up watches on the islands of Cos, Calino, Simi, Giaros and Stampalia, but had to withdraw with some narrow escapes when the Germans reoccupied them. Cos contained the only airfield, at Antimachia, and was defended by the 1st Battalion of the RAF Regiment who supported two Spitfire squadrons: No. 7 Squadron, South African Air Force, and No. 74 Squadron RAF. There was also an Italian garrison of 3,600 men, although their will to fight was questionable.

By 29 September, as a result of bombing raids, the airfield on Cos became inoperable, with a number of aircraft destroyed on the ground. On 3 October the Germans landed their invasion force, followed by paratroopers dropping south of the airfield. The ensuing battle lasted two days, with the British losing 65 killed and 1,388 men captured, including their commander Lieutenant-Colonel

For transport around the islands local caiques were used. Manned by the Royal Navy, they were known as Levant Schooner Flotilla. Photo: Merle Fogden.

L. R. F. Kenyon. The Germans lost only 14 killed. The Italian commander, Colonel Felice Leggio, and 101 of his officers were executed for siding with the British, and 3,145 of his men were taken prisoner.

Ian Judge witnessed the invasion of Cos from Calino (also known as Kalymnos, about 6 kilometres from Cos) where R1 Patrol and the SBS had established a watch. It was early in the morning and Judge had left his camp because he was feeling ill with stomach trouble. He was sitting on the sea wall relieving himself when he was disturbed by the sound of gunfire and explosions, then looking out across the water he spotted German ships heading for Cos. Quickly finishing his business he ran back to inform his comrades. The invasion was followed by much air activity and the men had to view the disheartening sight of the defending Spitfires being shot down one by one.

It was decided that this would be a good time for the patrol to withdraw, so they headed through the village to the northern end of the island. One member, Trooper Colin Kidd, was a strong swimmer and suggested they should swim to Leros. Fortunately that option was not taken up as it was later discovered that there was a dangerous rip. Not long after an LSF caique arrived and took the men off.

The loss of Cos along with its two Spitfire squadrons was a major setback, as it was the only island from which fighter aircraft could operate to protect the sea and land forces in the Aegean. This also put the enemy in a greatly improved position to gain control of the rest of the islands. Eventually it would be the lack of adequate air cover that would lead to the failure of the whole Dodecanese operation.

Prior to the invasion of Cos, Captain R. A. Tinker with a composite patrol of 12 men landed on the small island of Pserimo, midway between Calino and Cos. They were investigating some mysterious signalling to Turkey from the island, which turned out to be a Greek agent working for the British. While the men were there, the German invasion fleet bound for Cos pulled into the island before dawn on 3 October and landed about 80 troops to establish a headquarters and dressing station. Quite unexpectedly they encountered Tinker's party who quickly sought cover on the high ground, while at the same time coming under fire from the escort ships. Enemy patrols searched the island that day and the next, resulting in one man, Corporal W. H. Burgess, being taken prisoner. The others managed to elude their pursuers and were taken off in the late afternoon of 4 October and returned to Calino.

After the fall of Cos, Calino was considered untenable, thereby all the British forces, including the LRDG, were withdrawn and returned to Leros. A week later the LRDG sent parties of two or three men back to the island to gather information about the enemy activity there. On one occasion a New Zealander, Sergeant R. D. Tant, was captured and taken to Cos, but escaped soon after and made his way to Turkey. He eventually returned to Leros after being missing for a fortnight. When that island was later overrun, the same company of German paratroopers who had captured him before made him prisoner again.

The LRDG continued their watches from the more outlying Cyclades Islands. Captain C. K. Saxton (an ex-All Black) and six men of T1 Patrol were taken by a LSF caique to set up a watch on the occupied island of Kithnos. There, a garrison of about 20 Germans operated a permanent observation post and radio direction-finding station. At first it was intended for T1 to stay a fortnight, but as the information they had gained proved so valuable it was decided to keep them there for a month. The enemy were aware of their presence, but Saxton's men avoided discovery by constantly changing hiding places and moving about only at night.

After a time the wireless batteries required charging. This was a noisy operation that could betray the watchers to the enemy. The problem was overcome when an LSF caique, that had returned to Kithnos with supplies, took Saxton and the wireless operator to a small island off Seriphos to recharge the batteries.

Meanwhile, Sergeant J. L. D. Davis who took temporary command of the observation post, spotted and reported two small convoys moving at night. Davis, who spoke Greek, was able to obtain from the local inhabitants information about enemy shipping movements and of their dispositions in the neighbouring islands. His conduct throughout the Aegean operations earned him the BEM. Long after the war Jack Davis devoted many years as secretary of the LRDG (NZ) Association.

Kithnos was well situated for observing the routes from Greece to Crete and the Dodecanese Islands. T1 Patrol, who kept a constant watch for shipping and aircraft, sighted a convoy passing between the Kithnos and Siros islands on the afternoon of 6 October, and reported by wireless its size, speed, air cover and probable route. The next day the Royal Navy, acting on the information received, sank a convoy off Stampalia consisting of six landing craft, an ammunition ship, and an armed trawler. It was a disaster for the Germans, as there remained only 90 survivors out of a total of 2,500 troops. The destruction of this force prevented the enemy from making an immediate assault on Leros. Having been relieved by T2, Saxton's patrol returned to Leros on 23 October, along with two Greeks who had helped them.

T2 Patrol, which consisted of five men under Second-Lieutenant M. W. Cross, were disembarked at Seriphos because that island was thought to be safer than Kithnos which the enemy patrolled with seaplanes. The Greeks helped the New Zealanders with hiding places and observation points. They also kept the patrol constantly informed about the movements of the enemy garrison of nearly 50 strong, based in the town about 6 kilometres away. The postmaster passed the information by telephone to a monastery and a priest would send a runner to T2's hideout.

The patrol observed an enemy airlift from Athens to Rhodes with four large flying boats escorted by seaplane fighters, and reported the times they passed over the island. Consequently, six Beaufighters shot down the flying boats when they appeared one day without their fighter escort. After spending three weeks on the island T2 was relieved by a British patrol and returned to Leros on 9 November with three Greeks who had aided them.

Seven men from R1 Patrol under Lieutenant D. J. Aitken, spent 17 days on Naxos, one of the largest of the Cyclades Islands. They confused the garrison of 650 Germans, who were aware of their presence, by making long cross-country treks. As with the other patrols, the locals gave every assistance. R1 reported a concen-

tration of shipping at Naxos harbour, which was raided soon after by the RAF. Two ships were sunk at the cost of two aircraft shot down. The pilot and navigator of a Beaufighter which crashed in the sea were rescued by the Greeks, given medical treatment and hidden. On 6 November the patrol smuggled them out when they left the island and returned to Leros.

Sergeant Jack Davis of T1 Patrol who received the BEM for his conduct in the Aegean operations. While coast watching, his patrol reported a German troop convoy heading for Leros, which resulted in the Royal Navy destroying eight vessels with great loss of life on the troop transports. After the war Davis devoted many years as the secretary of the LRDG (NZ) Association. Photo: Sharon Palmer.

THE ASSAULT ON LEVITA

The Royal Navy considered the German occupied island of Levita to be of importance as a valuable observation post. It was thought to be garrisoned by only a handful of men, therefore the commander of 234 Brigade ordered the LRDG to capture the island. The plan was to destroy the radar and weather station, overwhelm the garrison, hold the island for the day and be picked up by a motor launch the following day. Major Guild and Captain Tinker urged that a reconnaissance should be made first before an assault force was landed, but they were told because of time factors permission to do so would not granted.

It was decided to attack with 48 men under the command of Captain J. R. Olivey, whose B Squadron party included Y2 with part of S1 Patrol; and A Squadron under Lieutenant J. M. Sutherland, which comprised of 22 men from R1, R2 and T2 Patrols. The R2 men had been withdrawn from manning the coastal battery on Mount Scumbardo, in southern Leros.

In case the enemy should be occupying both ends of Levita, B Squadron was to land to the west of the port, which is on the south coast, and the New Zealanders to the east. The objective was to reach the high central ground overlooking the harbour. Motor launches were to take the men to the landing area and off load them into small collapsible craft called "Folboats". These wooden and rubberised canvas-covered boats were delivered on the deck of a destroyer that had been under air attack on its way to Leros. Hence when they were received by the LRDG they were peppered with shrapnel holes and much time was spent repairing them with sticking plaster before the landing exercises could begin.

The force had four infantry wireless sets for inter-communication between the two parties and the launches, with a larger set being used for communication with Leros. Unfortu-

nately when they were about to leave at dusk on 23 October it was discovered that the A Squadron set had not been "netted in" with the others. At that late stage there was nothing that could be done, except try and improvise something on the way to the island.

The sea was rough for the Aegean and most of the men were badly seasick before they reached Levita. In the darkness it took a long time to float and board the Folboats from the tossing launch. Also, being loaded down with arms and equipment added to the difficulties, with one man slipping on the scramble net and falling head first into a boat, almost capsizing it in the heavy swell. But eventually at 2200hrs they landed on the dark rugged coast. The boats were collapsed and hidden, therewith the men recovered their gear from the rocks and dragged it up a cliff face.

After the force had disembarked, the motor launches were to fire upon a house in the centre of the island thought to be occupied by the enemy. Instead they entered an inlet and gave covering fire from their light and heavy machine-guns upon a small hut on the ridge in front of A Squadron. This proved to serve no purpose other than to alert the garrison of the landing. Sutherland told his wireless operator to try to communicate with Olivey, but at no stage was he able to do so. As the men moved towards the ridge they came under machine-gun fire from the vicinity of their landing place. This kept them pinned down over open ground until they were able to gather together and rush the gun position, which they captured with a dozen prisoners. In the attack Trooper H. L. Mallet was severely wounded by a grenade, and despite the best efforts of the medical orderly Private B. Steedman, he later died.

The New Zealanders continued the advance against the German dugouts on the high ground, which included machine-gun and light mortar emplacements. Progress was slow as the defences were hard to distinguish against the rocks. Yet by 0500hrs the ridge was secured with 35 prisoners being taken. Though in doing so, Trooper R. G. Haddow was wounded in the stomach, and Trooper A. J. Penhall was badly injured when a stick grenade burst in his face. Several others suffered minor wounds.

When dawn broke four seaplanes were seen to take off from Levita harbour. The New Zealanders, who overlooked the harbour from the ridge, opened fire and for a moment it seemed that Trooper L. G. Doel had put a seaplane out of action with his Bren gun, but cautiously it had moved out of range and took off after some delay. But within the hour, these aircraft, followed by eight Stukas, appeared overhead and strafed the position. The men sought cover and returned fire with no obvious effect.

B Squadron had encountered no resistance on landing and hence were able to advance to within 450 metres of the enemy headquarters by dawn and heard the fighting on the other side of the island. Had the radios worked, Sutherland would have contacted Olivey advising him of his situation and B Squadron could have advanced without fear of firing on their own A Squadron. The Germans, who received reinforcements during the day, isolated the New Zealanders on the ridge with machine-gun and mortar fire, supported by air attacks from Stuka and JU 88 dive bombers. Meanwhile most of B Squadron's party were now being subjected to heavy machine-gun and mortar fire, plus air attacks from Stukas and seaplanes. By the end of the day Olivey's squadron was encircled and most of his men captured.

The enemy then concentrated all his forces against A Squadron, which was holding three positions on the ridge. Sutherland was established on an exposed site on top overlooking the harbour. He was accompanied by his wireless operator, a medical orderly with the wounded, three or four other men, plus a large body of prisoners.

Sergeant E. J. Dobson was in a central position in charge of the bulk of the men, who were armed with a solitary Bren gun, a Thompson submachine-gun and rifles. Further away on higher ground Corporal J. E. Gill led a smaller third party. They were all short of food and out of water.

Trooper J. T. Bowler, accompanied by a German POW, together with the runner from Gill to Sutherland, Trooper D. Davidson, volunteered to make their way to the landing place to obtain some water and reconnoitre the situation. But they never returned and were presumed killed or captured. Bowler's body was later recovered, but Davidson was never found. He was posted as missing, presumed killed, and may have possibly fallen into one of the island's many deep, rocky crevasses.

In the afternoon Sutherland's position was under steady mortar and air attack, with his defensive movements being hampered by the 35 prisoners and the wounded. By late afternoon the condition of Troopers Haddow and Penhall had badly deteriorated, therefore on his own initiative Private B. Steedman the medical orderly arranged with the Germans to surrender them under a white flag.

Two trips were made to deliver the men to a boat waiting at an inlet, where they were handed over to a German NCO. Steedman also gave himself up so he could stay with the wounded. Haddow later recovered as a POW, but Penhall died the next day in an Athens hospital and was buried by the Germans with a full guard of honour.

The NCO told the other men who were assisting while under truce, that about 12 of Olivey's force had already been captured and more Stukas were on their way from Rhodes. As the party made its way back they could see small groups of Germans making their own way along the eastern edge of the island, supported by low flying planes. They reported this information on their return.

Sutherland's men had expended their ammunition and were now employing captured weapons, including a mortar and a machine-gun. The enemy were so close that the position was being bombarded with rifle grenades. At dusk, Sutherland decided to surrender to save further bloodshed. They had no food, water or ammunition, and there was nothing to be gained by holding on. A white flag was displayed and a German prisoner was sent out to inform his advancing comrades. All the weapons were gathered and thrown over the cliff into the sea. The prisoners they had captured earlier in the day were then invited to take command, consequently the New Zealanders were taken to the German HQ where they met up with most of B Squadron. Corporal Gill and three others managed to avoid the enemy for four days by hiding among the rocks. But they were unable to attract the attention of a rescue launch that circled the island and as they were without food and water had to give themselves up.

With instructions to evacuate the force from Levita, the newly appointed commanding officer of the LRDG, Lieutenant-Colonel J. R. Easonsmith, arrived by launch during the night of 24–25 October, but found only Captain Olivey, Captain R. P. Lawson the medical officer, and seven men of B Squadron at the rendezvous.

The following night Olivey returned with Major Guild to search for the missing men, but nobody was found. This ill-conceived operation cost B Squadron one man killed (Gunner S. Federman), with A Squadron losing three killed or died of wounds, and one man missing. All the rest became prisoners of war.

It was later discovered that Levita had been used as a base for the forthcoming attack on Leros. Had a reconnaissance been allowed to take place this disaster may not have happened. The New Zealand Squadron had lost more men in one day than they had in three years in the desert. In total the LRDG lost 40 men on Levita, including all the New Zealanders who had landed on the island.

Easonsmith called a meeting with the senior officers of A and B Squadrons about the future of the LRDG. It was recommended that with the exception of the patrols in the Cyclades Islands watching for the movement of enemy invasion forces, the Group should return to the Middle East to train reinforcements and reform. On 31 October Major Guild left by destroyer for Egypt to endeavour to have the LRDG withdrawn. When he arrived he learned that the New Zealand Government was planning to recall A Squadron which had been consigned to an operational role in the Aegean without official approval.

The Government required that it was to be consulted first before its troops were committed to a new theatre of war. The Commander-in-Chief Middle East, General Sir Henry Wilson, stated that it was impossible to replace the New Zealand Squadron at such short notice, and asked that it could remain with the LRDG until replacements could be trained. This was agreed to, and the New Zealanders were to be pulled out as soon as the tactical situation allowed.

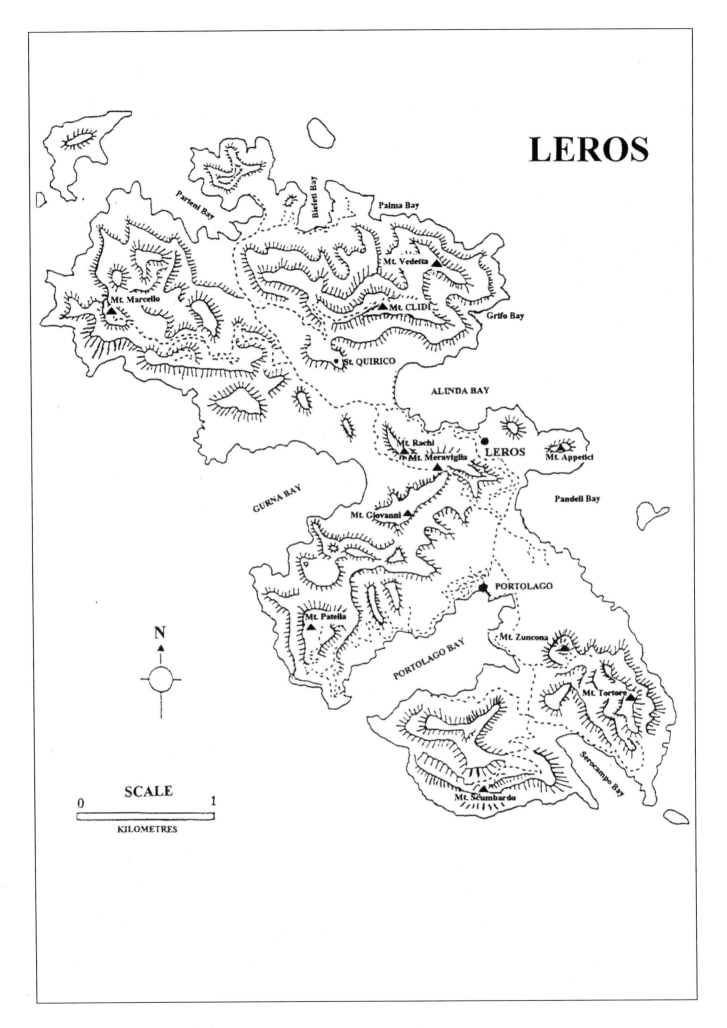

LEROS

Parteni Bay

Bufeti Bay

Palma Bay

Mt. Vedetta

Mt. Marcello

Mt. CLIDI

Grifo Bay

St. QUIRICO

ALINDA BAY

Mt. Rachi

Mt. Meraviglia

LEROS

Mt. Appetici

GURNA BAY

Pandell Bay

Mt. Giovanni

PORTOLAGO

N

Mt. Patella

Mt. Zuncona

PORTOLAGO BAY

Mt. Tortore

SCALE

0   1

Mt. Scumbardo

Serocampo Bay

KILOMETRES

THE BATTLE FOR LEROS

Before the invasion of Leros began only part of A Squadron had been withdrawn. Lieutenant D. J. Aitken with 20 men from R1 Patrol and A Squadron Headquarters, left for Palestine by destroyer on 7 November. R2 Patrol, reconstituted with eight New Zealanders and two Englishmen under Second-Lieutenant R. F. White, relieved T1 at the San Giorgio coastal-defence battery position on Mount Scumbardo where they also supervised some 60 Italian gunners. T1 moved on to an olive grove on the northern side of Alinda Bay and were joined by T2 when they returned from Seriphos the next day. In addition to the Raiding Forces, at the height of the battle there were nearly 4,000 regular British troops on the island (The King's Own Royal Regiment, Royal Irish Fusiliers, Royal West Kents and Royal East Kents, plus support units). Fortress HQ 234 Brigade, HQ LRDG and the Italian HQ were located in tunnels hewn out of solid rock on Mount Meraviglia.

From 4 October Leros was subjected to regular bombing attacks with both the port and coastal batteries being among the main targets. With little or no opposition often 60 or more aircraft took part in these raids. For example, when the troops withdrew from Calino they sailed to Leros at night and in anticipation of air raids they unloaded and removed the stores from the wharf before daylight. This precaution paid off, because at 5.30 am 55 dive-bombers began an attack on the port that lasted four hours. An Italian gunboat and several small craft were sunk, plus buildings and installations destroyed.

Private Ian Judge of R1 Patrol recalled an amusing incident that took place after one of these raids. He and Trooper Cecil Mason had sought shelter in a culvert where they experienced the deafening noise and concussion of exploding bombs followed by strafing. When it was all over they just sat there for a time to gather their senses. Then suddenly Mason spat out his false teeth and exclaimed, *"If you buggers don't stop chattering I'll throw you away"*! Satisfied that his teeth were now behaving themselves he put them back in and left the culvert to view the damage.

During these raids the civilians also suffered, many of whom were killed or injured. For example when Stukas

The 6-inch gun battery on Mount Scumbardo, Leros. Other batteries were mounted on high points about the island and manned by Italian gunners under LRDG supervision. Though subject to air and land attacks, most saw good service up to the fall of Leros.
Photo: Merle Fogden.

Portolago, the port of Leros with its good natural sheltered harbour. It had been used by the Italians as a seaplane and naval base.
Photo: Merle Fogden.

were dive bombing two Motor Torpedo Boats in the harbour, the bombs missed, hitting the water and the town. Private Judge was in the vicinity and heard the sound of screaming coming from a wrecked house. He rushed over and found a young girl whose leg was nearly severed by a bomb blast. He immediately picked her up and carried her to the local hospital which was fortunately nearby. Ian Judge said he still recalls today the gruesome sound of the surgeon's saw cutting through the remains of the child's leg. He returned to Leros for a visit in 1989 and inquired about the girl. The locals gladdened him with the good news that she had survived her ordeal and was now living in Athens.

On 8 October the gun battery on Mount Marcello, in the north-east where Y2 Patrol was stationed, was put out of action by Stuka attacks. The next day the battery at Mount Zuncona, to the east of Portolago Bay, manned by R1 under Lieutenant D. J. Aitken, was also knocked out, causing his patrol to be withdrawn to A Squadron HQ. These gun positions were especially targeted as they posed a threat to the invasion force. This was first proven on 10 October when German landing craft were observed entering the bays of Calino. Consequently, the following day the coastal batteries shelled the enemy from Leros.

When R1 Patrol and the Italian gunners were stationed at the guns on Mount Zuncona they had to garrison themselves in the discomfort of surrounding caves. After a time the men were running short of rations and water, though the latter could be obtained from a spring further down the hill. But the rations were to prove a greater challenge. In Portolago there was a NAAFI supply store that had been cordoned off because it was now "home" to an unexploded bomb. Seeing that as no real obstacle, Private Judge, accompanied by Gunner Doug "Shorty" McDonald, volunteered to trek down from the hills at night, enter the store and steal back their own

rations. They weren't too concerned about the unexploded bomb, figuring that if it hadn't gone off on impact it was unlikely to explode while they were there.

One evening, the patrol had run out of cigarettes, which were considered essential supplies as they were helpful in suppressing hunger pangs and calming the nerves. The call went out for Judge and McDonald to obtain some of these "essentials" while on their next visit to the store. Soon after they set off down the hill entered the building and in the darkness grabbed some tins of Capstan, amongst other things. On their return, after the long trek up the hill they found that all they had was pipe tobacco and not cigarettes. Judge possessed the only pipe so he cleaned it out, stoked it up and passed it around. The men could now relax, enjoying a smoke as they sat in their cave.

Despite the delays imposed by the RAF and Royal Navy, the Germans had assembled an invasion force at Cos and Calino for the assault on Leros. At dawn, 12 November, after two days of heavy bombing they landed 500 men on the north-east coast of the island. They gained possession of the high ground between Palma and Grifo Bays, including Mount Vedetta, but were held throughout the day by the 4th Royal East Kents (the "Buffs") and patrols of B Squadron. Another 150 troops landed at Pandeli Bay to the south east of Leros town. Having received information of a possible parachute attack, Captain Saxton's T1 Patrol moved inland from Alinda Bay and was joined by a British patrol and some SBS troops, to make a force of over 30 strong.

Early in the afternoon of 12 November, 35 Junkers-52 transport planes, escorted by Stukas, seaplanes and other aircraft, approached from a low altitude from the west and dropped 500 paratroops. They landed on the narrow strip of land between Gurna and Alinda Bays where they were engaged immediately by Allied troops in the area, including the composite LRDG/SBS group. One Ju 52 was shot down, while many parachutists were killed descending under heavy fire. Also due to the steep rocky terrain others, having landed safely, had difficulty recovering their supply containers that were dropped separately. A number of these were found and welcomed by the defenders as they contained food, weapons and ammunition, all of which were much in need. The fighting was particularly fierce on the Rachi ridge, but the enemy held their ground and eventually isolated the northern sector from the rest of the island. Major A. Redfern of B Squadron, who led the LRDG in this action, was killed.

On 13 November, 15 Ju 52s arrived overhead with more paratroops to reinforce their hard-pressed comrades on Rachi ridge. The aircraft were buffeted by high winds and greeted with anti-aircraft fire. Private Les Nicholls of T Patrol recalled that as the planes were disgorging their human cargoes, he witnessed a horrible sight that is still vivid in his memory today. A Ju 52 flew low overhead, and probably due to either its low altitude or damage to the static release cable, a whole stick of about 18 paratroopers jumped without their chutes opening. They fell to their deaths, smashed against the rocks within 100 metres of T Patrol's position. Gusty winds led to others being lost as they were blown out to sea. Furthermore, two transports were shot down over Alinda Bay.

Meanwhile, in the north-east on Mount Clidi, Captain J. R. Olivey with his S1 Patrol supporting the Italian gunners were firing their three 6-inch coastal batteries at approaching German troop landing craft escorted by destroyers. One landing craft was hit and sunk, yet the others were lucky as they were protected by a hill as they approached the shore, though the destroyers were still able to bombard the gun sites. S1 Patrol then had to redirect their guns and fire over open sights at the advancing infantry.

The enemy eventually overwhelmed the batteries, but not before Olivey and his men managed to disable the guns as they withdrew. The next day the "Buffs" and the LRDG patrols from the north recaptured the emplacements, but their position became tenuous as they were now subject to regular air attacks by the Luftwaffe.

Second-Lieutenant White's R2 Patrol on Scumbardo directed their 6-inch guns to shoot not only at enemy shipping but also landwards against targets to the north of Rachi and on Appectici. The shells passed over the Allied HQ on Meraviglia with only a few metres to spare, with some

accurate shooting being reported at a jetty in Alinda Bay. Further positions were engaged, including an old Crusader castle near Leros town, until the last day of battle when they ran out of ammunition. Frank White recalled that guns were ex-British naval, very accurate and well handled by the Italians. He also said he felt sorry for his gunnery officer because he was sure the Italian was later captured and executed.

One New Zealander, Private Don Gregory, who was delivering a message to the emplacement, walked near a 6-inch gun as it was fired. He was blown off his feet and his hearing was impaired for several days. Gregory considered himself very lucky because had he been any closer the concussion from the blast may have killed him.

Virtually unopposed, the Luftwaffe flew hundreds of sorties over the island. There was no Allied fighter cover, and due to the lack of ammunition, little anti-aircraft opposition, although 16 enemy aircraft were claimed by the 12 40mm Bofors AA guns on the island (these, along with four 25-pounder field guns were also used against ground targets). The Stukas had not enjoyed such success since the early days of the Blitzkrieg. Their old dive-bombing techniques demoralized the troops, sunk or damaged Allied ships and knocked

out gun emplacements. As the Germans took hold, the defender's communications became erratic, making control and movement difficult. With the troops becoming more weary the fighting deteriorated into small skirmishes. To help overcome fatigue some of the men were issued with Benzedrine tablets (an amphetamine) which would keep them alert for up to 24 hours. Ian Judge said that while on those pills you could have a 15 minute sleep and then wake up feeling that you had just had a full night's rest.

R1 Patrol had sailed for Palestine two days before the invasion of Leros, leaving Private Judge behind with LRDG HQ. He was lean and fit and was therefore attached as a messenger. While sheltering in the HQ communications room during an air raid he recalled being entertained by an English signaller who had managed to tune into the attacking Stuka squadron's radio frequency. The operator was telling the crews in very colourful language what he thought of them, that they weren't welcome and they should go back from whence they came. Undeterred, the Stuka crews were too busy enjoying their unopposed dive-bombing to heed the Englishman's message.

At dawn on 16 November the enemy launched a heavy air and ground attack against Meraviglia. Lt-Col. J. R.

The British radio operator Signalman Bill Smith, attached to R1 Patrol, overlook0s Leros from his dugout. Later this position was put out of action by Stuka dive bombing attacks. Photo: Merle Fogden.

Having reached Turkey after escaping Leros, LRDG and regular soldiers are now safely aboard a minesweeper heading for Haifa in Palestine. On the left are New Zealanders J. D. L Davis, C. A. Yaxley and M. D. Richardson. Captain C. K. Saxton of T1 Patrol is at right rear.
Photo: Ken Johnson.

Easonsmith, accompanied by several LRDG men, reconnoitred Leros town to evaluate the situation around the approaches to Fortress HQ. At first there were no enemy sightings but later when they returned before midnight to make a second reconnaissance, the Germans had established themselves in the town. The party was ambushed and Easonsmith (believed by veterans to be riding a bicycle at the time) was killed by a sniper's bullet. An attempt was made to rally the troops for a counter-attack, but with disrupted communications, low morale and exhaustion, any organized resistance soon succumbed to the overwhelming odds.

Late in the afternoon, Fortress HQ and HQ LRDG destroyed their documents and wireless equipment then withdrew to Portolago. Before the British force commander Brigadier R. A. Tilney could escape, he was surprised by grenade and automatic fire as members of the elite German Brandenberg Regiment broke into the fortress tunnel. He was captured and at about 6pm that evening was obliged to surrender Leros to the enemy commander General Friedrich Wilhelm Muller. The news was taken to all parts of the island by a number of German and British officers travelling in a jeep.

The LRDG patrols in the north were cut off from their HQ in the south. Major the Earl of Jellicoe had taken command of the composite LRDG/SBS group, which were manning machine-gun positions on the northern coast should the enemy land further troops there. When the news of the capitulation was received at about midnight, the men in the vicinity were rounded up with the aid of two jeeps. They refused to surrender and continued fighting or evading the enemy until they could escape the island.

A party of about 25, including T1 and T2 Patrols, took possession of an Italian caique and a small motor boat and sailed to little island north of Leros where they hid during the day. They reached Bodrum in Turkey the next night and joined an old minesweeper in which they made a three day voyage down the Turkish coast and across to Haifa in Palestine. Private Judge was returning through the hills after delivering a message when he met several soldiers from the Royal Irish Fusiliers. He was invited to join them as they had found a small boat to escape the island with. Judge was out of ammunition and the Germans seemed to be everywhere, he decided to take up the chance to get away. They successfully reached Turkey in a row boat after stopping overnight at a small island on the way.

After the surrender, most of Headquarters LRDG dispersed in the south near Mount Patella. Colonel Prendergast, Captain Croucher, Captain Tinker and several others, including two men from R2 Patrol, hid on Mount Tortore. The remainder of R2 escaped that night in two parties. Colonel Prendergast's party remained hidden on Leros until 22 November when they were evacuated by a RAF air-sea rescue launch.

When the island surrendered, the LRDG had 123 men on it, of these about 70 escaped in the ensuing weeks. In the end only two men of A Squadron were captured on Leros. Also over several days Major D. L. Lloyd Owen was able to organize, with the use of caiques, the rescue of several hundred British troops.

Second-Lieutenant Frank White was based on Mount Scumbardo when he received a wireless message from HQ stating that Leros had fallen. White related his escape as follows. When it was dark, he and five others (S. Kerr, G. F. McDowell, two English signalmen, B. Morrison and L. Thurgood, and Lieutenant Pavlidies, a Greek officer attached to the British) gathered what was needed and headed down the mountain to find a rowing boat sunk in Serocampo Bay. Fortunately the Greek, when he had first landed in Leros, had the foresight to go round to all the little harbours and sink a small boat in each of them. He did this because he knew that the

Germans would disable any vessel they saw, to prevent escapees leaving the island. The men found the submerged boat and began to bail it out while Pavlidies recovered some oars that he had previously hidden in the hillside. All this time the Italians on the headland across the bay were still playing their searchlights round, so when the light passed, the men had to stop what they were doing in case someone saw them. At about 10.00pm the lights were finally switched off as the surrender of the island was now almost complete. The party then set off very quietly down the harbour and headed out to sea.

With only one man being able to row at a time, turns were taken, as White navigated towards the Turkish coast, guided by the stars. The next morning they pulled into a little island called Pharmakonisi where they camouflaged the vessel and had a rest. Soon two Greeks appeared and were asked it they could obtain a mast to fit the boat. By cutting down the rocky island's only tree a mast was produced and with the aid of an old tent a sail was erected. The Greeks were each given a rifle in exchange for their kindness.

That evening, after resting for a good part of the day, the men continued their voyage this time under the ease of sail. Frank White had previously been taking Benzedrine tablets to keep awake, but now as they headed for the coast he was able to enjoy the best sleep he had ever had. When he was awoken they were sailing under fairly steep cliffs and thought they had reached Calino, but they had in fact arrived on the Turkish coast. On the way in their boat they were nearly capsized by the wake of a British destroyer. The men could hear voices on board so they yelled at the ship, but in the darkness they were neither heard nor seen. Foreign vessels were allowed to remain for 12 hours within three miles of Turkish territorial waters, which was why the destroyer came to be there in the first place. It was probably going in to pick up men who had escaped from Leros.

White's party landed on the coast of Turkey and prepared a meal, after which they rowed further up the bay until they came to a little village. The Greek officer was able to speak Turkish, so with the help of the local policeman, donkeys were provided to assist the men. They wrapped their weapons and few possessions in blankets, packed them on the donkeys and set out on a four-hour trek across the peninsula to Bodrum. When the party arrived they were entertained by the British Consul who offered a welcome beer and a meal, after which he said to them, *"You see that boat with the plank down, just go there and walk on. The rest of your men are already on board."*

They boarded a British MTB and met up with others who had escaped from Leros. The vessel headed back up the coast staying within neutral waters. Ahead of them were prisoners being transported in captured German boats. Following some distance behind, in the hope the small convoy would drift outside the three mile limit, were German naval ships. The men could see the lights of Rhodes as they passed at night and eventually a little further up the coast the pursuing Kriegsmarine finally gave up. When the Royal Navy felt it was safe, the boats sailed across to Haifa, where the troops celebrated their escape.

In all, some 3,200 British and 5,320 Italians were taken prisoner. Another 357 British troops had been killed, including 157 men who had drowned en route to Leros. The LRDG lost five, including its commander. The Germans suffered 246 killed and 162 missing. The commander of the Italian Aegean Islands, Admiral Luigi Campioni, along with Admiral Luigi Mascherpa, the Italian commander on Leros, were both executed by the Germans in March 1944.

Throughout the campaign the Royal Navy also suffered severe losses. In addition to the *Queen Olga* and the *Intrepid*, other ships sunk included the destroyers *Panther, Harworth, Eclipse* and *Dulverton*. Damaged beyond repair was the cruiser *Carlisle*, and the destroyer *Adrias* was forced to beach in Turkey. The destroyer *Rockwood* had been damaged by remote-controlled glider bombs.

On 26 November 1943, General Freyberg sent a report to the New Zealand Minister of Defence in regard to the Dodecanese operations, part of which included the following:

The outcome of the operations in the Aegean has been a serious blow to us all, as you can imagine. It was touch and go on Leros but in the end air supremacy won. We took the risk when we went in September, but we had hoped to follow up with an attack on Rhodes.

Every effort was made to strengthen our position in the Aegean and it was decided to try and hold on in view of the very valuable diversion it caused to the enemy's main effort in Italy and Russia. The force diverted included up to 400 aircraft, also 6000 highly trained troops for the assault, and others for garrisoning the islands he was forced to occupy by our raiding. One third of the enemy shipping in the Aegean was sunk and the Axis supply line to Rhodes interrupted for two months.

The LRDG were used as outposts for raiding and patrolling in enemy-held islands, a task for which they are ideally suited. Their operations were of the greatest value, and all the evidence proves that they were a serious thorn in the enemy's side, whilst the information given by their outposts proved invaluable to all services.

Second Lieutenant F. R. White's escape party lands in Turkey after sailing from Leros. Photo: Merle Fogden.

FINAL DAYS

The Dodecanese operation proved to be the last action the New Zealand squadron undertook with the LRDG. After that debacle they transferred to a new LRDG base at Azzib, north of Haifa in Palestine, to rest and re-organize. On orders from the New Zealand government, A Squadron was to disband on 31 December 1943. However, prior to this, the Christmas celebration was somewhat prolonged because there was practically a party every night as the Kiwis recalled special times and exchanged sad farewells with their British and Rhodesian comrades.

After the squadron was finally wound up in Cairo on 15 January 1944 most of its members, if they did not go home on furlough, spent time at the New Zealand Armoured Corps Training Depot in Egypt and were posted as reinforcements to the Divisional Cavalry with the 2nd New Zealand Division in Italy.

By December 1943 the Group, under the command of Lieutenant-Colonel David Lloyd Owen, was reorganized into two squadrons each of eight patrols consisting of one officer and 10 men. To replace the New Zealanders, a Rhodesian squadron was formed, under the command of the New Zealand-born Ken Lazarus. He had already earned much credit as a surveyor in mapping the Libyan deserts, and later as a patrol

commander. After the war he changed his surname to Lawrence. The British squadron was com-manded by Moir Stormonth-Darling. To ensure that the LRDG did not lose its high level of expertise, General Freyberg allowed Lloyd Owen to

retain several long serving A Squad-ron members. Initially they were Tony Browne, Ron Tinker, Dick Croucher and Jack Aitken, along with Len Hawkins who was a fitter employed in the workshops. Later Ron Landon-Lane, Paddy McLauchlan and Merlyn Craw also rejoined. All of these men had already served the group with much distinction.

Farewell celebrations, December 1943. S. Kerr (left) and T. Collins hold up a decorated blanket marking the A Squadron's departure from the LRDG—Kia ora (a Maori greeting) and happy days as the "Kiwi" leaves the scorpion.
Photo: Merle Fogden.

Azzib, Palestine 1943. A Squadron members relax awaiting their disbandment orders. Left to right: J. L. D. Davis, C. Kidd, D. O. Beale, J. Emslie, ?, M. F. Fogden, M. D. Richardson.
Photo: Merle Fogden.

LRDG mountain warfare training base, Gran Sasso mountains, Italy, 1944. Photo: Merlyn Craw.

LRDG members resting after a skiing exercise. This was in stark contrast to the heat and dryness of the desert. Photo: Merlyn Craw.

It was by pure chance that Craw came to serve with the unit once again. Having been a POW for a year, he escaped in September 1943 and was helped through the enemy lines by some Italian civilians. After spending six months at home on furlough, he was back in Italy with his original unit, the Divisional Cavalry. At first they operated armoured cars and light tanks, but in 1944 were later converted to infantry. During this reorganization Craw was promised Rome leave, yet it was reneged on and he was ordered to return to New Zealand. Disgruntled, he and a fellow sergeant left the truck that was to take them to Bari and decided to hitch-

Many New Zealand ex-LRDG members went on to serve in Italy with the NZ Divisional Cavalry. Here Sergeant M. F. Fogden commands a Staghound armoured car, Italy 1944. Photo: Merle Fogden.

hike. While on their travels they arrived in the area where Craw's Italian friends lived, the ones who had risked their lives helping him after he had escaped. He felt close to these people and enjoyed their hospitality for some time before moving on.

After being AWOL for nearly six weeks Craw eventually arrived in Rome, though without a leave pass he could no go to the New Zealand club or anywhere else for a comfortable bed. Luckily before long he saw a jeep in the street displaying a scorpion sign. Craw made himself known to the LRDG men and hitched a ride to a ski lodge in the Gran Sasso mountains, about 80 kilometres north of the capital. It was the same place from where the German commando Otto Skorzeny and his small raiding party had daringly uplifted Mussolini in September 1943. The British Squadron were now using it as a mountain warfare training base. That night they had a party and Craw was invited to rejoin the unit. Having nowhere else to go, he agreed and interestingly was never brought to account to the NZ Division for his unauthorized leave.

Two new bases were established at Bari and Rodi in southern Italy. Bari was the main operational HQ till the end of the war and it was from there that most of the missions were planned and directed. Rodi, though a long way from Bari, was a good site for base communications and a quiet place for the men to rest after operations. By May 1944, after months of diverse and specialized training, including parachuting, mountain warfare, skiing, how to operate in snow conditions, and the handling of pack mules and small boats, they were ready for the first of many intrusions into enemy occupied territory. Their initial actions were behind the lines in Italy and from then on till the end of the war, patrols operated in Yugoslavia, Albania, Greece, the Dalmatian Islands, Istria and Croatia.

The Group maintained its intelligence-gathering and reconnaissance role, but also operated with local Partisans

Captain Ron Tinker's wedding day, Senagalia, Italy. 14 April 1945. His New Zealand wife Frances had been serving as a nurse. The best man was Lieutenant Ron Landon-Lane. Both of these men were original LRP members and had remained with the LRDG until it was disbanded in 1945. Photo: Richard Williams.

in many sabotage hit-and-run actions. For example, Jack Aitken worked closely with the Partisans in Albania. The LRDG set up coast watches to report on enemy shipping targets for Allied naval and air commands and planned, often in conjunction with the Special Boat Service, small scale raids against enemy shipping in harbours and island garrisons. Objectives were reached either by parachute or by sea—the latter usually being preferred because there was less risk to men and equipment. By the middle of September 1944 there was a total of 18 different parties on various tasks stretching from the north-east corner of Italy through Yugoslavia and Albania to Greece. The organization and control of these operations was complex and their success did not only lay with the men in the field, but also in the care and skill of the planners at HQ.

The New Zealand officers attached to the Group, though often involved in staff duties, also participated in behind the line operations as did the Group Commander himself. On one occasion while on a mission, Lloyd Owen parachuted into Albania at night and unfortunately fractured his spine on landing. Captain Ron Tinker who accompanied him took over command and continued the assignment. He was later joined by a fellow New Zealander, Captain Paddy McLauchlan, who parachuted in with additional explosives for demolition work. A radio message was transmitted to base requesting medical assistance for their injured Commander. The Group's doctor, Michael Parsons, arrived soon after by parachute. He encased Lloyd Owen's spine in plaster and made him as comfortable as possible. However, it was several weeks before they were able to make the three-day trek to the coast to be safely evacuated by sea. Meanwhile, the medical officer was gainfully employed caring for a patrol member with malaria and treating sick and wounded Partisans.

Sometimes the conditions in which the patrols operated watches or established forward positions could be very trying. They would live in makeshift shelters of drafty farm sheds, in caves and amongst rocks or trees, which usually meant that for most of the time they were cold or damp and uncomfortable. Fleas or lice were common and the men often suffered from sores because they were never clean. Burdened with heavy packs they trekked in the freezing snow of winter or in the summer heat, over rocky passes and through thick forest and scrub, always keeping a low profile and evading the enemy. Despite these often difficult conditions the men were well trained and hardy and in true LRDG tradition stoically got on with the job, though at times they must have longed for the ease of motoring in the warm open space of the desert. The unit's title, the Long Range Desert Group, must have seemed a little curious to their Partisan allies who fought alongside them in the mountains and forests.

For operations around the Dalmatian islands the LRDG could not always rely on the Navy for assistance at short notice, hence they obtained their own transport—a motor fishing vessel, the MFV *La Palma*. It was stripped of all unnecessary superstructure and armed with a variety of deck-mounted weapons, which later included a 20mm Oerlikon and a 2-pounder gun. The vessel had a large carrying capacity for men, stores and equipment, including the ability to lash a jeep to the deck. Captain Alan Denniff was the skipper, with a crew of nine.

Later, another boat was added to the fleet, the MFV *Kufra*, an 80 tonne schooner which Captain Dick Croucher converted into a mobile headquarters. It was equipped with a sophisticated communication system capable of keeping in touch with the LRDG bases of Bari and Rodi. They were also able to intercept all signals to and from any patrols that were operating. Croucher, being ex-Merchant Marine (Union Steamship Co.) as well as the Group's Intelligence Officer, was appropriately made the skipper. Both these robust

vessels with their LRDG crews performed much valuable work. A Waco liaison aircraft was still in service and flown by Captain Trevor Barker, so along with the Group's vessels it was probably one of the few special forces units in World War 2 that could boast its own Air Force and Navy!

In Europe the Group had completed over 100 successful operations by the time the war had ended. Allied Force HQ recommended that the LRDG should continue its role in the Far East. Consequently, on 16 June 1945 they were ordered as a unit back to England where they were to regroup and go on leave before being sent to Asia. There was even talk of operating in the Gobi desert. However, a week later Lloyd Owen received a War Office signal stating that the LRDG was to be disbanded. The next six weeks were spent carrying out the disbandment order. The unit officially ceased to exist on 1 August 1945.

What began as Ralph Bagnold's small reconnaissance force which included Ron Tinker and Dick Croucher on the first trip, served five years and 14 days and in relation to their numbers had made a significant contribution to the war in their diverse areas of operations. This was reflected in a comment made during the desert campaign by the commander of the Afrika Korps, Field Marshall Erwin Rommel, who said *"The LRDG cause us more damage than any other unit of their size."*

In July 1945 General Freyberg sent a letter to Lloyd Owen recalling the value of the Group's work, part of which stated:

> *It is sad news that the LRDG is to be disbanded. Nobody realizes better than I do the extent to which their work contributed to the success of the North African campaign, and it will always be a source of pride and satisfaction in 2 NZEF that New Zealanders were able to play in your long series of brilliant operations.*

POSTWAR YEARS

LRDG Reunion, Whangarei, NZ, 1973.
Back row, left to right:
Don Gregory, Ian Judge, Dick Ramsay.
Middle, left: Fraser McLeod, Lloyd Doel, Cyril Dornbush, Dan Farmer, Bob Ellis, Claude Naden, Jim Reid, Alex Yaxley, Denis Bassett, Clarke Waetford, Alf Saunders, Dave Burnnand, Walter Ellingham, Tom McLelland.
Front row, left: Norm Campbell, Frank Stone, Fred Kendall, ?, Tommy McDonald, Ron Moore, Bluey Grimsey, Alf Ferguson, Wink Adams, DougMcDonald.
Photo: Ian Judge.

The Long Range Desert Group (New Zealand) Association held its first meeting on 14 July 1946. C. S. "Bing" Morris was nominated president and 85 members attended. Since then a reunion has been held every year alternating between the North and South Islands. Because the majority of members lived in rural areas this enabled them to attend a gathering at least once in every two years without incurring extensive travel. In 1956 they became one of the first returned servicemen organisations to invite wives to their reunions which provided for a closer support network within the membership.

Because the patrols were so small, close kinships grew and developed as the men were reliant on each other for their survival. One weak link in the team could compromise a whole mission or the welfare of the unit. Reunions are a special time of camaraderie for those who had been through so much together. As Merlyn Craw put it:

Many veterans can't talk to those who were not in the war, because they weren't there and will never really understand how, and why things were. I will never forget it, there were men who may have saved my life, or I may have saved theirs. It's probably not obvious to anybody else, but the bond between us remains till we are gone.

As time passes the numbers attending reunions naturally decline. In April 1998 the veterans celebrated the 50th reunion of the LRDG (NZ) Association at Burnham Military Camp near Christchurch. As part of the commemoration, a weeping dwarf cedar was planted at the camp along with the placement of a brass plaque marking the reunion. The tree is the only one of its genus in New Zealand. It is of the type that grew in the Cedars of Lebanon where the LRDG trained in 1943.

The LRDG Association in Britain have commemorated the Group at the

National Memorial Arboretum which is located at Alrewas in Staffordshire. Covering about 250 acres, it is the largest permanent tribute to the British Army where campaigns, regiments and corps are represented by trees. The RAF and the Royal and Merchant Navies are also included. Dedicated to the LRDG, a Cedar of Lebanon has been planted in a very prominent position in the Army Grove, significantly next to a Scots pine honouring the SAS.

Of about the 325 New Zealanders who served in the unit, 60 were still in the Association at the time of writing this work. The body maintains close links with the British and Zimbabwean (Southern Rhodesian) Associations. Every year the British LRDG Association produces a newsletter which includes annual reports and anecdotes encompassing the three groups. although after 55 years they have decided by the end of the year 2000 to wind up their association, as attrition and infirmity has finally taken its toll.

Since the war a number of LRDG men have written their stories, notably Ralph Bagnold, Bill Kennedy Shaw, David Lloyd Owen, Michael Crichton-Stuart and Alastair Timpson. The Group's activities have been recorded in many publications including official histories, books on special forces, journals, magazines, and even war comics. Apart from newspaper articles, as far as the author is aware, there have been no published accounts written by New Zealand LRDG members about their time in the unit, although several veterans have collated stories and kept diaries. Others have related some incredible experiences that would make worthy subjects for a book in their own right.

There is very little archival film footage featuring the LRDG. A rare example seen by the author was taken by Merlyn Craw who operated a personal cine camera. Unfortunately most of his films had been lost or destroyed. On one occasion when he recorded the journey over the Sand Seas on the way to the Barce raid, the exposed film was given to Captain P. L. Arnold, an officer of the Heavy Section, whose trucks had supplied fuel dumps for the trip. On their return journey Arnold was killed when his vehicle ran over an Italian "coffin" mine. Merlyn, who was captured after the Barce raid, never saw his films again.

The only movie about the LRDG was released in 1958, called *The Sea of Sand*, a classic British black and white war film, typical of the era. Television in the 1960s also presented a series called *Rat Patrol*, which was loosely based on the adventures of the SAS and LRDG. It showed heroic Americans in the back of jeeps shooting up dozens of enemy aircraft parked in the desert. The BBC had to cancel the showing of the series in Britain as they received so many complaints from original "desert rats" about the gross inaccuracy and lack of British characters in the story.

In recent years military vehicle collectors in several countries have put together a number of reconstructed LRDG 30cwt Chevrolets and Fords, along with jeeps. Based on this theme, it gives enthusiasts the opportunity to collect and dress the vehicles up with a variety of weapons and equipment to suit their individual taste. Examples are to be seen in the USA, England, Australia and New Zealand. The only known surviving original LRDG truck is a Chevrolet WB 30cwt, the *Waikaha*, which is on display at the Imperial War Museum in London.

Interestingly, the USA is the home of the LRDG Preservation Society, founded by Jack Valenti. He heads a body of enthusiasts committed to keeping the history of the Group alive by way of historical research, also by acquiring associated equipment and artefacts and by recreating LRDG vehicles. They display a superbly-reconstructed 1942 Chevrolet 30cwt which features the markings of a New Zealand T1 Patrol truck, T8 *Tirau II*. It was built by Rick Butler in Northern California, after having to gather parts from Canada, England and Australia. The public get the opportunity to see the society's work, as the vehicle is often exhibited at militaria or military vehicle collector shows throughout America. Their next project is to recreate a LRDG Chevrolet radio truck.

At least two fine examples of LRDG vehicles can be seen in Great Britain. One is a Ford F30 30cwt, representing the Yeomanry Y2 Patrol truck Y6 *Aramis*, constructed as a joint venture by Paul Lincoln and Clinton Long. They were honoured to have it displayed at the British LRDG Association reunion in 1996. The other is a 1942 Chevrolet showing the T1 Patrol markings of T6, *Te Anau II*, the only truck to survive the Barce raid. This was built by Adrian Brown, who won the "Best Vehicle of the Show" award at the Biggin Hill Battle of Britain Show in 1997.

In New Zealand, Allan Davies of Christchurch constructed a LRDG truck using two 1942 Chevrolets and a 3 ton truck. The vehicle was exhibited at the QE II Army Memorial Museum at Waiouru for about three years. This one also displays the T1 Patrol markings of T6, *Te Anau II*. The vehicle was a feature at the 1996 LRDG reunion in Christchurch. Though not an original, the veterans enjoyed seeing one of their old "war-horses" again. They thought it was wonderful that someone had gone to all that trouble to re-create part of their history. Allan has several other LRDG projects under way, including a 1939 Chevrolet WB 30cwt, and a jeep. In addition, he plans to restore a Model T Ford in the style used by Bagnold in his pre-war desert explorations.

Another New Zealand couple, Ross and Leonie Hopkins of Hamilton, head a family of military vehicle enthusiasts who have in their collection a reconstructed 1942 Chevrolet painted in Rhodesian S Patrol markings with the name *Salisbury*. This has been displayed at two reunions, 1994 at Hamilton and 2000 at Matamata. Also at the 2000 reunion was a 1942 Willys, outfitted as an LRDG jeep, mounting .30 and .50 Brownings. It was authentically put together by Owen Gillingham. Wherever these unique vehicles are exhibited alongside the LRDG veterans, it inevitably attracts much media attention, helping to make the public aware of this small, yet fascinating World War 2 special force.

In light of the foregoing, the history of this amazing unit will continue to be of interest long after its members have passed on. It has been wonderful that a number of veterans who have reached their late seventies or early eighties were prepared to share so many of their wartime experiences with the author. In some cases they recounted stories which up until now they have not even been able to tell their families. Other memories recalled were either too unpalatable or distressing for them to want to be published. This has been respected. These are the personal scars of war that most veterans carry somewhere in their subconscious.

Though a British unit, these "Kiwi Scorpions" deserve a special mention in New Zealand's military chronicles. To serve in the cause of freedom they travelled far from home to a remote and arid land, where through their own ingenuity and indefatigable spirit they achieved some incredible results from such a small resource. They can be proud of their achievements and the LRDG's place in history.

EARLY OPERATIONS

During the 2800 km. covered between CAIRO and ZOUAR the only serious mechanical breakdowns were the breaking of a rear axle of a Ford which has been towed to ZOUAR pending repair, and the loss near ZOUAR of one 30-cwt Chevrolet which was also towed in and stripped of serviceable parts.

The force was accompanied from CAIRO by SHEIKH ABD EL GALIL SLIF EN NASSER, for many years the leader of Arab resistance to Italian penetration of the FEZZAN. Sh.ABD EL GALIL was very well received by the native population amongst whom he has a great reputation as a fighter, and when the news of his visit reaches the Italians it should cause them much uneasiness. The opportunity was also taken to spread propaganda material among local inhabitants. At present, however, little effective co-operation can be expected from the Fezzan inhabitants. They have been completely disarmed and all the nomad Arab tribes who formed the back bone of resistance to the Italians have been moved away from the interior nearer to the coast.

Lieut-Colonel.
Cmdg. Long Range Desert Group.

January 31. 1941.

Left: The final chapter of a report on the Fezzan campaign, signed by Bagnold, January 1941. LRDG shoulder title. Source: John Daymond collection.

Below: Against a map of North Africa are some of the essentials for desert navigation. Left; a Star Atlas chart, magnetic compass, and an Astro-Fix training manual. Also shown are New Zealand, Popski's Private Army, and LRDG shoulder titles, a NZ Army 'Onward' badge, an LRDG sidecap, and Egyptian and Italian banknotes.
John Daymond collection.

NAVIGATION

TRANSPORT

Left: The green T Patrol flag, which was usually flown on the vehicles of the commanders and their 2ICs.
Michael Shepherd collection.

Right: The Chevrolet WB 30cwt Waikaha, as it was found in the Egyptian Sand Sea in 1980. It was later recovered and returned to Britain. The vehicle is now displayed at the Imperial War Museum, London.
Photo: LRDG (NZ) Assn.

EQUIPMENT & SUPPLIES

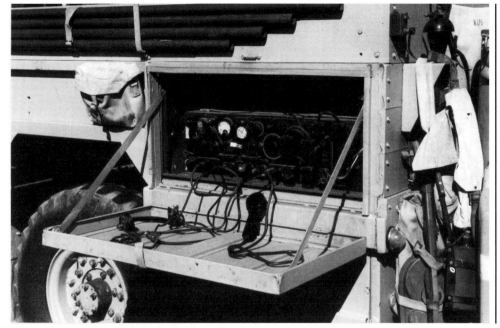

Left: A reconstructed 1942 Chevrolet wireless truck showing the No. 11 radio in position, and above that are seen the Wyndom aerial support poles. When erected, transmissions over great distances could be achieved. The vehicle is owned by Ross Hopkins of Hamilton, NZ.
Photo: Brendan O'Carroll

Above left: Unloading stores and equipment. The man on the left is carrying a jerrycan, in front of that is the 2 gallon water tin. On the right, a Shell petrol box containing two 4 gallon tins of fuel is being carried. The officer in front is armed with a Thompson sub-machine gun.
Photo: Reconstruction, Brendan O'Carroll.

Above right: A 1 gallon (4.5 litres) "SRD" (Service Rum, Diluted) rum jar, dated 1940. Packed in sawdust, two of these fitted into a special wooden box for safe carriage. Each man received a daily rum issue, usually in the evening to relax after a hard day on patrol.
Brendan O'Carroll collection.

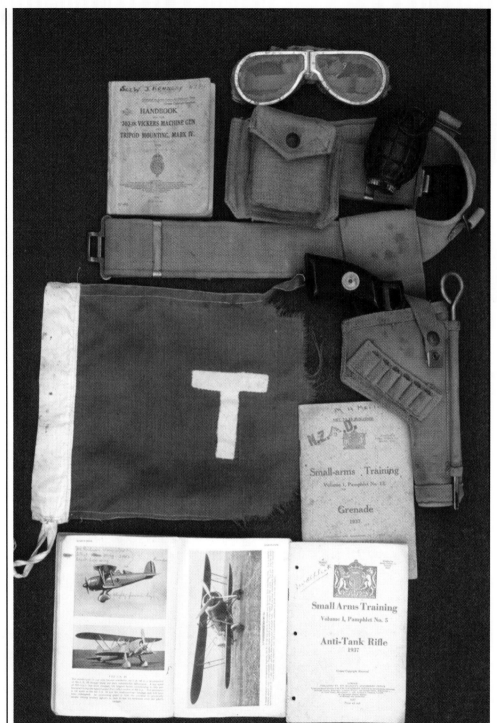

Personal equipment and manuals. From top: sand goggles, essential for protecting the eyes from the dust and glare of the sun; a 1937 Pat. web belt with an RTR Pat. open-top holster containing a .38 Enfield Mk. 1 revolver; a No. 36M hand grenade (these were either thrown or projected from grenade discharger cups); the T Patrol commander's flag; weapons training manuals and an aircraft recognition book (opened on the page showing the Italian CR42 fighters, which were sometimes encountered by the patrols). Brendan O'Carroll collection.

WEAPONS

Above: A New Zealand patrol member wearing the issue keffiyeh headdress and shouldering a .303 Lewis gun. This was the first weapon employed by the patrols, and though WWI vintage some were still being used up to late 1942. Photo: Reconstruction, Brendan O'Carroll.

*Above: New Zealand patrol members with a .55 Boys Mk. 1 anti-tank rifle. The officer holds the 5-round box magazine in one hand and the cleaning rod in the other. The troops considered the weapon useless as the patrols avoided, or rarely confronted, armoured vehicles. By 1942 additional machine-guns had replaced the Boys.
Photo: Reconstruction, Brendan O'Carroll.*

*Left: New Zealand patrol members prepare their 2-inch mortar for firing on an enemy position.
Photo: Reconstruction, Brendan O'Carroll.*

Right: A New Zealand patrol member poses with his .45 Thompson sub-machine gun. This example is fitted with a 50 round drum magazine. These weapons were standard issue to LRDG patrols. Beside him is a Shell petrol case which contained two 4-gallon tins.
Photo: Reconstruction, Brendan O'Carroll.

DRESS & INSIGNIA

Above left: A New Zealand patrol member enjoys a beer. The LRDG issue keffiyeh was mustard coloured and held in place with a black agal . Photo: Reconstruction, Brendan O'Carroll.

Left: New Zealand patrol member 1942. He wears the "Lemonsqueezer" felt hat with the puggaree of the NZ Infantry, and a brass LRDG badge. The hat badge was worn as a matter of personal choice on all types of headdress, including balaclavas. He is also displaying his red against navy blue LRDG shoulder titles. Photo: Reconstruction, Brendan O'Carroll.

Above right: New Zealand patrol members dressed for the cold. The officer on the left wears an Officer's Warm coat and carries a .45 Thompson sub-machine gun. The trooper on the right is wearing a World War 1-pattern greatcoat—these were common with the early patrols as they were still standard issue when the men left for overseas in 1940. The sand goggles on his Lemonsqueezer hat were essential desert wear, especially when travelling. He is armed with a captured German MP40 9mm sub-machine-gun. It was not unusual for the LRDG to use captured weapons. Photo: Reconstruction, Brendan O'Carroll.

NZ LRDG officer, Aegean operations, 1943. By this time the RTR Pat. beret had replaced the keffiyeh as the official headdress. He wears battledress displaying the late pattern NEW ZEALAND/LRDG shoulder title.
Photo: Reconstruction, Brendan O'Carroll.

Right: A pair of cloth LRDG shoulder titles, cap badge, and paybook cover of Trooper B. F. Shepherd, T Patrol. Shepherd collection.

Far right: Combined LRDG/ NZ shoulder title. The weave of the lettering was often crude or uneven. Most of the titles were made in Egypt. Photo: John Daymond.

Above: A brass LRDG shoulder title. The cloth titles were more commonly worn.

Left: NZ "Onward" badge. In the early days these were commonly worn by New Zealander patrol members, with the LRDG badge being reserved for leave or at base. By 1943 the unit's badge had become more regular wear.

Above: Battledress of Sergeant M. H. Craw, circa 1945. It displays the late pattern LRDG/NZ shoulder title. In 1944, while attached to the unit's British squadron, he completed his parachute course and was issued the SAS "wings" as seen above his stripes—this was probably because the LRDG was considered a "special force". His medal ribbons from left to right are; Military Medal, 1939-45 Star, Africa Star, Italy Star, 1939-45 War Medal.
Photo: Brendan O'Carroll.

Right: The silver Long Range Patrol badge. It was unofficial, and created in early 1941 to mark the existence of the LRP prior to the Guards joining the unit when it was reformed as the LRDG. A good proportion of the badges were made featuring a gilded scorpion, but being a only a gold wash it soon wore off. Around 90 were manufactured before the men destroyed the die themselves. Though it was sometimes worn as a hat badge while at base or on leave, most were sent home to friends and family. Paul Farmer collection.

Above: Typical Arab silver hallmark as sometimes seen on the reverse of LRP badges. Not all were stamped, and there was a variation in marks.

The official brass LRDG badge was produced in early 1942. The first issues tended to be cast, whereas later the sharper, struck examples became more evident. Also there was a variation in quality, finish and design of the scorpion and circle. Illustrated are: left, a struck and cut out badge; centre, LRP badge for size comparison and right, a cast badge. The diameter of the brass badge averaged around 33mm. The dimensions of the LRP badge was a 24mm circle diameter, the scroll 25mm across, and from top to bottom 30mm. Paul Farmer collection. The hallmark impression can be seen on the rim of the LRP badge. The brass badges were not usually marked.

A silver LRDG badge. These were made as "sweetheart" badges for girlfriends or wives. They were also produced in gold or gold plated. "SILVER" and an Arab hallmark can be clearly seen on the reverse.
Alan Hay collection.

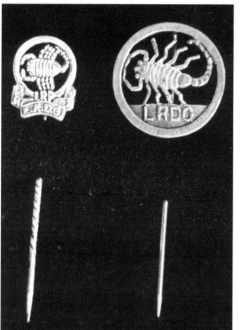

Silver stick pins of the LRP and the LRDG (NZ) Association.
Paul Farmer collection.

Bronze lapel badge marking the 50th reunion of the LRDG (NZ) Association. Manufactured by Hansen & Berry Ltd, Auckland, NZ in 1998.
Brendan O'Carroll collection.

Reproduction LRDG badges produced in white alloy and bronze. These were made in the 1970s by Russell King Badges for the British LRDG Association.
Robert Miles collection.

Brass ashtray engraved with an LRP badge. Other items such as engraved shell cases, tie pins or rings could be produced in Cairo featuring LRP/LRDG insignia. Ian Hamilton collection.

Army kitbag marked "J. Emslie 7364" with a red painted scorpion above the letters LRDG. Alongside is a .45 Thompson sub-machine gun, a standard LRDG weapon. Brendan O'Carroll collection.

Above: Laid out against the cloth of a keffiyeh and an Italian flag are the war souvenirs of one LRDG veteran. Left to right: Agal and pipe, LRDG titles and badge, SAS cap badge, "dog" tags, pocket knife, various German and Italian insignia, paybooks, and a cigarette case.
Shepherd collection.

Left: An officer wears a sheepskin-lined coat and is armed with a captured German 9mm MP40 sub-machine gun. The man on the right is also dressed against the cold, with his balaclava and WW1 pattern greatcoat. He carries a .38 Webley revolver in a RTR pattern open-top holster.
Photo: Reconstruction, Brendan O'Carroll.

WITH THE SAS

Above: Patrol members interrogate a captured Italian prisoner. Note the typical LRDG variety of uniform and headdress. The prisoner wears the sand painted Model 1933 steel helmet and his tropical field tunic displays the collar patches of the Pavia Division (17th Infantry Division). Photo: Reconstruction, Brendan O'Carroll.

Left: The winged dagger cap badge of the SAS. This example was a gift to a T Patrol gunner from a grateful L Detachment SAS member who had been picked up by the LRDG after a successful mission. Shepherd collection.

DESERT SURVIVAL

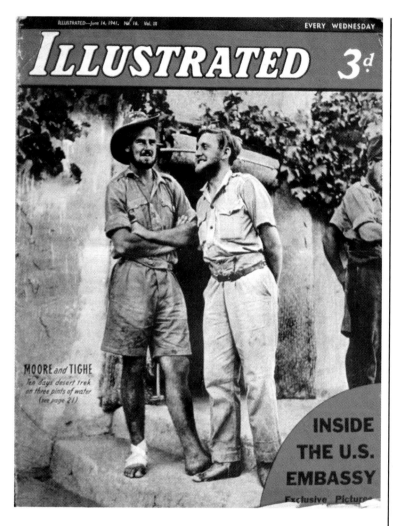

The Illustrated *magazine dated 14 June 1941, described the epic journey of Trooper Moore and his companions. The cover featured Moore on the left, alongside RAOC fitter A. Tighe.*
Merlyn Craw Collection.

TAXI SERVICE

An LRDG sergeant relaxes with a member of Popski's Private Army after they had returned from a successful combined operation. The LRDG guided both the SAS and PPA to their targets and brought them home again. Eventually these units adopted their own transport.
Photo: Reconstruction, Brendan O'Carroll.

THE BARCE RAID

LRDG (NZ) reunion, April 1999. Amongst the Barce raid veterans. From left to right: Alan Hay, the son of Euan Hay who rescued Keith Yealands from a burning truck in Barce town; Keith Tippett, MM; the author; Keith Yealands, OBE (postwar); and Merlyn Craw, MM. Photo: Brendan O'Carroll.

A brass plaque, which was placed next to a weeping dwarf cedar tree, commemorates the 50th reunion of the LRDG (NZ) Association. The reunion was held in April 1998 at Burnham Military Camp near Christchurch, NZ. Photo: Ian Judge.

Ian Judge, Secretary of LRDG (NZ) Association, April 2000. He and his wife Peggy (the Treasurer) are kept busy looking after the welfare of the veterans, organizing reunions and dealing with much correspondence. Photo: Brendan O'Carroll.

Above: LRDG reunion, Christchurch, NZ, April 1996.
Back left: Don Gregory, Alex Yaxley, Des Beale Williams, Les Nicholls, Sam Lucas, Alf Saunders, Bill Whimp,
Doug McDonald, Tommy McDonald (at wheel), Ian Gold, Ian Judge (sitting), Merv Curtis.
Front left: Richard Williams, Les Donaldson, Basil Green-street, Alan Nutt, Vern Goodwin, Laurie Lilley.
The truck is a Chevrolet reconstruction built by Alan Davies of Christchurch.
Photo: Ian Judge.

LRDG reunion Hamilton, NZ, 1999. Left to right: Frank White, Clarke Waetford, Ian Judge, Laurie Lilley. Photo taken as they prepare for a wreath laying ceremony. Photo: Brendan O'Carroll.

LRDG reunion Hamilton, NZ, 1994. Left: Dave Burnnard, Fred Kendall, Buster Gibb. Three of the original LRP/ LRDG veterans sitting in a reconstructed Chevrolet owned by Ross Hopkins of Hamilton. Photo: Ian Judge.

A reconstructed Ford F30 representing the Yeomanry Patrol truck Y6, Aramis. This superb example was built in Britain by Paul Lincoln and Clinton Long. Photo: Jack Valenti.

Reconstructed 1942 Chevrolet 30 cwt truck of the LRDG Preservation Society, USA. Put together by Rick Butler and Jack Valenti, the President of the Society. It features the markings of a New Zealand T Patrol truck, T8, Tirau II. This vehicle and related artifacts are often displayed at militaria, or military vehicle collector shows in USA, promoting much interest in the LRDG. Photo: Jack Valenti.

A 1942 Chevrolet displaying the markings of T1 Patrol truck, T6, Te Anau II, the sole surviving truck of the Barce raid, 1942. Built by Adrian Brown, it won the "Best Vehicle of Show" award at the Biggin Hill Battle of Britain show in 1997. Photo: Jack Valenti.

Right: A reconstructed 1942 Chevrolet 1533X2 wireless truck presented in Rhodesian S Patrol markings. Named "Salisbury" S5, it is owned by Ross and Leonie Hopkins of Hamilton, NZ. It was displayed at the LRDG (NZ) Association reunion in 2000. Photo: Brendan O'Carroll.

SOURCES AND RECOMMENDED READING

BAGNOLD, Lieutant-Colonel R., *Long Range Desert Group Training Notes*, 15 January 1941.

CLAYTON, Peter, *Desert Explorer: A Biography of Colonel P. A. Clayton*, Zerzura Press, 1998.

CRICHTON-STUART, Michael, *G Patrol,* William Kimber, 1958.

COWLES, Virginia, *The Phantom Major,* Collins. 1958.

FOSTER, Kate, compiled by, *An Ordinary Man: Memoirs of Frank White*, 1999.

JAMES, Malcolm, *Born of the Desert,* Collins, 1945.

JENNER, Bob and LIST, David,*The Long Range Desert Group,* Osprey Vanguard 36, 1983.

KAY, R. L., *Long Range Desert Group in Libya 1940-1941,* 1949, NZ Official History.

KAY, R. L., *The Long Range Desert Group in the Mediterranean,* 1950, NZ Official History.

KENNEDY SHAW, W. B., *Long Range Desert Group*, Collins, 1945.

KENNEDY SHAW, W. B., *Long Range Desert Group*, Revised edition, Landsborough Publications Ltd, Published as Four Square Book, 1959.

LLOYD OWEN, David, *Providence Their Guide*, Harrap, 1980.

LLOYD OWEN, David, *The Desert My Dwelling Place*, Cassell, 1957.

PENIAKOFF, Vladimir, *Popski's Private Army*, Jonathan Cape, 1950.

SANDERS, James, *Desert Patrols. New Zealanders with the LRDG*, Wilson and Horton, 1976.

SAUNDERS, Alf, *Collected LRDG stories*, Unpublished.

SCHENK, Dr. Peter, "The Battle for Leros", *After the Battle*, Issue No. 90, 1995.

WARNER, PHIIP, *The Special Boat Squadron*, Sphere Books, 1983.

Prelude to Battle: New Zealanders in the First Libyan Campaign, Army Board, Wellington, 1942.

Official History of New Zealand in the Second World War, Documents; Volumes 1 and 2, Department of Internal Affairs, 1951.

Nominal Rolls and Establishment Lists of the LRDG, Dated: 1 December 1940, 28 December 1940, 31 March 1941, March 1942, March 1943, June 1943, held by the LRDG (NZ) Association

New Zealand Expeditionary Force Nominal Rolls 1939–1945, (Embarkations) E. V. Paul, Government Printer, Wellington, 1941 to 1945.

Annual British and New Zealand LRDG Association Newsletters, Various publication dates. Kindly loaned by LRDG (NZ) Association.

Personal diary of Jack Davis, T Patrol. Excerpts loaned by the LRDG (NZ) Association.

Personal diary of Frank Jopling, T Patrol. Kindly loaned by the LRDG (NZ) Association with permission from Irene Jopling.

Personal diary of Dick Lewis, T Patrol. Kindly loaned by the LRDG (NZ) Association with permission from Ngaire Lewis.

National Archives of New Zealand, LRDG Interviews, Conducted by WO2 R. L. Kay, at HQ A (NZ) Sqn. LRDG, 3 May 1943. Participants: S/Sgt. Archie McLeod, Workshops Section; WO2 W. Hough, Signals Troop, LRDG; L/Cpl Mick Allen, Gunner/Medical Orderly; Capt. D. Barrett, QM/Adjutant LRDG.

Radio NZ Archives. Interviews of NZ LRDG members recorded by the mobile unit of the Broadcasting Service in 1941 and 1942. Participants: L. B. Ballantyne, F. B. Edmundson, J. R. Shepherd, L. H. Browne, T. B. McNeil, C. W. Eyre, E. W. R. Kitney, E. B. Smith, C. H. B.Croucher, I. H. McInnes, L. J. Hawkins, P. L. Garland, E. Sanders, F. W. Jopling.

Taped interviews recorded by the author with the following veterans: S. D. "Snow" Parker, November 1997, Merlyn Craw, June 1998, Ian Judge, August 1998, A. D. "Buster" Gibb, December 1998, Keith Tippett, December 1998, Clarke Waetford (recorded by son Charlie Waetford), 1999.

APPENDIX I

NEW ZEALAND ROLL OF HONOUR

LRDG, NORTH AFRICA

BEECH, Corporal F. R. — Killed in action 31/01/1941.

HEWSON, Sergeant C. D. — Killed in action 11/01/1941.

O'MALLEY, Lance-Corporal N. — Killed in action 18/11/1942.

McIVER, Trooper L. A. — POW 23/11/1941; wounded in battle between Russians and Germans 09/02/1945, died of wounds while POW 16/02/1945.

RODERICK, Lance-Corporal L. — POW 31/01/1941; later escaped, and joined Italian Partisans. Killed in action 6/04/1944 while leading a Partisan attack.

LRDG, A (NZ) SQUADRON, DODECANESE ISLANDS

MALLETT, Trooper H. L. — Died of wounds 24/10/1943.

BOWLER, Trooper J. T. — Killed in action 24/10/1943.

DAVIDSON, Trooper D. — Missing presumed killed, 24/10/1943.

PENHALL, Trooper A. J. — POW 25/10/1943, died of wounds 28/10/1943.

DOBSON, Sergeant E. J. — POW 28/10/1943, died while POW 6/04/1945.

APPENDIX II

COMMANDERS OF NEW ZEALAND PATROLS

LRP Patrols   "R"   Captain D. G. STEELE (2 NZEF)

                 "T"   Captain P. A. CLAYTON (BIC)
                                   Captain L. B. BALLANTYNE (2 NZEF)

                 "W"   Captain E. C. MITFORD (RTR)

LRDG Patrols "R1"   Captain J. R. EASONSMITH (RTR)
                                     Captain A. I. GUILD (2 NZEF)
                                   Captain L. H. BROWNE (2 NZEF)
                                   Lieutenant K. F. McLAUCHLAN (2 NZEF)
                                   Lieutenant D. J. AITKEN (2 NZEF)

                 "R2"   Lieutenant C. H. CROUCHER (2 NZEF)
                                     Lieutenant J. R. TALBOT (2 NZEF)
                                   Captain K. H. LAZARUS (RE)
                                   Lieutenant R. F. WHITE (2 NZEF)
                                   Lieutenant J. M. SUTHERLAND (2 NZEF)

                 "T1"   Captain L. B. BALLANTYNE (2 NZEF)
                                     Lieutenant J. E. CRISP (2 NZEF)
                                   Captain N. P. WILDER (2 NZEF)
                                   Captain C. K. SAXTON (2 NZEF)

                 "T2"   Captain C. S. MORRIS (2 NZEF)
                                   Captain N.P. WILDER (2 NZEF)
                                   Captain A. D. N. HUNTER (RTR)
                                   Lieutenant A. R. CRAMOND (2 NZEF)
                                   Captain R. A. TINKER (2 NZEF)
                                   Lieutenant M. W. CROSS (2 NZEF)

APPENDIX III

HONOURS AND AWARDS TO NEW ZEALANDERS IN THE LRDG

Distinguished Service Order	WILDER, Captain N. P.
Order of the British Empire	STEELE, Major D. G.
Member of the British Empire	BARRETT, Lieutenant D:
Military Cross	BROWNE, Captain L. H.
	MORRIS, Lieutenant C. S.
	SUTHERLAND, Lieutenant J. H.
	TINKER, Captain R. A.
Distinguished Conduct Medal	BASSETT, Trooper D. M.
	BROWNE, Corporal L. H.
	MOORE, Trooper R. J.
Military Medal	BROWN, Private F. R.
	CRAW, Corporal M. H.
	DOBSON, Trooper T. B.
	DORNBUSH, Private C.
	ELLIS, Trooper E.
	GARVEN, Corporal G. C.
	McINNES, Trooper I. H.
	SANDERS, Gunner E.
	TINKER, Corporal R. A.
	TIPPETT, Trooper K. E.
	WAETFORD, Corporal C.
	WILLCOX, Trooper L. A.
British Empire Medal	McLEOD, Sergeant A. F.
	DAVIS, Sergeant J. L. D.
Mentioned in Dispatches	AITKEN, Major D. J.
	BALL, Sergeant C. G.
	BALLANTYNE, Captain L. B.
	BARRETT, Lieutenant D. (twice)
	BEECH, Corporal F. R.
	CROUCHER, Captain C. H. B. (three mentions)
	HAMMOND, Trooper M. E.
	DAVISON, Corporal G. L.
	HARCOURT, Trooper E.
	KENDALL, Corporal F.
	LANDON-LANE, Sergeant R. J.
	MATHER, Trooper L. F.
	McGARRY, Trooper T. J.
	McINNES, Private D. J.
	McINNES, Sergeant I. H.
	McNEIL, Private T. B.
	McQUEEN, Lieutenant R. B.
	MOORE, Trooper R. J.
	SAXTON, Captain C. K.
	SHEPHERD, Sergeant J. R.
	SPOTSWOOD, Private R. O.
	STEELE, Major D. G.
	TINKER, Corporal R. A.

APPENDIX IV

LRDG: ROLL OF NEW ZEALAND OFFICERS

NAME	RANK ON LEAVING	PARENT UNIT
AITKEN, D. J. (Jack)	Lieutenant	NZ Div Cav
BALLANTYNE, L.B. (Bruce)	Major	NZ Div Cav
BARKER, R. F. T. (Trevor)	Captain	NZ Div Cav
BARRETT, D. (Shorty)	Captain	NZ Div Cav
BROWNE, L. H. (Tony)	Captain	NZ ASC
CRAMOND, A. R. (Reg)	Lieutenant	27 (MG) Bn
CRISP, J. E. (Jack)	Lieutenant	27 (MG) Bn
CROSS, M. W. (Merv)	Lieutenant	27 (MG) Bn
CROUCHER, C. H. B. (Dick)	Captain	27 (MG) Bn
COSTELLO, P. (Paddy)	2nd Lieutenant	NZ Inf
EDMONDSON, F. B. (Frank)	Captain	NZMC
ELLINGHAM, S. W. (Walter)	Lieutenant	NZ Div Cav
GUILD, A. D. (Alistair)	Major	NZ Div Cav
HUTCHINSON, E. Y. M. (York)	Lieutenant	27 (MG) Bn
LANDON-LANE, R. J. (Ron)	2nd Lieutenant	NZ Div Cav
MORRIS, C. S. (Bing)	Major	NZ Div Cav
McQUEEN, R. B. (Ralph)	Lieutenant	NZ Div Cav
McLAUCHLAN, K. F. (Paddy)	Captain	NZE
ROSS, D. I. (Don)	Lieutenant	NZ Div Cav
STEELE, D. G. (Don)	Major	27 (MG) Bn
SUTHERLAND, J. H. (Jim)	Captain	NZ DIV CAV
SUTHERLAND, J .M. (Jack)	Lieutenant	NZ Inf
SAXTON, C. K. (Charlie)	Lieutenant	NZ Inf
TINKER, R. A. (Ron)	Captain	27 (MG) Bn
TALBOT, J. R. (Roly)	Lieutenant	NZ Div Cav
WILDER, N. P. (Nick)	Captain	NZ Div Cav
WHITE, R. F. (Frank)	Lieutenant	NZ Div Cav

APPENDIX V

NOMINAL ROLL OF NEW ZEALANDERS WHO SERVED WITH THE LRP/LRDG

NAME	SERVICE NUMBER (Where known)	COMMENT
Adams, D. J.	1055	LRP
Adams, W. R.	1074	LRP
Aislabie, W. P.	1014	LRP
Aitken, D. J.	5461	
Baldwin, I.	1184	LRP
Ball, C. G.	7423	LRP
Ballantyne, L. B.	1398	LRP
Bambery, W. R.	36935	
Barber, J. A.	25477	
Barker, R. F. T.	35299	
Barrett, D.	1062	LRP
Bassett, D. M.	12518	
Beale, D. O.	41386	
Beech, F. R.	1093	LRP
Bourgeois, V. C.	600725	
Bowler, J. T.	36701	
Boys, A.	21906	
Brown, F. R.	8753	LRP
Brown, F. S.	1127	
Browne, L. H.	4444	LRP
Burgess, W. H.	14351	
Burke, P. J.	17545	
Burnnand, W. D.	1179	LRP
Butler, W. G.	1189	LRP
Cameron, E. A.	21910	
Cameron, W.	17605	
Campbell, K.	7881	LRP
Campbell, L. T.	1153	
Campbell, M. C.	16441	
Campbell, N. R.	12071	
Carter, E. G.	1131	LRP
Chaney, M. F.	277074	
Church, M. H.	452224	
Cleaver, H. H.	1195	LRP
Clemens, D. L.	453283	
Coates, J.	8816	LRP
Collett, C.	—	
Collins, T.	238590	
Connell, E. M.	60075	
Connelly, A.	22494	
Cosgrove, F. W.	25536	
Costello, P.	—	
Cowles, H. W.	246536	
Crabbe, R. H.	83381	
Cramond, A. R.	23051	
Craw, M. H.	37112	
Crawford, A. B.	15263	
Crisp, J. E.	7689	
Cross, M. W.	32358	
Crossley, J.	—	
Croucher, C. H. B.	8803	LRP

Curtis, M. W.	9660	LRP
Dalziel, L. D.	47528	
Dale, A.	1595	
Dale, A. R.	240198	
Dally, A. E.	16453	
Davies, J.	1302	LRP
Davies, R. C.	12515	
Davis, J. L. D.	37293	
Davidson, A. G.	13721	
Davidson, D.	—	
Davison, R. A.	17874	
Davison, G. L.	1349	LRP
Davoren, J. A. E.	23966	
Dean, L. G.	37710	
Derrett, W. A.	25542	
Dobson, D. G.	406306	
Dobson, E. J.	12958	
Dobson, T. B.	1203	
Dodunski, A. F.	1204	LRP
Doel, L. G.	64961	
Donaldson, L.	17790	
Dornbush, C. A.	29533	
Duncan, J. E.	—	
Edmundson, F. B.	991	LRP
Ellingham, S. W.	30972	
Ellis, E.	16503	
Ellis, L. A.	1135	LRP
Ellis, N.	254649	
Ellis, R.	—	
Emeny, A. V.	600980	
Emslie, J.	7364	LRP
Eyles, J. W.	1100	LRP
Eyre, C. W.	1305	LRP
Faithful, W. G.	31838	
Fanning, V. S.	13822	
Farmer, D.	261630	
Ferguson, A. G.	2441	
Ferguson, I. C.	1371	LRP
Finnigan, C. F.	17619	
Fisher, C. L.	14106	
Fleming, D. A.	498419	
Fogarty, D. M.	1121	
Fogden, M. F.	14621	
Forbes, W. D. S.	35079	
Franks, J. A.	21991	
Franks, R.	—	
Frost, L. H.	37166	
Garland, P. L.	1366	LRP
Garrett, J. L.	264863	
Garven, G. C.	1307	LRP
Gedye, N. M.	283269	
Gerrard, W. G.	16606	
Gibb, A. D.	1373	LRP
Gibbons, J.	—	
Giles, J.	—	
Gill, J.E.	35836	
Gilmore, J. P.	28615	
Gold, I.	—	
Goodall, F. H.	16362	

Goodwin, V. C.	266720	
Gorringe, E. F.	7834	
Gorringe, R. O.	1211	LRP
Greason, J.	—	
Greenstreet, B. W.	63246	
Gregory, D. N.	299172	
Grimsey, C. O.	551	LRP
Guild, A. I.	12740	
Haddow, R. G.	295641	
Hamilton, W. J.	7082	LRP
Hammond, M. E.	1104	LRP
Hankins, A. E.	7891	LRP
Hare, R. E. J.	37607	
Hardyment, C. H.	3267	
Harcourt, E.	7346	LRP
Hawkins, L. J.	7377	LRP
Hay, R. E.	15302	
Hayes, R. D.	17526	
Heard, V. J.	29568	
Hewetson, H. P.	29197	
Hewson, C. D.	1030	LRP
Hiscoke, A. P.	29572	
Hobson, N. W.	14324	
Holland, H. T. R.	34194	
Hood, A. W.	1041	LRP
Houston, J. W.	227417	
Hughes, L. T.	3862	LRP
Hunter, M. A.	36035	
Hutchinson, E. Y. M.	34264	
Ineson, K. C. J.	9484	
Jacobs, K.S.	—	
Jacobson, G.	—	
Jalfon, H. H.	466354	
James, W.	—	
Job, A. J.	508	LRP
Johnstone, L. R. B.	1141	
Jones, J. H.	8326	
Jopling, F. W.	1314	LRP
Joss, P. M.	7411	LRP
Judge, I. J.	439721	
Kearns, P.	1105	
Kelly, K.	17625	
Kendall, F.	1019	LRP
Kerr, S.	17527	
Kidd, C.	17169	
Kidd, S. J.	9318	LRP
Kitney, E. W. R.	3863	LRP
Knowles, G. S. D.	500082	
Knudsen, K. E.	74685	
Lamb, G.	—	
Lambert, B. W.	417495	
Landon-Lane, R. J.	1292	LRP
Larkin, R.	33123	
Larsen, L.A.	9910	
Lawson, S.J.	229864	
Lennox, F.	—	
Lennox, G. M.	636103	
Lewis, D. A.	45398	
Lewis, R. W. N.	12053	

Lilley, L. H.	243424	
Lord, H.	2856	
Loughnan, H. M.	15718	
Lucas, J. C.	16007	
Macassey, J. L. P.	15250	
Macready, D. M.	14543	
Mackay, H. D.	17668	
MacLellan, G. I.	9313	LRP
Magee, J. B.	17547	
Mallett, H. L.	16545	
Martin, A. C.	21956	
Mason, C. B.	17764	
Mather, L. F.	1250	LRP
McBean, R.	17652	
McCallum, F. R.	35950	
McCallum, I. C.	—	
McCorkindale, A.	2676	LRP
McConachie, C. I.	36922	
McCulloch, I. G.	12001	
McDonald, D. O.	63248	
McDonald, T.	1075	
McDowell, G. F.	288538	
McGarry, T. J.	1214	LRP
McGarvey, O. S.	429798	
McGregor, P.	7089	LRP
McHardy, T.	—	
McInnes, D. J.	9651	
McInnes, I. H.	1052	LRP
McIntyre, J. S.	231244	
McIver, L. A.	37404	
McKay, F. R.	375621	
McKay, H. L. W.	66148	
McKay, W. M.	—	
McKeon, D. M.	—	
McKenzie, C. B.	17536	
McKeown, F. J. W.	14063	
McLauchlan, K. F.	2257	
McLelland, T.	431916	
McLeod, A. F.	3388	LRP
McLeod, D. C.	32434	
McLeod, R. F.	439511	
McNeil, T. B.	1253	LRP
McQueen, R. B.	1401	LRP
Middlebrook, L. J.	32400	
Milburn, T. A.	17850	
Milne, J. C.	37873	
Mitford, P. V.	12002	
Mooney, P.	33099	
Moore, R. J.	1248	LRP
Morgan, R. J.	3688	
Morris, C. S.	1072	
Murphy, F. J.	1251	
Munro, D.	13174	
Murdoch, A. A.	17450	
Naden, C. H.	427515	
Nelson, G. H.	7497	LRP
Nelson, J. B.	2020	LRP
Nicholls, L. R.	632843	

Nutt, A. H. C.	14550	
O'Keefe, J. R.	1257	
O'Malley, N.	16372	
Ormond, A. R. W.	1256	LRP
Parker, S. D.	21963	
Parker, N. J.	40597	
Parkes, G. C.	1383	LRP
Partington, H.	38422	
Payne, L.	29781	
Penhall, A. J.	565573	
Pickering, C.	398476	
Pope, J. F.	630676	
Porter, R. T.	14265	
Potter, F. P.	32678	
Proctor, W. A.	9744	
Rail, W. H.	1262	
Ramsay, R. A.	1325	
Rawson, R.	8809	LRP
Reid, E. E.	432081	
Reid, J. L.	31121	
Reid, P. G.	31046	
Renwick, A. P.	13380	
Respinger, A. E.	594	LRP
Rhodes, F. D.	1331	LRP
Richards, J.	1357	LRP
Richardson, M. D.	16450	
Ritchie, T. E.	29441	
Roberts, N.	632851	
Robinson, F. M.	33508	
Rodgers, R. K.	16671	
Roderick, L.	1113	LRP
Rollinson, N. J.	1168	LRP
Ross, D. I.	30855	
Russell, E. T.	7381	LRP
Sadgrove, A. D.	8825	LRP
Sanders, E.	598	LRP
Saunders, A. M.	1329	LRP
Saxton, C. K.	13930	
Scott, L. D.	250977	
Schaab, J. L.	1169	LRP
Shaw, A. G.	—	
Shepherd, B. F.	5365	
Shepherd, J. R.	1328	LRP
Simonsen, J. M.	46071	
Simpson, R. A.	29613	
Smith, E. B.	1065	LRP
Smith, G. T.	29792	
Smith, R. C.	20841	
Spain, V. C.	1149	LRP
Spedding, A. J.	1023	LRP
Spotswood, R. O.	7748	LRP
Steedman, B.	38212	
Steele, D. G.	8855	LRP
Stewart, A. M. D.	12054	
Stewart, K.	—	
Stewart, M. W.	14355	
Steveman, G.	—	
Stone, F. R.	68106	

Stuart, J. B.	23751	
Stutterd, E. C.	24964	
Sutherland, G. M.	16484	
Sutherland, J. H.	1013	LRP
Sutherland, J. M.	37905	
Talbot, J. R.	1037	
Tant, R. D.	16650	
Taylor, J. H. E.	61512	
Thompson, J. H.	37409	
Tilbury, H.	—	
Tinker, R. A.	7483	LRP
Tippett, K. E.	20441	
Tomlinson, D. J.	17292	
Treadwell, C. J.	38169	
Treanor, R. A.	445101	
Tyler, F. W.	24346	
Vincent, A.	16913	
Vining, L. J.	37287	
Waetford, C.	3420	LRP
Waetford, E. B.	25415	
Walsh, M. C.	41535	
Walsh, T. E.	28796	
Warbrick, D. P.	21884	
Watkins, A. R.	67070	
Watson, A.	—	
Wells, T.	—	
Wheeler, D. E.	38671	
Whimp, S. W.	63251	
Whitaker, F. J.	7717	
White, R. F.	1174	
Wilder, N. P.	21988	
Willcox, L. A.	1290	LRP
Williams, R. R.	7670	
Williamson, J. M.	8760	
Wilson, A.	1390	
Wright, O. W.	29935	
Wrigley, F. M.	82870	
Wynne, J. E.	1151	LRP
Yates, A.	—	
Yaxley, C. A.	17155	
Yealands, K.	10736	
Zimmerman, J.	1392	LRP

NOTE: This roll has been compiled from records held by the NZ LRDG Association.

Their records include those who joined after the desert campaign, but did not show Service Nos. The numbers are not listed where the author has been unable to confirm them.

Any members not included, would only be those who served a very short time.

APPENDIX VI

PATROL FORMATION AND PERSONNEL

VEHICLES	PERSONNEL	ARMS

RIGHT HALF PATROL

A (HQ) TROOP (GREEN)

No. 1. 15cwt	1 Officer O.C. patrol 1 Driver	1 Vickers gun
No. 2. 30cwt	1 Navigator 1 W/T operator	1 Lewis gun 1 A/T rifle

B TROOP (BLACK)

No. 3. 30cwt	1 L/Sgt or Cpl i/c troop 1 Gunner 1 Driver	1 Vickers gun
No. 4. 30cwt	1 W/T operator 1 gunner	1 Lewis gun 1 A/T rifle
No. 5. 30cwt	1 Fitter 1 Gunner 1 Driver	1 Lewis gun

LEFT HALF PATROL

C TROOP (YELLOW)

No. 6. 30cwt	1 Sergeant i/c Troop 1 Gunner 1 Driver	1 Vickers gun
No. 7. 30cwt	2 Bofors Gunners 1 Driver	1 Bofors gun
No. 8. 30cwt	2 Gunners 1 Driver	1 Lewis gun 1 A/T rifle

D TROOP (RED)

No. 9. 30cwt	1 Navigator 1 Gunner 1 Driver	1 Lewis gun
No. 10. 30cwt	1 Fitter 1 Gunner 1 Driver	1 Lewis gun 1 A/T rifle
No. 11. 30cwt	1 Officer 2 i/c patrol 1 Gunner 1 Driver	1 Vickers gun

Establishment of a Fighting Patrol as at January 1941:

Captain	1
Subaltern	1
Sergeant	1
Corporals	3
L/Corporals	3
Privates	21
Operators (att)	2
Total	32

APPENDIX VII

NEW ZEALAND PATROL TRUCK NAMES*

W PATROL

Waihi, Waiti, Waikaha, Waikato, Waima, Waipa, Wainui, Waitoma, Waitemata, Wanaka, Waiariki, Wairoa, Waiora, Waitotara.

T PATROL

Te Anau, Te Ariki, Te Aroha, Te Auti, Te Aute, Te Awa, Te Hai, Te Hau, Te Pa, Te Paki, Te Puke, Te Rangi, Te Roti, Te Taniwha, Te Wanaka, Taipo, Taupo, Tirau, Tutira.

R PATROL

Rotoma, Rotoehu, Rotoiti, Rotorua, Rotoroa, Rotoairo, Rotokawa, Rotomahana, Rotowhero, Rotokakahi, Rotowaro, Rotowai.

NB: Listed are those known to the author. It may be incomplete.

APPENDIX VIII

T1 PATROL MEMBERS WHO PARTICIPATED IN THE BARCE RAID, AND THOSE CAPTURED, SEPTEMBER 1942

Captain Nick Wilder	
Corporal Merlyn Craw	POW
Lance-Corporal Alan Nutt	POW
Trooper Keith Tippett	
Trooper Wally Rail	
Trooper Tom Milburn	POW
Trooper Frank Jopling	POW
Trooper Derek Parker	
Trooper Euan Hay	POW
Trooper Bruce Dobson	
Trooper Peter Burke	
Trooper Peter Mitford	
Trooper Mick Holland	POW
Trooper Keith Yealands	POW
Trooper Sandy Vincent	
Private Jack Davis	
Private David Warbrick	
Gunner Edgar Sanders	